REFLECTIONS ON MY LIFE AND WRITINGS

THE NOTEBOOKS OF PAUL BRUNTON
(VOLUME 8)

REFLECTIONS ON MY LIFE AND WRITINGS

PAUL BRUNTON
(1898–1981)

An in-depth study of
category number twelve
from the notebooks

Published for the
PAUL BRUNTON PHILOSOPHIC FOUNDATION
by Larson Publications

International Standard Book Number (cloth) 0-943914-28-0
International Standard Book Number (paper) 0-943914-29-9
International Standard Book Number (series, cloth) 0-943914-17-5
International Standard Book Number (series, paper) 0-943914-23-X
Library of Congress Catalog Card Number: 87-80402

Manufactured in the United States of America

Published for the
Paul Brunton Philosophic Foundation
by
Larson Publications
4936 Route 414
Burdett, New York 14818

Distributed to the trade by
Kampmann and Company
9 East 40 Street
New York, New York 10016

88 90 91 89 87
2 4 6 8 10 9 7 5 3 1

The works of Dr. Brunton

A Search in Secret India
The Secret Path
A Search in Secret Egypt
A Message from Arunachala
A Hermit in the Himalayas
The Quest of the Overself
The Inner Reality
(*also titled* Discover Yourself)
Indian Philosophy and Modern Culture
The Hidden Teaching Beyond Yoga
The Wisdom of the Overself
The Spiritual Crisis of Man

Published posthumously

Essays on the Quest

CONTENTS

EDITORS' INTRODUCTION

Reflections on My Life and Writing is a mosaic of autobiographical excerpts from Paul Brunton's personal notebooks. The eighth volume in *The Notebooks of Paul Brunton*, it brings together a variety of the author's most personal thoughts and observations.

Though his readership numbers in the millions, Paul Brunton (1898–1981) was an intensely private and naturally unassuming man. He continually sought for effective ways to bring his ideas to the public mind and keep his own personality at a low profile. When pressed to describe himself, he usually said that he was a "researcher"—which he defined as "one who creates new knowledge."

Maturing with a century that brought more changes than the previous thousand years, he witnessed the advent of the automobile, the airplane, radio, television, and nuclear power, and devoted his life to a path of spiritual discovery suitable for this epoch of turmoil and transition. This role took him on many journeys into the soul, across the centuries, and around the world in an extraordinary quest for Truth. In the course of these journeys, he occasionally paused to record his private impressions of himself, his works, and people or places he encountered.

The inner and outer aspects of this quietly paradoxical individual were remarkably different from one another. Inwardly, Paul Brunton was a tirelessly exacting scholar and researcher of philosophical and religious ideas and practices. Outwardly, he dedicated himself to sharing his hard-earned understanding in the simplest, most inspiring and nontechnical form he could develop. In him, the poet's reverence for beauty and the scientist's reverence for truth demanded the creation of a mutually satisfying common language. The process gave birth to a voice that bridges an earlier and a future time.

The outer man traveled widely to drink deeply of a world-dispersed wisdom this century had largely chosen to ignore. The inner man, in love with the beauty of what a human being can become, envisioned a scientifically literate human community that would eventually rediscover and creatively reintegrate the values of its own spiritual heritage. As the scholar-researcher matured and the poet-mystic deepened, a thoroughly modern philosopher emerged. Long before other writers now well-known arose in the 1950s to focus attention on specific Eastern teachings, Paul Brunton's "exotic" books had awakened hundreds of thousands of the curious, the confused, and the sincere to the rich treasures of the Oriental mind. He is undeniably one of the individuals to whom the current popularity of the East-West cultural and philosophical movement is most indebted.

Although philosophically at ease with the necessary presence of the ego, P.B. was uninterested in its gaudy manifestations and preferred to direct his uncannily perceptive intelligence to the variety of topics comprising his definition of philosophy. It is quite possible, therefore, that he would disapprove of this volume; at the very least he would dislike its focus on his personality and his personal opinions of himself and others.

And yet these pages reveal much of him: his humor, his anguish over the world situation, his admiration for great individuals, his disenchantment with the egotism so often found under the robes of the "holy ones," and his assessment of the value and imperfections of his own work. They provide at least partial answers to questions such as: What transformed a London-born journalist into such a successful interpreter and popularizer of Oriental wisdom and mystical techniques? Why did he deliberately undo much of his own worldly success and seek relative anonymity for the last thirty years of his life? How did he avoid the fate of so many of his contemporaries—that of becoming a guru surrounded by one circle of adulating disciples and another circle of vehement critics? What was the destiny that linked his cycles of inner and outer growth with the development of the East-West cultural movement itself? What is the relevance for us of life's unusual experiment with him?

Chapter one consists of two essays that summarize P.B.'s literary and mystical development up to the time they were written, in the early to middle 1950s. Chapter two considers the problem of bringing vitally needed education to bear upon the weakened spiritual condition of modern culture, and the need for a fresh approach to philosophy in response to the crisis. In the third chapter, P.B. reflects on the awakening of his own consciousness to the presence of the Overself, and the responsibilities that awareness required of him. The fourth chapter reviews lessons and achievements in the path of all seekers of spiritual truth; it describes some of P.B.'s own struggles to externalize the inner wisdom he had acquired. In the fifth chapter, P.B. reviews his literary life. He examines his books, his audience of critics and admirers, his own method and writing style, and looks beyond the written work to the less apparent but more powerful communication through silence. Finally, in the last chapter, P.B. takes a look at himself and at a few of the many places and people he encountered in his busy life, along with thoughts on a few other topics.

There is, however, a serious problem of chronology: very few of the notes in the notebooks bear dates indicating when they were written. The vast majority of them are impossible to date accurately. It is clear that the two essays forming the first chapter were written while the author was in his mid-fifties. Many of the paras also seem to have been written after the publication of *The Spiritual Crisis of Man* (1952) and before 1963, the year that brought a profound deepening that visibly affected all his subsequent work and writing. We hope, therefore, that the two essays will serve as a sort of landmark by which readers may be able to estimate whether a given statement is from an earlier or later period of his life.

What is most clear is that very little of the personal material available in *The Notebooks* dates from the later years. It seems that his disinclination to speak about himself eventually had its way.

Further information about *The Notebooks* series and related activities may be obtained by writing the

Paul Brunton Philosophic Foundation
P.O. Box 89
Hector, New York 14841

Reflections
on my Life
and Writings

This book has been wrought around many moods and it is the work of several years, so that it might seem in places as though it were the production of two or three different hands. I could have omitted some chapters because they might be thought to break the harmony of the whole, and because they sound a note not so certain or happy as I have generally sought to give forth. But I prefer to let them stay as showing something in the way of growth, and to let them stand as milestones where I had camped for a while but have long since passed by. Some of the subsequent paragraphs were indeed written so long ago that I can hardly claim identity with the author, such are the changes which the years bring.

1
TWO ESSAYS

I take a look at my own life. It seems an invisible cinema is flickering past my mind's eye, giving me back my record with vivid luminosity. Spool after spool of pictures unlooses itself in front of my eyes, stirring the past with both bitter and pleasant memories that had long fallen into oblivion. Yet as I concentrate upon each detail when it appears, I am astonished to notice how these forgotten scenes swiftly take on again the veridic note of immediate reality. It is an uncomfortable thought that hours lived with such supreme urgency or such overwhelming emotion as some of which now appear before me, ultimately fade off into the same neutral tint as feebler ones. Moreover the unwinding reel of the years turns more and more hastily as one gets older. Such is the perishable stuff of existence. 'Tis all a mental construction, a tissue of ephemeral ideas!

And yet the years have not been irrevocably lost. I amused myself with scribbling mystical books to bore materialistic people, playing with queer thoughts which were thrown up into the air and caught on the tip of my pen. I have tried to rescue from the vanished past, perhaps before it got too late, bygone impressions, unusual adventures, inspired moments, exotic ideas, half-felt intuitions, and new-found truths—and then to turn them into written sheets. Thus ten books have successively been born and thus my own recollections and reflections have been given out to a larger audience than myself. Despite my flippant description of them, it is a fact that the fundamental motive which inspired their creation was service.

They have effected their purpose, for thousands of people have testified to the benefit received from reading these books and to the solace gotten from dwelling on their ideas. Sometimes I wrote for the ordinary reader, sometimes for the extraordinary one. If *A Search in Secret India* and *A Search in Secret Egypt* did not tire the brains of many novel readers, *The Hidden Teaching Beyond Yoga* and *The Wisdom of the Overself* did constitute a doctrinal construction which attracted only the few who felt such a need. Some of my earlier work will continue to stand by itself but the rest may serve as an introduction to the more substantial work presented in those two volumes, *The Hidden Teaching Beyond Yoga* and *The Wisdom of the Overself.* Fate earlier settled that these writings should become known rapidly, either in the English original or in European and Indian translations, to waiting readers who are so scattered that they can be found in most countries of the five continents, from far Japan to distant Chile. They belong to white, yellow, brown, and black races. They vary from half-literate workmen to highly cultured scholars.

Not a few have indicated that new doors to higher living had thus been opened to them. Judged by the tranquillizing influence they seem to exert on troubled minds and the unusual information which they endeavour to carry to perplexed ones, it is clear that those books were worth their labour. And when people write and tell the author that his books have beneficially shaken up their ideas or produced a radically altered outlook on life, he cannot but begin to have faith anew in the mysterious power of the pen and its ancient ally, ink. "Wondrous, indeed, is a true book . . . talismanic and the strange symbolism thaumaturgic, for it can persuade men" exclaims Carlyle in powerful and picturesque words. Nevertheless I cannot presume to take the popularity of these books as a certificate for myself but rather as a certificate of the importance which is now beginning to be assigned to these subjects in the West.

They performed the much-needed service of carrying encouragement to those aspiring individuals who most need it, who are struggling to live mentally in a more exalted ethical environment than the one in which they live physically. They inspired and stimulated even while they instructed. They were to become both refuge and guide to those who would rescue life from aimlessness and save a few really worthwhile hours from its moth-like impermanence.

Not that I have ever been satisfied with what has been done—knowing only too well its numerous defects—but it has been done usually under difficult circumstances and against great pressure of time and therefore represents only what was possible at the time, quite apart from the further defects imposed by my personal limitations. Nevertheless it is unlikely that any recognition of my research work or creative efforts will come from official quarters. The task which destiny set me was too unusual for that. I do not write for those who would sit philosophy in an academic chair but for those who would apply it to life. In any case the world of stuffy official presentations, of morning-coat solemnity and bourgeois conventionality is not my world.

There were difficult circumstances in my personal life: the vicissitudes of frequent travel, the labours of constant and ever-widening research, the enervation and illnesses of tropical climates, the ever-present need of carrying on unremittingly with literary work which succeeds in reaching thousands where correspondence reaches but a relative few.

They were aggravated by the fact that I am by nature lazy, although I have so far driven mind and body with a hard will born out of a sense of rigid duty. I have a kindred and congenial spirit in Charles Lamb who, always the last to arrive for his work at the old East India Company's office, excused himself by saying that he was always the first to leave. My temperament is such that I would prefer to spend my days doing nothing harder than lying stretched at ease on a Persian carpet bespread with several cushions, drinking a cup of the fragrant Chinese shrub or Mocha herb, wrapping my mind up in a Sufi shawl of coloured poesy and hearing all the while a continuous stream of European classical music.

I have consistently and frankly made it plain, both in the prefaces to certain books and during the course of personal interviews, that I have no desire to set myself up as a spiritual teacher and consequently no desire to acquire a following. I do not regard myself as a holy man or a saint or a sage or anything of that sort and consequently cannot honestly permit readers to regard me as such. Let others bear those dubious honours; a less ambitious if more worldly existence suffices for me. I write mystic and philosophic books not because I possess a spiritual status beyond that of others but partly because I possess a spiritual experience which is unlike that of others and partly because I wish to do a little good with my pen, if I may, rather than let it be hired out to the much more lucrative but less satisfying work which is repeatedly offered me. If I write about some of my own mystic experiences, it is only to show what benefits I have myself received from the pursuit of yoga. This is done because I know that an effective way to persuade some of my fellows to adopt meditation practices is to relate them to personal life. The egotistical style has been deliberately adopted. Such a personal style however is out of place in purely metaphysical works where an impersonal detached and dry manner is more apposite. That I recognize the truth of this axiom may be verified on examining my two latest books. I wrote always for those who are still, like myself, at the humbler level of aspiration. I do not claim any greater weight for my statements than any student may accord to another student's. But nevertheless the fact remains that I have been a specially privileged one.

Certain it is that I found myself possessed of an equipment to carry this special task such as few in the West of whose existence I am aware also possessed. Fate has provided me with exceptional opportunities whilst determination has provided me with a unique life-experience. Whether it be correct or not the fact remains that I have drunk deeply of doctrines that have been left like a legacy out of Asia's past. As a simple statement of fact and without pandering to vanity, it may be noted that Prince Mussooree Shum Shere of Nepal, himself an advanced practitioner of yoga and familiar with all the leading yogis of the Himalayan world, has set down these words: "I am convinced that Brunton is one of the chosen instruments to interpret the half-lost wisdom of the East."

Asiatic and African mystics, yogis and learned men, and even rare sages of whose eminence and existence the West still knows little or nothing have given me their confidence, confided much of their knowledge and secrets to my care, and sent me forth from their presence with their uttered benediction to mediate between Orient and Occident. I have thus had several teachers, yet could become the pupil of none; I have studied the tenets of several schools, but could become enslaved by none. In obedience to an inner compulsion and intermittent premonition whose justification became quite clear as destiny unfolded, I have ever maintained a sacred independence amidst all such relations, a detached loyalty, and have considered Truth a goddess above all mortals and hence alone to be worshipped. This attitude brought me painful emotional conflicts during the period of my growth and provoked others to malicious misunderstandings, but it has finally and fully proved its worth. For my loftiest, strangest, most significant, and most elevating mystic experiences occurred before I had ever met a single teacher, before I had even set foot on Asiatic soil. Through them I was really reborn. But alas! in my youth and novitiate I could not understand them. I was dazzled by the light and so continued to grope as though I were still in the dark. Now at long last I have brought my mystic and philosophic wandering to an anchor. Henceforth I owe intellectual allegiance and mystical obedience to no man.

And if I abhor the thought of forming a cult and making disciples, this is not to say that I abhor the thought of assisting my fellow man to find something of what I have already found. And if I refuse to set myself up as a sage when I am myself but a student, this is not to say that there are not always those who know even less than oneself and who may profitably share a few of my own crumbs. For no one can come into even partial comprehension of the Overself which supports the existence of all living creatures and continue to sit smugly in self-centered enjoyment of his knowledge and egoistic enjoyment of his peace. It is only ascetic mystics who touch their inner self without also touching the inner self of the universe who can do that. But he who has even begun to perceive that the basis of his own individual being is one and the same, wholly identical, with that of all other individual beings is no longer a mystic. For him the ultimate unity of all humanity—secret and not obvious though it be—is nevertheless a fact, and he has to reorder his own life accordingly. It will not be possible for him to dismiss from his mind the melancholy case of those who aspire to a wiser and better life. They will haunt his heart like wraiths and he will not get free of them, go where he will, be it into the loneliest solitude or the busiest city. Their service becomes his inescapable duty.

2

My Initiations into the Overself

After years of hesitation and reluctance, I include this chapter of a chronicle of personal mystical experience. The first intention had been to write it in old age and to publish it anonymously or perhaps posthumously. But I find that old age keeps on being before me, that instead of being more than half a century old I have simply lived for more than half a century, and that this task might as well be done now as later. There are still other chapters of this kind which will have to be written one day, but their concern is chiefly with cosmic mysteries rather than with personal experience, although the unveiling of those mysteries could not have happened except as a direct result of such experience. But since those subjects do not pertain to the present book, for they are on a plane that is more ethereal and less material, I have omitted them.

The reluctance to put in the present chapter arises partly because it touches private, intimate, and sacred moments, and partly because it will necessarily be so prolific in first-person pronouns that it will sound far too egotistic. Its very virtue may appear as its vanity. But I know from wide experience that such a narration will help those who are already seeking the Overself to recognize certain important signs on their own way, to learn where the correct path should lead them, and, above all, to confirm them in the necessity of hope. I believe, too, that it may give those who are not questers but ordinary people more faith that God does exist and more trust in the ultimate beneficence of God's World-Idea. If it serves also in such ways, it can only do a little good to write and release this record.

Although a writer never really knows how much good or how much harm his work does (for the reports of its results are few and far between), if his aim is to serve he need not be concerned about those results. He would do his best and find peace in the thought that man and fate will take care of them. So I follow the practice and counsel of an old Greek monk,

Callistus Telicudes, who wrote: "One ought not to keep what is learned by Meditation, but one should make notes of it and circulate the writings for the use of others." This is why I communicate these inner experiences to those who might be helped, to those who might receive more vision of and more belief in life itself.

Before I reached the threshold of manhood and after six months of unwavering daily practice of meditation and eighteen months of burning aspiration for the Spiritual Self, I underwent a series of mystical ecstasies. During them I attained a kind of elementary consciousness of it.

If anyone could imagine a consciousness which does not objectify anything but remains in its own native purity, a happiness beyond which it is impossible to go, and a self which is unvaryingly one and the same, he would have the correct idea of the Overself.

There are not a few persons who have known infrequent occasions when their ordinary mentality seems to lapse, when their feeling for beauty and goodness seems to expand enormously, and when their worldly cynicism falls away into abeyance for a short time. The place may seem perfect for this experience, but it may also seem quite the opposite—such as a noisy metropolitan street. There are many other persons who have known the beauty of a great musical symphony and felt its power to draw the emotions into a vortex of delight or grandeur. Such persons can more easily imagine what this rapturous emotional mystical experience is like. But they may not know that under the ordinary human consciousness there is a hidden region whence these aesthetic feelings are drawn.

It was certainly the most blissful time I had ever had until then. I saw how transient and how shallow was earthly pleasure by comparison with the real happiness to be found in this deeper Self. Before my illumination the solitary scenes of Nature's grandeur usually served as my greatest form of inspiration. I could become so absorbed in admiring such beauty that I would feel swallowed up in it for a period of time and fall into a tranquil state. After my illumination I no longer became totally absorbed in such scenes. They remained something separate from me: I was detached from them. The emotional exaltation they aroused was less or lower than the peace and joy I felt in the Overself. Yet this spatial detachment did not prevent me from enjoying nature, art, and music to an even greater and more satisfying extent than previously. The detachment gave me freedom, release from some personal limitations, and enabled me to feel and understand beauty in a larger and deeper way. I even became more attentive to detail.

The glamour and the freshness of those mystical ecstasies subsided within three or four weeks and vanished. But the awareness kindled by them remained for three years. I then met an advanced mystic—an expatriate American living in Europe—who told me that I was near the point where I could advance to the next and higher degree of illumination and that, at such a period, most aspirants undergo certain tests before they succeed in gaining the degree.

He was right. I underwent the tests very soon after and failed in them— failed so miserably that I fell headlong down and lost even the spiritual consciousness which I had previously possessed. The period which followed was a terrible one, a veritable "dark night of the soul" through which I had to struggle slowly and painfully for another three years. During all that period there was neither time nor capacity to practise meditation, nor was I inclined to sustain aspiration.

It is at times necessary to give a man a shock to show him what he is really like. This is usually done by friends, sometimes by enemies, and occasionally by the Master. It is always done by life itself. The experience is painful, but, if its lessons are sufficiently taken to heart, the debt owed to it is a large one. It arouses the man to do what will save him from avoidable sufferings in the future by stimulating him to remove their causes within himself. One day I was faced with an unexpected event which gave me a tremendous shock. The emergency called for all the wisdom and strength and determination I could muster in order to deal with it. I succeeded in doing so and was drastically aroused in the process. In this way I shook myself out of the spiritual depression and, in a somewhat desultory manner, took up again the practice of meditation as well as occasional attempts at self-improvement. This transition period was succeeded by another when I acted more resolutely and worked more diligently. I laid down a program for regular daily meditation, practised even more intensively, and tried harder to improve myself than I had done for years. There suddenly came a feeling of impending momentous discovery. Six weeks later, I found myself plunged for two hours one evening (which was twice as long as the period allotted each day to the practice) in the deepest mental withdrawnness for me at the time. I felt I had come home after an all-too-long and dishonourable absence like a prodigal son. During that memorable session, I recovered once more the degree of consciousness which I had enjoyed in the earlier period of my Quest, although there was more knowledge and understanding this time. I could see more clearly that there was a definite preordained pattern in my life and in the lives of others: all the chief events had some kind of inner meaning in them; all could teach some lesson which if learned would lead to spiritual growth. To discern these lessons, we have to develop a more mature emotional attitude in our relations with others and also a stronger character. We have to get ourselves out of our selves and look at each situation, momentarily at least, the way the other person involved in it looks at it. Then we have to seek true justice for all and not be selfish.

In the course of that evening's inner work, I found that my thoughts were being definitely directed along a certain course by some impulsion which was not altogether my own. It led me to retrace briefly the past history of my spiritual career and, especially, to examine carefully the point where I missed my step and lost my path. I analysed the reasons for this mishap until they were perfectly clear and taken deeply to heart. Then I was led to build up imaginatively a picture of what might have happened had I successfully passed the tests. I was also led to see that each man or woman who had been brought by life into short or long association with me had borne a silent message or embodied a hidden test, or else was someone to be helped or served in a way which would reveal itself in time. That Presence which was and yet was not myself told me inwardly how, through all the frustration and confusion which had filled the second cycle of my spiritual career, it had never left me but had remained beside me waiting for the time when my own efforts to find my way back would unite with its magnetic drawing power to liberate me. I was told that there was in this a great lesson—the necessity of hope—which I ought to communicate to the aspirants I would meet later who were spending fruitless barren years of spiritual seeking, and who were becoming discouraged at the lack of results. Inexperienced travellers on this path often find that their early enthusiasm wanes and then the journey becomes tedious. For working upon themselves, changing improving and developing the moral mental and emotional material they must use is so slow an affair, so poor in visible results, that it tends to stifle buoyancy and enfeeble determination. Perhaps there will also be periods of harsh testing when resentment doubt or rebellion against the Quest will appear within themselves. So I had to instill the lesson of never abandoning the belief that the struggle was worthwhile, of always trusting in the eventuality of Grace, and of living in the memory of their past uplifted moments. Those who are intimidated by the Quest's difficulties ought to be stimulated by its rewards. They should take to heart the truth that no spiritual darkness is a permanent one, and that at no time are they really lost, deserted, or fallen creatures. If their will weakens or their light clouds, it is an inevitable part or result of their imperfect nature as well as of their unfinished development. But it is also a condition which must right itself with further experience, evolutionary pressure, or unexpected Grace.

When my meditation seemed to have ended a great store of strength poured into me. Indeed, it was so overwhelming as to appear irresistible. I felt that every obstacle could be overcome by its support and help, and that I merely had to stretch out my hand to gain victory. Suddenly I saw a vision in which a duplicate of myself was pushing a huge boulder away from the entrance to a cave. I knew instinctively that the boulder was a symbol for the lower self and that the cave was a symbol for the Higher Self. I could feel a change working rapidly in my character and personality, bringing me closer to the ideal which I held. I succeeded at last in rolling away the boulder and, with that, attained a certain degree of self-mastery which from that moment onward remained with me. I felt that I could never again fall below that degree, that it was no more possible to do so than it was for the hatched chicken to return to the egg.

I stood at the entrance to the cave and looked inside. I found it to be full of light, dazzlingly brilliant by comparison with the murky gloom outside it. The power to enter the cave was not given to me, only to stand at the entrance and gaze inside. I understood that the inner work necessary to gain this power would constitute the next cycle of my labours.

The vision came to an end and with it I realized that a man does not become truly humble until he has first seen himself as truly great. The glimpse of his Higher Self throws a powerful light by reaction upon his darker one. He discovers how simple, how ignorant, how weak, and how arrogant he is and has been. If the discovery brings him to the ground, it also stimulates him to resolve to remake himself in the image of the ideal. With the shaming contrast between the animal and the angelic in him, as well as between the human and the Divine, he is penetrated through and through with the need of imposing the Higher Will forcefully upon the lower one.

The years which succeeded this vision were years of development and growth. One of the most interesting new phenomena of that period came about occasionally when I was entering into or emerging from the deeper states of meditation. Out of the silent recesses of my being there came forth utterance—yet no form was to be seen and no one was there, nor did any vision come with it! This was the mystery—that speech came into existence without a speaker. It was the activity of vocal intuition, a Presence which spoke to the inner ear and not to the outer. It must not be confused with the hearing of audible voices such as mediums and psychics are supposed to hear. It was nothing of that kind. This was one's Spiritual Self speaking to one's human self. I suppose it was what the German mystics of the sixteenth century called "The Interior Word" and what the medieval saints of the Catholic church meant when they claimed that God talked to them. It was definite, commanding, forceful, insistent, and authoritative. If it gave an order, it gave also the power needed to carry out the order.

Yet it was not the intuition associated with everyday existence as an occasional phenomena, for that is usually a mental first impression or a silent feeling. That intuition may well be the faint beginnings of this Voice, which I like to call the Voice of the Overself.

I felt that I could put the utmost confidence in its guidance wherever it led me, even if it led directly to loss of every material possession, to sacrifice of every human relationship, and to the renunciation of every professional ambition.

The place where I heard this Voice became ever after a holy sanctuary, an oasis of peace, and a citadel of strength to which I could return or retreat whenever I was alone, or whenever a crisis of the outer world was impending. People think too often that they have to travel to distant places for wisdom or teaching. They fail to recognize that it is not only within themselves—this wisdom or this teaching—but that it will never be found anywhere else. The echo of some other person's wisdom will never take its place.

To find the holy Presence by withdrawing from the world temporarily into meditation was much easier than to find it while busy in the world. That was a different task. To go on from there until it became a fixed phenomenon was still harder. It may help others to learn how I did this. I had entered into a session which combined prayer with meditation. Although I assumed the usual physical position and it was the customary hour for the evening practice of meditation, actually I gave myself up to my feelings and spoke silently from the heart in fervent prayer. I addressed my words to the Overself and related how I had come evening after evening to this inner tryst, and I emphasized that it was aspiration and the attraction of love which had drawn me away from every other activity to spend more than an hour in this one. I admitted that an uplifting spiritual experience had often been the result, but I complained that the end of each session was the end of the experience. The next day had to be spent in ordinary consciousness like the day of any other person uninterested in the Quest. I had taken up the practice of exercises in constant recollection as well as exercises in declarative muttering, but to no result; they were not my path. I still got so immersed in work or talk or whatever I happened to be doing that I forgot the practice and failed to carry it off.

It became obvious that if I depended on myself, on my own poor and feeble power, the effort could not end in anything but failure. There was no hope for progress unless the Overself came to my rescue and, out of its Grace, brought about the desired state. I asked ardently for its help; indeed, I begged for it and lamented that life was worthless unless it could be lived continuously in that state. I carried on this one-way conversation in a lovingly familiar yet humbly beseeching tone.

A response came at last. I felt myself being carried down deeper into my inner being until a level of rich consciousness was touched. It required great intensity of purpose, great resolution of will, and extreme power of concentration to remain on that level, so I summoned up these resources and succeeded in remaining. After a while I was instructed by the inner Voice to form a mental picture of a duplicate of myself at work, in talk or travel, or in any other activity likely to be entered during the following day. In this picture I was to keep hold of the awareness in which I was now held and not to let my attention wander from it for even a minute. I was particularly guided to include such occasions or contacts where I was likely to be provoked by annoyance, irritation, overconcentration on work, and excessive physical activity into forgetfulness.

Thus the first step was to make the desired state come true in imagination. This could not be done without the fullest trust that it would do so, and without the fullest consent of my logical mind that it could do so. The second step was to identify myself imaginatively with the ideal state during the day as often as I could remember to do it, and during formal meditation periods as intensely as I could force the mind into doing it. In the first step I had to project a picture of myself as active in the outer world, to put forth a thought-form which would incubate for a period of time like an egg. I had not merely to think about that desired state from present conditions but also—indeed, rather—to think from it. I had to determine my outlook by it as if it were already an actuality and to imitate all the characteristics and qualities it had. I was not to gaze up to the idea, but to gaze down from it.

In the second step the ideal had to be knitted into me as if by a magic spell. I had to play the wizard and enchant myself into first seeing and then being what I aspired to become.

At first it was not possible to retain that peaceful state continuously. It would fade away intermittently. Both to prevent that from happening and to make the needed conditions to sustain its presence, the practice of this exercise in creative imagination became necessary. I found the exercise a valuable one for use in meditation practices of later years and so pass it on for the benefit of others.

Even then I knew that the effort required was too great for me, that imaginative power alone was too insufficient for such a result to be achieved without Grace. If I had to depend on myself, on my poor little human self, the end of it would be merely an illusion which would one day be harshly dispelled or a dream from which I would one day rudely awake. The imagination by itself was not capable of bringing such an exalted state into actual realization, but the imagination plus Grace was capable.

When the ego works on its own self, its willingness is reluctant and its power is limited. When Grace works inside the ego, its participation is joyous and its power is unpredictable. Does Divine Grace exist? Orthodox theology makes an arbitrary fact of it and does not correctly present it. Yet it is reasonable in theory and verified by experience that it comes down to meet and mingle with human aspiration. But it is also a fact that such a desirable consciousness is not likely to happen if the aspirant fails to fulfil the conditions controlling its appearance.

On the day when its long awaited dawn reddened my sky I certainly had no doubts that it was at work because I could directly feel its inner movements as soon as I started to meditate. I was perfectly aware of a swift change from the ordinary to the deeper level and of the inward pull which are signs of its action and which repeated themselves many times in other meditations.

In the result, the state of divided being—the state of disunion in the heart—which had been my general state and which is necessarily the general state of all seekers, began to vanish. Instead of two opposing forces being ever at war within myself, the actual and the ideal, there began to appear only a single controlling force. This led in turn to a great happiness which made unnecessary all the constant searching for happiness in outside things, circumstances, or persons—a searching which is one of the causes of this self-division. I felt that the desires and attachments I had cared about so greatly, anguished over and worried for, were not important at all in themselves but only in the spiritual lesson to which they led in the end. All the little desires, all the personal yearnings, are really God-desire. At first it is unconscious but with the growth of understanding it becomes conscious. It is then that the will turns around to start on the Quest, and that the desiring heart which had been looking and hungering for things outside itself starts to look within itself.

In this emptying of self, of fears and desires, the anxiety or relation about the results of their activity is also emptied. At the same time there is the certainty that they will be taken care of in the World-Mind's providence.

By carrying out these exercises and then consciously forming the habit of carrying their results into the everyday life and routine, I came in time to keep the peace all day long. This was certainly a great reward for all the years of toil and effort which preceded it. But it also brought certain responsibilities to myself and to others.

Once identified with the Cause of the True Self, how could anyone ever betray it by expressing any of the uglier traits and baser qualities which belong to the lower self? Once it is discovered that all that is noblest in every human aspiration comes from this sacred Source, how could one go along with one's ignoble tendencies?

Negatively, one could not raise one's hand or open one's lips to injure a fellow being. One could not be antagonistic to him even in thought. Positively, one had to practise an active goodwill toward all living creatures.

Because of the sweetness which pervaded my heart, the world looked different and it was not difficult to restrain those ignobler tendencies. I was perfectly conscious of the fact that I was Spirit and that my neighbour, however outwardly repulsive he might be, was Spirit too. When I looked at anyone I saw his outer person as a mere surface appearance. Within it, in his heart region, there was a calm centre of divine peace. It remained unchanged no matter how educated the surface self was and untarnished no matter how evil that self acted.

I no longer looked either for the worst in him or for the good in him but accepted him just as he was for that was the way he was. Never again could I condemn him too harshly. Each person I met was indeed a part of my own consciousness. I automatically and sympathetically identified myself with him or with anyone from whom I received a letter. I entered metaphorically into his shoes and shared his outlook, hopes, understanding, and, even, limitations. My enemy was explained too: how and why he could not help being so. In this immense sympathetic sweep, I even ventured to justify him against me.

The time came when this attitude developed to an extreme. I did not know how to stop losing myself in the process of absorbing the other man into my own entity, so that he became a part of it, too often an incongruous part. What he thought or felt was reflected in my own consciousness like an image in a mirror. So if he told me something which did not correspond to the thought in his mind I immediately became aware of his discrepancy. It was sympathy lifted to a degree which amounted to empathy.

This faculty brought many unpleasant registrations to my mind and began to make life intolerable. Not until some time later, when I had had enough of it, was I told and taught by the Interior Word that the condition was only a preliminary one and now needed to be brought under strict control. I was warned that I did not need to effect harmony with others on the plane of their ego. Help was given me for the cure of this condition but I, on my part, had to make a positive exercise of the will for many months and a definite withdrawal of attention from others as well. Gradually these phenomena disappeared until I became quite free of them.

Although I did not get any cosmic revelation in those days, I did feel in a general way that behind the universe there was extreme beneficence, that whatever happened had its place in the Infinite Purpose. No event was merely a chance one. The Infinite Wisdom was behind all human life and fortune. I felt that this applied just as much to so-called evil events and calamitous happenings if only we could interpret them correctly. This strongly intuitive feeling made me happy and I wanted to share it with others and to get them to rise above their own experience into it.

But paradoxically I did not feel any necessity to talk to them, even to friends, about these new experiences unless they themselves were seeking the inner life. On the contrary, it seemed sacrilegious to divulge promiscuously what had happened to me. So I deliberately concealed the fact of their existence. This was because I soon found that to preach truth to the mass of people was of no use. They could not grasp it and it was better to be silent about it except to those few who were themselves on the verge of the Quest. I was taught inwardly, and confirmed by disappointment, that people stand on different levels of moral character, intuitive comprehension, and purpose in life, and I was warned to cease to try to proselytize, and to let the unready go their way while I went mine.

The supreme lesson of all experience must first be learned by undergoing experience itself. There was no other way at that stage. What could I do for those who would not seek themselves, but only objects outside themselves? They sought to impose more and more fetters on their minds and hearts; I to point out the way which could lead to a free and fetterless existence. The two directions were directly opposite one another. My time could be more usefully occupied with those who, having experienced the results of travel in the one and satiated or disenchanted with these results, were at last ready for travel in the other direction.

I prayed to become a clear channel for the unhindered flow of inspiration, goodness, and truth to such persons, to those who were seeking for these things. As regards the unreceptive majority, I found it was more practical just to let the feeling of beneficence reflect itself through me to them as sincere goodwill and outward kindness. In some way and at some future time, the Spirit from which these two emanated would touch their subconscious being and affect them, help them or uplift them when eventually it succeeded in rising to the conscious mind. The result might be slight or great, but it was certain.

During the years which elapsed, nothing dislodged me from those attitudes. If I would no longer try to push the truth upon others, neither would I let them push me out of it; and if they tried to, I could only silently smile at their foolish arguments. Experience itself was better than their arguments. I preferred to believe in the awareness which always remained with me than in the merely theoretical reasons for its non-existence.

It ought now to be made clear that these two initiations were mystical ones and not philosophic. They enabled one to see the inner meaning of his own life, but not of all life. They concerned the "I" and gave knowledge of the True Self. They did not concern the universe and the human relation to it. Those subjects belonged to the field of a philosophic initiation which came much later and was my fourth in line. That was an event which interpreted all other events. While still including the mystical initiation, there was blended into it the fuller perception of a Cosmic Knowledge.

I discovered that there are progressive degrees of the mystical initiation leading to progressive degrees of the Cosmic one in turn. I have no experience beyond the first of the Cosmic degrees. Yet even that slight unveiling taught me that the immense mystery which surrounds us will ever remain a mystery. The human entity is not competent to cope with more than a very limited degree of knowledge and still remain human. There is an iron ring around what it can know, a ring that we cannot pass beyond.

What I went through in these initiations may fairly be described as finding the True self—that impersonal part of us which is covered over and effectively hidden by the personal ego. But the second time I found it in a very different way from that of the first, when the discovery had been tremendously emotional, excitedly rapturous, and ebulliently joyous. The second discovery was quiet, strong, and poised. This does not mean that it did not bring an intense glowing satisfaction: but all feeling was perfectly controlled by the sense of dominant will, of the higher purpose fulfilling itself rigidly. Indeed, I learned later that one of the tests of the greater enlightenment is the extraordinary calm in which it happens—a calm like the one which follows the violent monsoon storm in the tropics. To write that this inner peace is perfect is no literary overstatement or emotional colouring, but an accurate factual description. "Come unto Me all ye that are weary and heavy laden and I will give you rest" is still as true today as when spoken by the Christ-Consciousness through Jesus nearly two thousand years ago.

In the first initiation I had only a vague notion of what was happening to me. This was partly because of its unfamiliarity, partly because I had little knowledge of the subject at the time, and partly because I lacked intellectual development at that early age. In the second one there was not only more understanding of the experience but better adjustment to it. Again, after the earlier experience, I found myself reverting to a child's simplicity, trust, and openness. But after the latter one there was a desire to add whatever discrimination, wisdom, and practicality that my experience and study had since been able to garner. These two tendencies existed side by side and seemed to accommodate each other without difficulty. There was no conflict between reason and intuition or between reason and faith.

Nor was this the only result of a paradoxical nature: there was another. When I lived in the Himalayas I felt especially during full-moon periods like the solitary inhabitant of an unpeopled planet. It is not easy even today to forget those unbelievable mountains where silence is total and absolute, where nature seems to be meditating and man seems to be intruding. When I shut my door on the bustling world and retire first within my room and then within myself, it is as if I again enter into that still Himalayan world. There is utter silence within me. If I engage in work at the desk or go out into the bustling streets and mingle with people, it is as though a current is flowing steadily and incessantly through my heart—the current of that same inner peaceful silence.

4

ve here given an account of a way of expressing spirituality in lif
s fit for our time; however ancient be this way, I have described i
tly because I speak a language and have to encounter environment
he ancients never spoke or encountered.

5

ke the most obscure truths easily intelligible, to translate the
mbol into plain communication, is a noble work.

6

o "demystify"—if the term may be invented—the hotch-potch,
es and the subtleties, the difficulties, the condensations and the
tions which fill this literature, and to render it readable.

7

pen times, when most information, many opinions, and much
ooner or later finds its way into print, lecture, and discussion,
need to torment oneself with study of writings, antique or
ich deliberately clothe ideas in fantastic forms, in baffling
r hide meaning under layers of meaninglessness.

8

once-abstruse truths of mentalism into works readable, un-
nd nontechnical—just as had been done with yoga—was a
made with enthusiasm but now, so many years later, its
ns even greater than it did then.

9

e who, stupefied by convention, do not comprehend that
he truth of these ideas is not to be settled by the fact that
in an informal vivid way rather than in a prim academic
down in this way because the custodians of philosophy
time-spirit and want to make them more accessible to
ey have been in the past. But this could not be done
sticism and metaphysics out of their verbal mummy-

10

anishing age of foolish imposture when man's evolu-
ands its very disappearance is the very reverse of my

11

once said to me in India: "Although we are writing
man in the street, nevertheless let them be philo-
netaphysically accurate even from the standpoint of

Now I come to a metaphysical result of the second initiation. In the earlier one, I seemed to expand the ego with love and delight. In the later one, I seemed to attenuate it with perception and revaluation. Just before it happened I felt that some drastic and highly important event was about to develop. When it did happen the feeling was soon explained. There was a sloughing off of the old self which was followed by a sense of immense relief. It was as if a tremendously heavy and burdensome topcoat had been thrown off my shoulders. The sense of being liberated was immeasurable. The ego's dominance was gone. I could see now how it had confined my thinking and dimmed my outlook.

It was simultaneously a kind of death and also a kind of birth—or rebirth—for in that life which was Essence I felt that the wishes, desires, attachments, and ambitions of the unreal self were futile, unnecessary, and vain. The entire existence to which they belonged was a dreamlike show, a passing cinema film. Those persons who were satisfied with such an existence were satisfied with a mere shadow of a shadow. They did not even suspect what the substance which cast the shadow really was, nor where it was, nor how to find it. This substance was the Infinite Life and Infinite Consciousness. It alone was real and eternal. Everything else was only a shadow-shape which merely reflected it. When later in the Near East an old Adept of the Hebrew Mystic Kabbala told me that its major text teaches that the Real Man lives like a sun in Heaven while only the shadow-man lives on earth, I immediately caught his meaning.

All the people I had ever known in the past or in the present, all the events of forgotten years as well as well-remembered ones, temporarily became nothing more than dreamlike figures in the mind, envisioned happenings in the consciousness, during this second initiation. If one of my own thoughts could suddenly become me, the thinker, the transformation would be something like the one which happens when the ego becomes the Overself. For I myself am nothing other than a thought in the Overself-Consciousness.

Yet that discovery delighted me. I did not seem to care. My surface individuality was going or perhaps was gone, but, somehow, something mysteriously remained that was anonymous, nameless, universal, and absolute. That was the immeasurably important Essence of me: not the other with the petty desires and little idiosyncrasies, which had wasted my time for years and distracted me from the true significance of my life. Here, in this impersonal Being, I really belonged, lived, and found happiness.

After this it was easy to see why people welcome the condition of deep dreamless sleep. This is not only for the obvious reason of physical and mental recuperation, but also because it frees them from personal being, offers them an escape from the world and its care. This same freedom entered into knowledge of the Overself, but with a difference that the same happiness which is derived from deep sleep is here consciously enjoyed. Such happiness is really inseparable from awareness of the Overself. The reward of giving up the ego-sense is the ability to live in the deepest part of one's deepest being—the Overself.

Thus it became clear from both these initiations that it was all-important to rid the mind of the ego, or rather, of its crushing tyranny. This could not be the result of a single and sudden act, nor of years of disciplinary toil, but of a combination of the one leading to the other, of the Long Path leading to what is called the Short Path.

Although it properly belongs to my experience of philosophic initiation, it is perhaps interesting to note at this point that in the deep meditations accompanying that initiation I went through a stage where the ego's consciousness was annihilated so utterly and where pure consciousness, not centered or divided in any way, was so overwhelming that God alone reigned as I AM. There was then no duality of person and Overself, no hint even of the cosmic mysteries involved in the vanished world's existence.

And that is really the Truth: there is no second entity or power. There is only God.

[Editors' note: The two essays that form this chapter were composed when the author was in his mid-fifties. People who knew him both during and after this period generally observe that the most significant phases of his development were yet to come, during his subsequent twenty-five years. Readers will find these essays helpful in estimating whether individual paras in the following pages date from earlier or later years.]

PHI

CONTEMPO

Grand truths and common spee

Born in the previous century, I
to those who are only one-third
only in a vastly changed world b
and the past. Perhaps there are
should be made. The first is th
hood, I too was a protester a
questions and doubts galore
became a seeker after truth
results that seem to me to

My writings are prim
verbal technicalities and
dull texts of professio
profits nobody excep
fashion in academic
at the work of Russe
were regarded as b
succeeded in win
succeeded in free

It seems to h
first inkling of
other people
sophic cultu

I ha
which
differe
which

To m
world-sy

I tried
the disguis
circumlocu

In these
knowledge
there is no
medieval, w
symbolism, o

To put the
derstandable, a
further effort I
importance see

There are thos
the question of t
they are set down
one. They are set
feel the democrati
the masses than th
without taking my
wrappings.

To help restore a
tion imperiously der
aim.

Dandapani, a guru,
popular works for the
sophically correct and

advanced students. Let us not mislead the masses while simplifying our
doctrine for them."

12

Blunt speech and plain writing have their place too, along with flowery
prose and poetic colour; but in this matter of secret paths and unfamiliar
quests and higher states of consciousness, they are even more indispensable than symbolic terms, metaphoric phrases, or enigmatic sentences.

13

In some of my later works I tried to clear up, through the aid of science
and plain language, many of the mysteries which have been locked up in
the old *Upanishads* beyond the understanding of modern people like ourselves.

14

The Indians have written the most important philosophic statement of
all—"All is Brahman"—which I have transposed, possibly to their frowns,
as "All is Mind." But one cannot go on repeating it all the time. There are
other statements which need to be made, less important but still much to
the point for us who have to live in the twentieth century.

15

In these writings it has been necessary to stress certain points and to pass
lightly over others; to develop certain features, because the writing is
primarily for a particular type of Western reader. The attempt was made to
interest in Indian wisdom the general reader of literature who is thoughtful and a seeker after knowledge. It was also written in an attempt to clarify
Indian wisdom for the few who are already interested in it, but who have
not the time, patience, or opportunity to go more deeply into it.

16

In order to help others it is sufficient to bring forward the religious and
mystical aspects of this teaching. Metaphysics gives an intellectual grasp of
the same thing that religion gets hold of through faith. Mysticism gives an
intuitive grasp of it and philosophy makes the individual wholly one with
it—in life as in thoughts, in conduct as in feeling. The religious man
believes in the truth of God's existence, the mystical man *feels* it intermittently within himself, the metaphysical man *learns* about it rationally, and
the philosophic man believes, feels, knows, and applies it in action everywhere and at every moment. The average person, however, is far from
philosophical and therefore is indifferent to philosophy's ideas. So it will
be enough at first to make known the religious and mystical ideals and
ideas.

17

The soul does not hunger for dry monographs, but for words that are *alive*, words that spring up from a profound devotion, inspiration, and dedication to the highest being. I have not the time nor the will to meander through a system of metaphysics—and neither, perhaps, has the average reader of today.

18

Perhaps my book may break a few of the glass houses of contemporary illusions.

19

There is always the temptation to *over*simplify such an obscure and complex subject. But to do this would be to fall into a snare and to take the reader with one.

20

This work of reinterpreting the universal and perennial mystical philosophy is not to be regarded as being the same as propagating the doctrines of some mystical Oriental cult.

21

Must a mystic walk about looking like an early Christian martyr? And write his books accordingly?

22

The introduction of artistic style in the exposition of philosophical truth need not necessarily attenuate that truth, if it is carefully done. That is my aim. After all, so many "dry" expositions already exist that a change may interest people who otherwise pass the subject by. Art can rouse interest in an uninteresting theme. The Oriental philosophies are expressed generally in too cryptic and complicated a style. Paul Deussen has pointed out the great value of the artistic style used by the Greeks in the presentation of their philosophies, as compared with the syllogistic systematizing method used by the Hindus.

23

New philosophers are afoot in the world today. New words for old thoughts.

24

I prefer to say lightly what our wise ones say laboriously and heavily; that does not mean that I am less sincere than they.

25

There are certain matters which will inevitably arise more readily in the mind of a Westerner than of an Oriental, merely because the life and needs of the two are different. Hence I felt justified in going further and making explicit what was implicit in the teachings.

26

I am striking out a path of my own. Therefore my latest writings will not please many who do not understand that in this way I am carrying forward the quest and not, as they wrongly believe, departing from it.

27

My aim is to popularize truth, if possible, yet I shall take care not to pay the price of dilution or distortion for such popularization.

28

If a spiritual message is to find any acceptance among the educated or half-educated younger generation of today, it will have to be presented in an intellectual manner. The only explanation of mysticism which will satisfy the world today is a scientific explanation. Hence I have tried to explain these doctrines in such a way that the reader who understands one of them may advance to the next in a logical development. I have offered to lead him up the steps of irresistible logic towards truth.

29

I tried to make this exposition of philosophical doctrines easier to read than those expositions which I myself had to read.

30

It is true that my writings represent a simplification of the philosophy of truth and that therefore they do not adequately cover the ground, but this is not to say that they represent a distortion of it.

31

This teaching is presented as an independent one because its intellectual form and external practices are being organically re-created afresh in the light of altered conditions due to human evolution as well as to meet the needs of twentieth-century civilization.

32

Must every writer express the profoundest spiritual experiences in the most tedious sentences he can find?

33

We shall set up no new gods. On the other hand, neither shall we acclaim or deny the gods of the past.

34

My work is not only to state the old wisdom but even more to clarify it. Hence my work is not expository but clarificatory.

35

We shall engage in no sterile polemics, nor invite men to winnow mere words. But those who seek new thoughts, finer experiences, and truer realizations will find this frontier open and free.

36

It would be an egoistic error for anyone to proclaim to our generation that he alone has found eternal laws, universal truths, and spiritual principles which the ancients did not know. But it would be only a simple statement of fact to say that P.B. was among the few writers in modern times to formulate these laws, truths, and principles in clear understandable language free from all mystery-mongering and cult-pushing.

37

We do not seek to shine in the firmament of literature. We do not compete for a place among great writers. It is enough for this pen if it can communicate something of the knowledge we have gleaned, the consciousness we have gained of the possibilities of a transcendental existence for men. If therefore we are accused, as we often are accused by academic metaphysicians, disdainful mystics, superior yogis, and highbrow literateurs, of being nothing better than a journalist, we humbly plead guilty. Only it should be added in fairness that we have something quite celestial to report. Are these writings less true because they refuse to wear the sedate dress of academic respectability or because they refuse to conform to the stiff obsolete and feeble style which is supposed to be natural for mystics, metaphysicians, and philosophers? Are they to be condemned, as some reviewers have condemned them, because their ideas are conceived and expressed with an almost journalistic plainness of appeal to the man in the street? If this is to be the era of the common man, if the war has brought his right to a fuller life to belated recognition, if the higher teachings of mysticism and philosophy are to be placed at last within his grasp, are we not serving him by striving to make the abstruse simple, the abstract understandable, and the metaphysical interesting?

38

I must plead for patience. But I do this only to clear the ground of the debris of ages and to unfold mysticism at its best in a coherent and clear manner—the heretofore little-known higher mysticism which is utterly beyond such taints, defects, and blemishes.

39

Even ancient wisdom will serve us, provided it be presented in a form that is adequate to the cultivated modern mind.

40

I have taken the abstruse Tibetan teachings, for instance, and shorn them of their formidable subtleties, their Oriental names and terms, their technical words and foreign phrases.

41

I have excavated some truths out of the Orient's past and published a portion of them, but I have rejected many more as unsuited to my time.

42

Although we have rigidly set our face against taxing the eyes of readers with unfamiliar Sanskrit, there is no reason why, if the English language has absorbed so many merely marketplace Asiatic words like "curry" and "bungalow," it should not also absorb a couple of valuable metaphysical words like "karma" and "yoga" which, in any case, have already been granted this new linguistic nationality by dozens of Western writers.

43

Moreover such is the misuse of philosophical terminology by those who would dilute it with religion and such is the misunderstanding of Sanskrit words which have passed through the alembic of theological pedants and theosophical pundits that we shall have to re-define afresh every important technical term as it appears. Nor shall we hesitate to invent new words if necessary to explain our meaning where the old ones fall short of it, for the dictionary is our servant, not our master. And every word will be an English one. We soon weary of reading an article whose solid English pages are stippled with unfamiliar unintelligible Sanskrit words. The West will not absorb Oriental wisdom unless it is entirely presented in Western language.

44

Here it is in explicit language—not trying to impress you with enigmas or stun you with paradoxes.

45

We have to take the truth about God out of the monastery and relate it to the world today, the nuclear physical knowledge of today, and the altered ways and views of today.

46

The most effective method of propagating spiritual truth in this modern age is undoubtedly the radio. The printed word can only be a secondary medium. But propaganda is not quite the same as education. Radio propaganda is the most effective of all methods for bringing new ideas to people who have never heard them before, and for inspiring individuals with right feeling and enthusiasm. But the printed word is necessary where deep thinking and repeated reflection are required in order to master difficult points. Therefore the awakening of unenlightened people and the encouragement of enlightened beginners to spiritual truth is best done through the radio, but the instruction and assistance of more advanced students is best done through the printed word. An adequate scheme should cover both methods. The printed word is essential chiefly for the intermediate and advanced students who are scattered in various parts of the world in loneliness and isolation and who have no personal teacher to instruct them.

47

The West not only needed instruction in the art of meditation, but it needed *specific* instruction.

48

I wanted those books, in their humble measure, to be a grace to others— or at least to serve them in some way.

49

I have attempted to make clear to the man in the street certain subtle and recondite matters which are usually difficult enough to make clear even to specialized students of them.

50

I have tried to put in plainer language that which was so long withheld from the majority of people because it was deemed to be too philosophic for their understanding.

51

In all this writing I have sought not to found the latest church but to formulate the oldest intuitions.

52

An extract from H.P. Blavatsky's *Lucifer* magazine: "If the voice of the mysteries has become silent for many ages in the West, if Eleusis, Memphis, Antium, Delphi, and Cresa have long been made the tombs of a Science once as colossal in the West as it is yet in the East, there are successors now being prepared for them. We are in 1887 and the nineteenth century is close to its death. The twentieth century has strange developments for humanity."

53

When I undertook to raise mysticism to sane acceptable and useful standards, I undertook a job which was crying out to be done.

54

I had to indulge the Western pride in its intellectualism and scientific achievement, or rather to seem to do so, while leading the Western reader to question its values and its deficiencies.

55

It had to be written at this point in the world's evolution, to lead people to look to God alone, not to organizations, churches, and half-illumined guides: hence the book could not have been written earlier.

56

The Western world does not want abstract metaphysics alone. It wants also tangible results, visible demonstration, and practical guidance. And because I wrote chiefly for my Western fellows, I endeavoured to bring this subject down from the rarefied atmosphere in which I found it in the East, and to make plain its bearing on common life.

The need for spiritual education

57

The books were written out of passionate feeling for truths and matters higher than those which ordinarily occupy people's minds. The hope was to make the readers feel something of what the writer felt and to establish the fact that there is a Reality beyond and behind existence, of which we are a part. The books had their own particular work to do. It was to awaken interest in it, to arouse the mind to the existence of man's higher goal, and to give both the impulse to search for truth and the urge to practise what the truth requires.

58

What seemed to be needed was to bring into mystical understanding and theory something of the precision which is so valuable a feature of modern science. Instead of getting lost in vague generalities or sentimental rhapsodies, as usually happened, a careful analysis of mystical technique and experience would surely be the most helpful service a writer on the subject could give his readers.

59

This kind of research has been a lifelong activity and not all the results have been reported. Perhaps it is because there is too much sectarianism in the atmosphere for a full, impartial, and free discussion. But the legacy of truth is needed, important, and at some unknown time it shall be made known.

60

I did not *seek* to become the formulator of such a unique and priceless message to mankind. Indeed knowing myself in weakness as well as strength, I naturally shrink from seeking such an immense responsibility and would rather have helped and served a worthier man to formulate the message. This is not to say that I underrate its value, its dignity, its public prestige. But all my previous attempts to evade the task having ended in failure, I now positively and affirmatively—no longer reluctantly and hesitantly—step forward to its accomplishment. I do so moreover with tranquil joy, for I am utterly convinced in the deepest recess of my heart, no less than in the logical thinking of my brain, that the teaching is so greatly needed in our time by those who have sought in vain for comprehensive elucidation of the problem of their existence, that I feel the help it will give them constitutes the best possible use of my energies, talents, and days in this incarnation.(P)

61

I have not planted in vain. My teachings have already borne a little fruit. Although I have refused to set myself up formally on the teacher's dais, nevertheless teaching has somehow been going on. Through books, letters, interviews, and even meditations, men and women have been guided, counselled, instructed, perhaps inspired, upon this age-old quest of the Overself.

62

"Help me through written words to meet their need: the seekers, the baffled, and the hopeless."—A Writer's Prayer by P.B.

63

For a great peace filled my heart. The white splendour of a hope that had seemed a mirage now flamed out of the lost years. It turned the dark past into a lighted avenue that led up the Hill of Patience to the House of Fulfilment. So stick to this quest with the iron determination not to stop until you have realized the truth. Don't worry about the remoteness of the goal; leave all the results to fate and do the best you can. With proper guidance, the goal can be brought infinitely nearer than it seems. Those who know truth want to share it—what else do they care for? Make up your mind and progress from can't to can!

64

I consider it a God-sent privilege to myself and a possible source of blessing to others if I use properly the opportunity of transmitting these revelations.

65

My special work is not public addresses nor private interviews. It is writing—not writing a constant stream of letters, but words which thousands shall read. It is writing about the Quest, arousing people to follow it, guiding those upon it, and explaining the goals at the end of it. My special parish is people who cannot find truth in any existing institution, cult, religion, sect, or creed and who, therefore, can attach themselves to none.

66

To what better use can I put my pen than to give others the assurance that there is a Mind behind the world, a purpose behind their lives?

67

I have withdrawn from the world and now live in retirement, which is not to say that I live in inactivity. But I find that I can help others with less misunderstanding and with more smoothness by confining my efforts to the inner worlds of being and the outer world of occasional writings than by personal intercourse with them. It is easy for me to be in the world and yet not of it. But it is hard for some critics who do not know me—a knowledge which cannot be gained merely by meeting my body, for I habitually screen myself with ordinariness—to understand how this can be.

68

I have a function to perform: the published work is only the first part of it. The other part is independent, creative, original, constructive.

69

In earlier years I communicated verbally through the printed symbols of a published book, but in later ones silently through the telepathic emanation of a felt divine presence. Anyone, anywhere in the English-speaking world might read the one if he cared to, no one could receive the other unless he cared to do so.

70

To bring these magnificent truths to bed upon homely paper was sacred service to them, a worthwhile duty to humanity, and an aesthetic joy to myself.

71

I write, first, because my mind seeks such expression, which gives me joy and peace, and second, to be of service to others.

72

This book of practical guidance became necessary when men and women, finding no real personal help in rhetorical books, no actual and positive result after reading so many sonorous pages, asked for it.

73

"My Initiations": (a) There is the additional reason of leaving a testimony since I am nearing the period when age and death are often friends.

There are others, either in this generation or in posterity, who will find themselves searching as I once searched, and to whom a clue, a map, a confirmation of the treasure's real existence may mean much.

(b) The time I spent analysing the delicate processes of meditation for the benefit of those who have yet to master its art, as well as the lengthy research and study made for the sake of developing theory and increasing knowledge, turned out later to be well spent, for the descriptions I was later able to give in published writings proved helpful to many who read them. And I see also that to record spiritual experiences and the steps leading to them with some of the detailed precision of a laboratory report may serve a useful purpose. It may guide those who are studying it as a new subject and encourage the seekers of a younger generation who are now pressing behind me.

74

The best of being a writer is the opportunity given to show man his true worth, to lift up his own idea of himself, to persuade him that trivial aims are not enough.

75

My inner labours do not express themselves wholly through these writings. Those who are intuitively sensitive to such ideas and personally sympathetic to their transmitter may be touched at times on a purely mental non-physical plane of being.

76

We must not shrink from revealing this, the most sacred of all experiences, if it adds one more testimony to divine existence. For in this age of materialism and scepticism, existentialism and nihilism, every affirmation of the opposite kind has increased value—even illumination must be shared with those still in darkness.

77

This book is made dedicate to that Sage of the Orient at whose behest these pages were written: to one incredibly wise and ceaselessly beneficent. And, further, I have wrapped this book in the bright orange-chrome coloured cloth even as you have wrapped your body in cloth of the same colour—the sannyasi's colour—the mark of one who has renounced the world as you have. And if the dealings of the cards of destiny bid me wear cloth of another hue, command me to mix and mingle with the world and help carry on its work, be assured that somewhere in the deep places of my heart, I have gathered all my desires into a little heap and offered them all unto the Nameless Higher Power.(P)

78

People feel the need of some kind of communion or communication with the Higher Power, be it ceremonial worship, verbal prayer, or silent meditation. One whose job is to state in words the possibility of such communion, to describe its actual realization, and to portray its supreme upliftings of emotion and sublime openings of consciousness is as needed by the world as is any other worker whose contribution is useful, worthwhile, or needed.

79

"You will raise an ancient statue, now lying half-buried in the sand, and reveal it as a thing of worth." This was the prediction made to me by Brother M.

80

There is no special urge to bring others to repent, but there is a feeling that as a writer one can be used to bring them to inner quietude. It will make them better and happier persons, and they need to know that it can be found, felt, established, and that the time accorded to the search could hardly be better used.

81

Turn the work of service entirely over to the Master, refuse to accept any personal responsibility for it. Do everything there in His name alone. Hand all these people over to him.

82

I have been telling others for years that their situations and experiences have meaning and purpose because all life has meaning and purpose. I garnered this lesson in my first flash of cosmic consciousness, but reason alone can tell us the same thing.

83

He is never really isolated from the world. For his thoughts do telepathically reach those who value them, his written letters and published words do constitute some kind of communication and even conversation.

84

He does not know and does not need to know the various personal problems of disciples as and when each one arises. This is because he does not assume the role of a *personal* master, hence does not pry into their mental and emotional states. This does not mean that he is not helping them. He does. But he is able to do so without opening the doors of his conscious mind. The subconscious doors are always open and through them there enters each disciple's call and there emerges his response.

85

He is not the conscious leader of any movement, and yet a following of grateful and reverent people whom he has helped, awakened, or healed trails behind him. He does not try to give them guidance directly and yet they do receive it, however incidentally.

86

It is the business of my books to act as awakeners rather than as teachers, to make people aware of their higher possibilities and of the obstacles or limitations within themselves which hinder their realization.

87

He is not a guru, so he does not take anyone under his care. But he is ever ready to give to others if the Power bids him give inner help.

88

These thoughts are the progeny of fact, strict and scientific. I am no poet, giving to airy nothings a local habitation and a name!

89

It is not without its use to others to affirm, in a materialistic age, that this spiritual self is a matter of personal experience rather than of mere theory. One need not necessarily make such affirmation out of vanity.

90

In many cases the Brunton books have been the start of their spiritual education. They have been awakened and given direction. Afterwards they go on to find teachers, schools.

91

Some may get from this reading not only the intellectual help necessary to understand difficult points but also the good fortune of a spiritual glimpse.

92

To raise the half-buried, half-petrified figure of meditation from the desert sand, expose and clean it, explain and publicize it—this was only a first task. To advance further and awaken the juniors who undertook this inner work to the truth of mentalism—this was a second task.

93

I refuse to write letters under pressure of business and hurry the words and sentences because of lack of time. I prefer to reduce the size of my letters, perhaps to a single paragraph, perhaps to a single sentence, maybe even a short phrase; but if these are pregnant with meaning they will suffice.

94

It is better to make himself silent for some seconds at the beginning of

the meeting—even though the other person is disconcerted by the silence—for then the host will receive a truer impression about the other's
mental and emotional condition and may also receive from a still higher
source some guidance as to how to deal with, and what to say to, the
guest, the questioner, or the contact.

95

Out of the tranquillity and beauty of deep meditation, I have plucked
for others a few exotic blossoms redolent with spiritual fragrance and offer
them in the hope that they may bring from the mysterious region of their
source some suggestion of the peace and truth I found there.

96

So I will play the part of the psychoanalyst for a moment and show the
world its own subconscious.

97

I have no intention of wandering into the uncertain realms of metaphysical morals nor of flying in a balloon into the clouds of moral metaphysics.

98

I am less concerned in this book with proving my propositions than
with laying them down and setting them firmly in our sight; for they are
their own justification and need little evidence to reveal their truth.

99

The book will render you a service, even without changing your life and
habits, by merely making you believe in the possibility of such a change.

100

I intend not only to leave marks on paper, but also on the foe of
materialism. I hope to throw several stupidities prone on the platform of
literary debate. I want to wield the two-edged sword of truth, whose
razor-edged and lancet-pointed thrusts may serve to do for the cause of
mysticism what several think but few say. I do not doubt but that I shall
carry off not a few carcasses of priestly rancour and pleasure-soaked
fatuities to the crematorium. But in donning the casque and visor and
hacking for the benefit of public enemies, I shall not forget to keep the
kindly smile and brotherly clasp for the benefit of private friends, the
followers of inward light, and for all men of goodwill.

101

I was allowed to enter several retreats and homes where these teachers
dwelt, and to stay or study for a while. They were the greatest seers and
mystics of these times, and the uniqueness of my privilege becomes clearer
every year—as none of the same high quality arise to replace them. This

autobiographical note with its seemingly egotistical details, is necessary to help explain why these books were written.

102

My writings were never intended to be didactic and I never intended to be a teacher. They serve the purpose of enabling me to *share* ideas, not to impose them.

103

My work is to awaken intuition and to instigate research. It is to affirm the precepts of truth as well as to argue the logic of it.

104

Readers of my books have occasionally written to me in the hope I can *prove* to them that the doctrines there presented are true. This I regret being unable to do. I can prepare a powerful case, and in some instances have tried to do so; but, like all cases, a trained mentality should be able to demolish them. This is as it must be, but it should be remembered that the powers of the logical intellect are—and must always remain—limited by the amount of factual material and experience available to it. There is only one way anyone can be certain of the truth of these statements. He must take to the Quest and keep on the Quest, until the Overself reveals itself to him. Indeed, more people know in their own personal histories the concrete proof of these statements than the public generally dreams of.

105

Experience alone may have already taught them several philosophic truths, but these writings may help people become more fully conscious of them. Such are the power and beauty of universal ideas that some people may arrive at them immediately by intuition as soon as the eyes read them on a printed page but others only ultimately after a long and toilsome course of study. Then there are those who will feel an intuitive response to these statements even where they cannot yield an intellectual one. Conversely, there are others who will yield intellectual assent although no inward stirring certifies their judgement. But all types will know that they have been lifted to higher levels of thought and conduct as a result.

106

I now want to help such keener spirits to move forward on the path and find a fuller life, that of truly universal being, that of the Overself as the ALL, and not merely as the sacred spirit in man.

107

If we point to the spiritual sphinx of our time, we at least attempt to answer its riddle.

108

I have never been in want of a subject on which to write. Philosophy is as wide as the world and its research has been my ruling power.

109

I conceded the truth of mysticism in order to lead the reader to give up his self-identification with the material body. I advocated the practice of yoga in order to discipline his mind into utter calmness and thus prepare it for the study of higher truths later on.

110

A book like this must necessarily savour somewhat of egoism in the writer, and that cannot be helped. The truth is that we all are egoists, only some are unpleasantly so while others retain a refined feeling of considerateness.

111

I have never thought of my book-writing as a branch of commerce; it has always been a part of my ideal of service.

112

I have several excuses for continuing to inflict my screeds upon the public. One of them has been well put by Arthur Machen: "When you are condemned by the gods to write," he said, "you can't leave off." Another is that I wrote down these creative ideas not only because of the wish to assist other seekers but also because of the struggle to work out my own intellectual salvation. Much of my writing has thus not only been an attempt at communication but also an effort to work out my personal salvation: I wrote for myself as well as for others. For, as explained in so many prefaces, I am only a student of these matters and not a master. In the words of Saint Paul, "I count not myself to have attained." This is partly why I seem to have fallen into inconsistency. But every growing thing is inconsistent with its former self. Consistency belongs to the cemetery alone. Between the time when I wrote the first book and the time when I wrote the tenth book, there was an advance in capacity and an evolution in outlook. The shift of emphasis and the transference of interest which my writings show are the natural result of fuller inner maturation and further outer experience.

The third excuse may appear less credible in a cynical and self-centered world. Yet it happens to be true. And it is true only because I feel the presence and command of the Overself continually beside me, not because of any virtue in my own self. But for this I would certainly be as cynical and self-centered as so many others. Grinding overwork has tyrannized my head and hands for years. I have long promised myself freedom, but know that I shall probably never take it. Yet freedom is already there, I have only to stretch forth my hand and it will lie within my grasp. Why then do I submit to unending slavery? The answer can be given in a single word— compassion! Those whose personal malice prevented them from believing this during my lifetime will have to believe it as soon as I have gone. And I shall not be sorry to go. But that is another story. If I can persuade or at least encourage some people to tread a higher path rather than a lower one, to look for guidance to spiritual rather than materialist sources, to think rightly about God as well as their fellows, it will make me feel that one of my life-tasks has been accomplished. So it is something real for me to want others to have it, too. Also, this realization seems to me to be just what we have been put on this earth to find—all the other activities such as earning a livelihood and feeding the body being merely the accessories which enable us to exist here in order to do so. I have written about it not to obtrude my own personality but in obedience to an overwhelming inner urge. The task itself is an inspiring one. It is not an exaggeration to say that sometimes I felt as if I were bringing humanity messages from another world. Starved souls have found nourishment in these pages that speak of the Overself. These writings have instructed some in the noble truths of philosophy and consoled others in the sad hours of affliction. They have propagated themselves over all the continents. However lightly and however imperfectly, their truths have entered the thoughts and their ideals have suffused the hearts of hundreds of thousands. I have tried to transmit aureoled concepts to my own generation, to lodge new-old spiritualizing tenets in its mind.

113

This book tells not only of what man did for himself but also of what Grace did for him.

114

I do not wish to clothe men in a new faith but rather to get them to stand as giants and shake off the ropes which keep them imprisoned. I want to get them to depend on a fourth dimensional life now that the old existence has utterly failed them.

115

Those earlier books were written not so much to convince others as to show the very real need of a contemplative life to be brought in to counterbalance the active one, not to lead people into monasteries and ashrams for the remainder of their lives as world-renunciates, but to lead them into themselves.

116

I conceive my work to be the blowing of smouldering coals of aspiration into burning flames of inspiration, expressible and visible in the end as altruistic action.

117

I would not trouble to disturb the calm repose of white paper with the following thoughts if misapprehensions concerning their subjects were not so widespread.

118

The work of securing reforms in the social economic and political spheres may seem desirable, but the philosopher feels (and knows) that he must leave all such activities to the men who can perceive nothing higher, nothing more important, than that. He is ironically aware that never before in human history were so many reformers at work as in the past hundred years, so many improvers of other men or of the environmental conditions around them, yet never before were so many menacing situations of appalling possibility the end result of all this work as is the case today. For himself, he thinks he can better use his limited time in seeking to learn and stating for others those higher laws of being which govern men. Without this knowledge they are merely blundering about in the dark and hurting themselves continually.

119

It is well to raise a literary statue to these few principles which the times have obscured and human weakness uncomprehended.

120

It is during such a time of general bewilderment and cultural crisis that we eagerly gaze at the horizon for new teachers who shall proclaim the eternal gospel of the divine significance and purpose of human existence, who shall lead us to the loftier hope and nobler faith without which we cannot live but merely exist as animals exist. Yet such teachers do not appear. It therefore behooves us, who are mere students, blundering wayfarers, to remain silent no longer, but speak, however stammeringly, the broken words whose truth we do know.

121

We prefer to open our holy war in a quiet way, rather than strike the air with the sword of argument to make much battle but little victory.

122

It gladdens me whenever he remembers that he has untiringly sustained men's faith that the divine soul, the Holy Ghost, does dwell in them.

123

What else can I do than drop some words into a mind willing to receive them?

124

Does not my own privacy require that I leave others alone and not try to take on their affairs or problems?

125

I felt that this was a primary task—that someone needed to call the attention of laymen, not only of theological students or religious aspirants, to this now uncommon, obscure, unfamiliar, and neglected yet important side of the spiritual life.

126

My writing is both a form of sharing knowledge and a way of teaching it at one and the same time. It is a response to my natural desire to pass on to others some ideas that have taken their place in my pattern of life-meaning, but it is also an attempt to explain and propagate those ideas for the benefit of these others.

127

It is not for me to lead men or organize movements. I can only stimulate intuition and arouse thought, inspire ideals and explain the higher laws.

128

Whatsoever I have done in the way of attempting to explain the inexplicable experiences of the Overself has been done against my own will and desire, even as my much more illustrious and ancient namesake sank his own personal prejudices and set out on the dangerous task of converting the Graeco-Roman world to the Christian gospel which he had himself discovered with such dramatic unexpectedness. The parallel runs still more closely, for just as Saint Paul confessed that he was going forth "as a liar yet telling the truth" so I feel that few will give credence to the plain records of divine experiences nowhere to be seen in the marketplace and of apparently supernatural phenomena nowhere to be found in the laboratory, which it has been my unsought task to write down. And if this comparison with one who after all was but a tent-maker by vocation be not too presumptuous, I have at least freed myself from the other man's preoccupation with calling men to follow Christ and to join the Christian church, for I call men to follow no other Christ than the quiet Christ-Self rooted deep in their hearts and to join no other church than the unseen one.

129

My work is curiously compounded of a thinker's and an expositor's, a mystic's and an interpreter's, a researcher's and a teacher's.

130

I am trying to found an independent school of thought and not a crystallized school of instruction, to lead the free and mystical tendencies of my time into a wider direction and not to take in hand the individuals displaying them.

Creative independence

131

I must say at once that I do not claim to represent any teacher anywhere of any time, nor orthodox system of religion or metaphysics, mysticism or occultism. None of the representatives of any, very old or more recent, can therefore rightly say that I am giving an incorrect exposition in this writing.

132

With more than forty years spent in these studies and with the observation of thousands of people engaged in their practical application, I have become familiar with most of the leading mystical ideas. What is better is that I have also watched results in practice all over the world. Out of this experience, certain definite conclusions have formed themselves and forced my acceptance. The fact that I belong to no special group, no particular religion, no separate organization, but keep my mind open for truth from any direction with complete independence, has doubtless helped the formulation of these conclusions.

133

I have no use for, so do not keep, my own birthday anniversaries; hence I see no reason for abandoning this view in regard to my friends' anniversaries. The only birthday I like to remember is not the conventional one which emphasizes awareness of the body nor the false one which identifies the "I" with it, but the true one which celebrates a spiritual illumination. That is a day not to be forgotten which awakened the mind to its timeless existence in Mind. Birth into the kingdom of heaven is the only anniversary worth troubling about.

134

I detest those long lingering hesitant and indecisive farewells: they irritate and annoy: they waste time uselessly: they are even worse when the performance is given in public or on the telephone. If there is no other way to take one's leave, no more reasonable and graceful form of exit, I prefer to bolt abruptly. It may appear unkind but it is better for everyone concerned in the end.

135

I could not endure the self-righteousness of those who live in the ashrams, for it was as ugly and hard as the pharisaic, as the self-righteousness of the narrow sects.

136

I held to my individual position, because I wrote and spoke about the necessity of a free search for truth; my position among the groups I visited and the teachers I listened to was an anomalous one.

137

Because my research is independent, because I have no ties to any cult, group, creed, or organization, I have been free to arrive at unbiased conclusions. When I *began* any study or investigation, I gave up my independence of judgement; but when I approached the end, I resumed it.

138

I am by nature a wanderer, a gypsy. But there is no utopian meaning behind my travels. I am not searching for any colony or monastery, group or co-operative, where all live harmoniously together in a paradisal relationship. Only young dreamers and naïve inexperienced enthusiasts look for such places in this world.

139

As a writer I have been my own master. As a student of truth I ended as my own guru.

140

Because I was not a monk, I was able to write for the general public— who also refuse to go so far as to take the vow.

141

Something seemed to ask me, "Do you want to have your ego catered to and pampered like a child, primarily seeking its outer comforts, or will you give up the ego altogether and find peace? The choice you make at this crossroads will also determine the outer fortunes coming to you."

142

Not all the techniques were learned from traditional sources. Some I was forced to originate in the endeavour to provide material suitable to modern seekers.

143

I have accumulated an experience in these matters that is unique.

144

Paul Brunton is trying to do something new. He went to India to learn from the most perceptive Indians, not to copy their followers. Yet the latter at times lack the wide tolerance of their teacher. Merely and politely to disagree with them is denounced as immense arrogance. "Who are you," these followers shout, "to dare to have an opinion contrary to the divine word of our Holy One?" Brunton has the highest regard affection and reverence for these Indian teachers, and especially for the ones who freely initiated him into their knowledge and inner circle. But this regard does not necessarily mean that he is obliged always to agree with them and always to think along with them. Indeed, they did not agree with each other. Those who might deem it ungracious of him to criticize their doctrines at certain points, should know that he speaks not only on his own personal behalf but also with certain sanctions—derived from the most ancient esoteric initiatory Oriental traditions—behind him. Paul Brunton also has something of his own to give. He cannot merely copy these others in living or echo them in writing. He too must be himself just as they were themselves. He may be their friend but he cannot be their follower. If it is for others to be that, he rejoices; but if he is to be true to the light which has come to him, he must shed it by himself, however small it be in contrast to theirs. He may be but a candle to the suns of other guides, but to hide it because their light is greater would be to disobey his own inner voice. There was a time when this same voice bade him give forth the message of a few among those he had sought out and studied with. He gladly did so. But now its bidding is different. He has to speak the Word which he alone can speak, for every individual is unique. Every man is born to be himself, to undergo a set of experiences which in their entirety no one else has undergone. He alone of all the human race has just the mental and emotional psyche which he has.(P)

145

Although I was already travelling the road to the self-discovery of these truths, it is true that an apparently fortuitous meeting with an extraordinary individual at Angkor saved me from some of the time and labour involved in this process. For he turned out to be an adept in the higher philosophy who had not only had a most unusual personal history but also a most unusual comprehension of the problems which were troubling me. He put me through strange initiatory experiences in a deserted temple and then, with a few brief explanations of the hidden teachings, placed the key to their solutions in my hands. But after all it was only a key to the door-chamber itself, and not the entire treasure. These I had to ferret out for myself. That is to say, I was given the principle but had to work out the details, develop the applications, and trace out the ramifications for myself. I was provided with a foundation but had to erect the super-structure by my own efforts. And all this has been a task for many years, a task upon which I am still engaged.(P)

146

I have attempted to think out anew, and on the basis of my own experience and not that of men who lived five thousand years ago, what should be the attitude of a normal modern man toward life. Such blessed independence may be scorned by some, but it is a birthright which I jealously guard.(P)

147

The conventionalists will be able to make nothing of a man whose nonconformity and intractability are entirely spiritual and therefore entirely inward. They will be able to make nothing of a man who belongs to no religious affiliation, no political party, yet who is more devout than any affiliate, more concerned with humanity's welfare than any politician.

148

We shall read these old texts not to treat them as final authorities but to verify our own thought, and we shall quote them only to illustrate it.

149

I have played the vivisector to a representative selection of these cults. Scalpel in hand, I examined their histories, their progenitors, and their followers.

150

Henceforth I shall give the full strength of my devotion not to any ashram or any personality in India's living present, but only to those great principles of truth which are expressed in the *Upanishads*, the *Bhagavad Gita*, and other books belonging to India's dead past.

151

Nevertheless, and paradoxically, this protracted and disappointing experience had been necessary for my spiritual education. I therefore thank Fate for having sent it to me. It strongly revealed the futility of expecting to find truth in an institution and not by one's own solitary striving. It delineated the limitations of discipleship as against the vital need for individual effort, for the disciple is often satisfied that he is progressing when he is merely copying his master by wearing the same clothes, eating the same food, and parrot-like uttering the same phrases. In this tropically enervated country it was a common and dangerous delusion that you had only to find a master and then sit down, basking in the sunshine of his presence, while he wafted you into Nirvana for evermore.

152

Half a century has passed since I went, Sunday morning after Sunday morning, to that quiet Quaker "Meeting-house," as the parishioners of that Buckinghamshire village called their church building. Here George Fox, William Penn, and other pioneer Friends also worshipped. A few months later I left England again to pursue those strange researches in the Orient which destiny had allotted me. Not since then have I been so faithful and regular in religious attendance, going only when the mood is on me, and even then irrespective of what creed that particular house of worship belongs to—be it mosque, church, or temple.

153

It is very different to criticize, not as an opponent or detractor, but as one who is himself a believer, who accepts the ideal, the practice, and the teaching but wants only to push them higher, farther, and wider, to make them more complete. It is unfortunate, and cannot be helped, if this makes me no believer in the orthodox sense.

154

I have witnessed with amazement the names and lives of yogis living in my own time becoming the source of unjustified legends.

155

The fierce independence I have maintained for so many years, the stubborn refusal to part with my freedom at the bidding of any cult or clique, has contributed, I believe, to my salvation.

156

Why should I trouble to drive a golf-ball or sit up nightly over a pack of printed cards? Was it for this that I was born? I am a yogi. I am busy with a game of a higher sort. "If a man does not keep pace with his companions," says Thoreau, "perhaps it is because he hears a different drummer. Let him step to the music which he hears, however measured or far away."

157

I have had opportunities to reach records and meet men not readily accessible to ordinary seekers.

158

He is one of those strange beings who prefers the fate of being a Crusoe among the crowd, a mystic who seeks the society of materialists, and a hermit who haunts the homely hearths of the metropolis.

159

He has had to take a line of his own and withdraw from crowded paths. No party, institution, or cult claim his allegiance. It is certainly a harder way to travel. There is, however, this consolation—that he is not exactly traversing a wilderness, that a few loyal hearts and discerning minds accompany him in such self-sought exile.

160

I have walked with these holy men through both shady mountain forests and steaming jungles, and learned a little of their notions.

161

Sometimes in the still night hours, while the others slept, we—the teacher and myself—could talk alone more privately.

162

I do not belong to any school any more than does my Master. I am an individualist.

163

In my verdant days I would wander around begging a few crumbs of Truth from the table of haughty mandarins who were far older than myself.

164

I had come across this wise man by accident. Therefore I would travel onwards and make some more accidents.

165

I think of myself as being, along with a few others, part of the spearhead of the modern trend in mysticism.

166

As I am an individual isolated from every party, movement, tradition, and sect, it would appear that my contribution to social betterment will be trivial and insignificant, a mere voice in the wilderness. In most other spheres of activity this would be true enough, but in the sphere of truth-seeking and truth-proclaiming it no longer holds good. For the very fact of being dissociated from every conventional influence, every orthodox and traditional group, sets one free to find and give out the truth in a way that these others cannot dare to follow. It raises the value of my results.

167

I believe in constructing my philosophy of life independently out of my own experience, not out of someone else's theories.

168

A man is known by the company he keeps away from! I saw that the Rubicon of my spiritual life had to be resolutely crossed and my boat burned behind me; that the last tight-holding threads of an entire cycle of outer and inner life had to be cut and cut forever.

169

I am no crusader for a queer cult or creed. My sole aim is to bring before my fellows some little-stressed points of worth in the ancient culture of mysticism, and if I support that culture so largely, I do so with a clear recognition of the frailties and follies into which many of its followers have sadly fallen. This temperate attitude towards the old learning and this critical reserve towards its degenerate successors will make me little acceptable to the narrow-minded. But I do not care. Truth is my aim and truth takes a wider orbit than any group of people with their little ideas.

170

If my starting point was the same as that of most other mystics around me, my finishing point was not. I was compelled by the nature of my experience to take a different and independent position. The change that was worked in me could not be kept out of my writings.

171

I am opposed to all forms of totalitarianism, communism, and regimentation. I have witnessed its consequences both under the communistic government and ashram management. I would not submit myself to it nor ask others to do so. Consequently, I am opposed to any colony or group organization being formed which might allow this to happen, whether under a leader with messianic complexes, or under a committee.

172

Louise Maunsell Field, writing a review of *A Search in Secret India* in a New York literary journal, once asked a pertinent question. She said: "The sympathetic reader, following Paul Brunton's experiences, his encounters with other Masters more or less resembling the Maharishee [Ramana Maharshi], cannot but wonder how much influence these Indian mystics have on the teeming millions of their fellow countrymen. Can the intensely spiritual, somewhat rarefied atmosphere wherein they live and move penetrate the lives and thoughts of those many others?" This same question kept on coming into my mind, too. I was forced in the end to give it a negative answer. But this very answer was one of the contributing causes which led me to seek and find the higher teaching.

173

A pundit guide was indispensable for study. It would be quite useless for me or even for the average educated Indian to approach India's literary heirloom and search for her subtlest traditional wisdom without the help of one of these scholarly exponents. Yet it would have been equally useless to place myself in the hands of the average conservative pundit, for he generally followed a cramped religious line or at best a scholastic approach to the question of truth, whereas I had now lost most of my interest in such an approach—although I readily granted its usefulness to others— and could only view things honestly from a rational and scientific angle. Both the selection of suitable texts and the quality of his interpretations would be coloured by the nature of his belief: he would expect me to swallow his whole pantheon of untenable superstitions, as well as many other matters that offered affronts to reason. The verbal protest of disbelief on my part would immediately certify me as unfit and unworthy to profit by his assistance and place me with the outcastes beyond the sacred shrine of his learning. Nor would I care to hurt the man's conscientiously held religious feelings in such a way. How then could I hope to find the books I cared for when he would disdain them for those that suited his personal taste?

174

Working at his own original ideas in an individual and distinctive way, such a person will go farther than the herd man. He can bring fresh helps, devise better techniques, and serve human uplift. The brave determination to go his independent way and not be a mere sheep ambling behind the group may cause him to lose in some matters but to gain in other ones.

175

I became a keen resurrectionist, with the ancient wisdom as the object of my activities. But all this was done as a freelance—independent of any school, group, or organization—and therefore without the bias or restraints, the prejudices or constrictions which follow them.

176

Having made a deep and full research, and having done so outside the limitations imposed by sect or school or guru, I started as an independent, but accepted several teachers on the way, who held different views, and have remained within this independence ever since.

177

I have no organization of any kind to sustain or advocate my teachings.

178

I am not a follower of any cult, Eastern or Western, although my creative, independent, and unorthodox synthesis stretches over the ideas of both hemispheres.

179

All these experiences, disheartening though they were at the time, were not without their useful results. For they aroused me to the folly of pursuing a path of servile imitation and awakened me to the necessity of starting on a path of creative independence.

180

From the knowledge picked up earlier and stored in his head or books, from the experiences of his present life made the subject of reflection, he had generated a kind of wisdom which supported him. From the old thoughts he had drawn out new ones. But the longing was for thought-free Peace, thought-transcending Being.

181

Whatever value there has been in my work of Oriental research, whatever virtue its results possess for the Western reader, derives mostly from the independence with which I approached it, from the lack of bias for or against any particular cult, religion, or school among the many to be found in the Orient.

The challenge of synthesis

182

Such a grand synthesis became the object of my intensive search the more I perceived the fragmentariness of available teachings and the more I discovered the limitations of accessible teachers. But I could not find it and in the end had to construct my own.

183

It is an error to assume that I am a propagandist for any new Western system or old Indian philosophy. The world's present need is not a new Western system of thought but Western *thinkers*; not an old Indian philosophy, but Indian *philosophers*.

184

This is not a personal teaching, peculiar to its author alone. Its fundamental tenets have been taught since the hoariest antiquity, in the Far, Middle, and Near East, as well as in the great Mediterranean cultures. It is true that they were not taught to the generality of people, but that was only because the latter had not reached the needed educational standard to understand and welcome it. It is true also that the author has adapted the teaching to the modern situation but that still leaves its essentials unchanged.

185

Once I took it upon myself to interpret Oriental mysticism to the West. Now after long experience and longer thought, I find it necessary to stand aside from all the dead and living sources of knowledge with which I had established contact, if I am not to misinterpret Oriental mysticism. I am compelled to walk in lonely isolation, even though I respect and honour not a few of those sources. What I learnt and assimilated from them stood finally before a bar of my own making. For I thought, felt, walked, worked, and lived in terms of a twentieth-century experience which, seek as I might, could not be found in its fullness among them. However satisfactory to others, their outlook was too restricted for me. Either they could not come down to the mental horizons of the people who surrounded me, or else they came down theoretically with their heads and not with their hearts. This does not mean that I question their immediate correctness; it means that I question their ultimate usefulness.

It would be as absurd to deduce that I am now inconsistently rejecting mysticism as it would be absurd to declare that I reject the first three letters of the alphabet, merely because I refuse to limit my writing to the combination of ABC alone. I am trying to say that the whole content of mysticism is not identifiable with what is ordinarily known as such; it exceeds the sphere of the latter to such an extent that I have preferred to return to the ancient custom and call it *philosophy*.(P)

186

They alone will comprehend the purport of this volume who can comprehend that it does not only seek to present the pabulum of an ancient system for modern consumption but that it has integrated its material with the wider knowledge that has come to mankind during the thousands of years which have passed since that system first appeared. Consequently we offer here not only a re-statement but also an entirely new and radically fresh world-view which could not have been reached historically earlier.

If we study the history of human culture we shall begin to discern signs of an orderly growth, a logical development of its body. Truth has had different meanings at different periods. This was inevitable because the human mind has been moving nearer and nearer to it, nearer and nearer to the grand ultimate goal. And when we watch the way knowledge has mounted up during the last three centuries we ought not to be surprised at the statement that the culmination of all this long historical process, the end of thousands of years of human search, is going to crystallize in the new East-West philosophy which it is the privilege of this century to formulate. Here alone can the relative interpretations of truth which have been discovered by former men, rise to the absolute wherein they merge and vanish. This means that although truth has always existed, its knowledge has only existed at different stages of development, that we are the fortunate inheritors of the results gathered by past thinkers, and still more that we are now called to complete the circle and formulate a finished system of philosophy which shall stand good for all time.

All the conflicting doctrines which have appeared in the past were not meaningless and not useless; they have played their part most usefully even where they seemed most contradictory. They were really in collaboration, not in opposition. We need not disdain to illustrate the highest abstract principles by the homeliest concrete anecdotes, and we may describe them as pieces in a jig-saw puzzle which can now be fitted together, for now we have the master pattern which is the secret of the whole. Hence all that is vital and valuable in earlier knowledge is contained in the East-West philosophy; only their fallacies have been shed. A full view of the universe now replaces all the partial views which were alone available before and which embodied merely single phases of the discovery of Truth. Thus the analytic movement which uncovered the various pieces of this world puzzle must now yield to a synthetic process of putting them together in a final united pattern. Culture, on this view, is the timeless truth appearing in the world of time and therefore in successive but progressive periods. Only now has it been able to utter its latest word. Only now does philosophy attain its maturest completion. Only now are we able to reap the fruit of seven thousand years of historical philosophy. Only now have we achieved a world-system, a universal doctrine which belongs to no particular place but to the planet. Knowledge has grown by analysis but shall finish by synthesis.(P)

187

Not one but several minds will be needed to labour at the metaphysical foundation of the twentieth-century structure of philosophy. I can claim the merit only of being among the earliest of these pioneers. There are others yet to appear who will unquestionably do better and more valuable work.(P)

188

Henceforth the background of this teaching will be, nay must be, a universal one. It shall resist those who would label it Eastern because they will not be able to deny its Western contents, form, and spirit. It shall resist those who would label it Western, because they too shall not be able to deny its Eastern roots and contents.(P)

189

Even my former books were mostly based on the old outlooks, the old limited viewpoints which the new knowledge transcends.

190

Whatever I owe to their traditions and however much I may have associated with their leading contemporaries, it is the conclusions of my physical and spiritual maturity which should surely count most now. And those conclusions differ in important theoretical and practical matters. I cannot therefore truly call myself an adherent of their schools or an exponent of Oriental yoga.

191

The unerring Wisdom of Providence separated me with pain and protest from limited standpoints, aroused me with shocks from India's glamour, only to unite me with pleasure and agreement to a global standpoint, illumine me with insights into real spirituality, remind me of the worth and need of Christ's message of love.

192

Although it is by no means a complete exposition, it is at least an indispensable foundation upon which such an exposition may later be set up by more competent hands. As such it may serve my contemporaries for the time being.

193

If I revolted against what was practically undesirable in Oriental tradition, it became inevitable that I should sooner or later pass also through a process of re-examination and revaluation of their metaphysical bases.

194

Such reputation as I may achieve will rest, I hope, much more on the philosophic system to be unfolded in this and future works, than on my rescue of yoga from disappearance with the disappearing old culture of the East.

195

The formulation of this grand synthesis is my chosen mission, both as a researcher and a writer.

196

The revelations which have come to mankind hitherto have been fragmentary rather than whole.

197

I wait and work for the hour when this Synthesis shall have articulated itself.

198

This work of synthesis will never be finished, for the materials which go into its making are never complete.

199

The new cultural synthesis that is to be created must include religion, mysticism, and metaphysics but must not stop with them. It sees that they are only a small part of the totality needed, albeit an important one.

200

I saw that I must work in full independence of all mystical schools, all Oriental traditions, while yet studying them sympathetically. I saw too that the combination of selected factors in their separate teachings was necessary as the resultant whole must be combined with my own personal revelation and reflection. Their theory and training, even the secret initiations given me by their masters, were not to be the finalized result but only the foundation for it. I saw that this would have to be the form in which I could best fulfil my own large aspirations as well as best give them what I had dedicated myself to give.

201

I came at last to the perception that the goal of a satisfying doctrine could only be reached if I taught myself something beyond what my teachers taught me. One thing became clear and that was the necessity of uniqueness in the synthesis which must be made. I had to remain utterly independent.

202

The experiences, the revelations, the inspirations, and the reflections of Asia's greatest minds have poured into this wisdom.

203

All my previous life and travel, all my researches and experiences have been leading up to this fuller and culminating revelation that I have been asked to communicate to the world of seekers.

204

Such a united system of knowledge and practice has been sorely lacking; here it is made available at last. When the old wisdom of the Orient is joined with the newer wisdom of the Occident, the century's need will be truly met.

205

He does not belong to the modern Occident, with its harsh strident materialism and glittering superficial soulless existence. He does not belong to the modern Orient, either, with its pitiful imitation of the West, its incredible superstitions and exaggerated piety, and its hybrid bewildered society.

206

Our group has become an organism, not an organization. It is a living growth, not a mechanical formation. It stands for the formulation of an East-West old-new outlook. Its books exist for the exposition of what is universally applicable in ancient knowledge, not in ancient foolishness, conjoined with what is worth keeping in modern civilization.

207

Thus, designed for helpful service and dedicated to human enlightenment, they have only begun to outline a grand system which unites in itself
the three aspects of intellectual quality, moral sublimity, and practical
applicability. They are the product of a profound historical necessity.

208

The reference to the three books mentioned in the second chapter of
The Hidden Teaching Beyond Yoga should not be misunderstood. They
were mentioned merely to illustrate one of the ways in which I was introduced to this teaching. There were other ways, too. And these three texts
contain only fragments of the hidden teaching; none is final or exhaustive.
Again, important aspects of it were not written down but have been
transmitted privately. Let nobody think I am engaged in any kind of
revival work. The circumstances and habits, the outlook and aspirations of
those who lived when these texts were written are quite foreign to us. It
would be as foolish to adopt such teaching in its entirety as it would be to
ignore it altogether. Today's need is not merely a synthesis of modern
scientific ideas with ancient mystical ones, not merely a dovetailing of
Oriental and Occidental teachings, but virtually a new creation to fit the
new age now about to dawn. I therefore do not advocate the study of old
Sanskrit texts as an essential goal but merely as an incidental means and
then only for those who like to do so. There are new forces penetrating
this planet's atmosphere today and they demand a new inspiration, new
thinking, and a new way of living. We have today what no previous
generation has ever possessed.

209

I am not a mere transcriber of Hindu thought. Some Hindus and their
Western converts who believed so once see their mistake now, and many
others will see it later before my pen is through with its job. I must
forestall any Indian critic here and now, by reminding them that I am
teaching this not as an Indian tradition but as a universal one. The present
fact is indeed that I no longer regard myself as an exponent of any particular ancient Indian system. I wish to speak only of such knowledge as lives
within me, as I have arrived at through my own thinking, experiment, and
research, but which is nevertheless firmly based upon a reformulation of
the hidden wisdom of Asia. I claim no special merit for original doctrine
but only for original synthesis of existing doctrines. My talents have been
employed in the direction of choice rather than invention. Yet this was no
small matter. If I escaped with my sanity it was only at the cost of gigantic

efforts which may render smooth the path of those who shall follow when I have gone. That which guided me through this labyrinth was the light of my own philosophic experience.

210

Three centuries ago there was created at the great monastery of Tashi-lhunpo a gilded figure of the then Grand Lama of Tibet. It was physically modelled and psychically magnetized in his presence. In the course of time the statuette belonged to the late (thirteenth) Grand Lama at Lhasa. Through a close friend of his, it passed into the possession of the writer. Now it sits silently on his desk, half-smiling at the bustling mechanically aided literary activities which are a vivid and visible symbol of the renewal of an age-old knowledge stirring out of long hibernation. Is there not a profound significance in this conjuncture of ancient Asiatic and modern Occidental attitudes? For these two currents of calm contemplation and practical service flow, I hope, through my pages towards a common goal and bring about in the hearts, minds, and actions of those who respond to it a better understanding of life's activity. Nevertheless my emphasis is modern because this iconoclastic century is compelled to live chiefly for the shining hour rather than the buried past.

211

My ultimate aim is to effect a synthesis of West-East thought. Truth is universal. The West has a good enough light of its own, and spiritual traditions that are fairly satisfactory for those who like them. It is purely a matter of personal temperament that I go East at times to pick up more pebbles of Truth.

212

Such is his independence that no group or party dare claim him. Thus he may seem to possess a merely personalist view. Yet the fact is he strives more than all others for a genuine and magnificent universalism. He is above the littlenesses of factional, partial, or sectarian views.

213

I do not belong to that small and sentimental band of avowed propagandists for Eastern culture. I have not forgotten and do not intend to forget the values I learned in the West.

214

My work has been to cut new patterns, clear untrodden paths, and clean blackened windows. It has been a pioneer's work, and has met with a pioneer's fate. Some have appreciated it but others have jeered at it.

215

All this was a kind of training, ripening the mind and broadening its experience for the task in which I have at last engaged myself—the intellectual shaping of a great synthesis and its transposition to the literary plane.

216

I conceived my work to be not only to reject, select, and fit together these various segments of the circle of truth, but also to provide the missing ones.

217

The desire of intelligent seekers in the West today is for a balanced doctrine and practical technique which will be free from all occult mystification or religious bigotry, which will satisfy the cravings of the heart and yet reconcile them with the conflicting claims of the head, and which will be suited to the needs of modern people. Is it not possible, out of the rich mystical and philosophic past of mankind and out of the creative resources of present-day human intelligence, boldly to bring to birth a comprehensive explanation of the world and a practical method of self-discovery, which can be followed by men and women who still work at their daily tasks in the world?

218

No one person has yet put the whole of philosophy together. I was privileged to receive its tradition in those limited circles where it has been kept alive by voice or pen; but what I received, in various places and under different masters, was separate fragments. My published views are founded partly on my experience and my own revelation, and partly on the authority of other and higher men.

3

ENCOUNTER WITH DESTINY

A *mysterious presence*

In these pages I have tried to tell how consciousness of God and how knowledge of God's value came to me.

2

As this work went forward, I felt and knew some presence in myself that took a part in its making. If I were to say that these pages were written by me, there would be an uneasy feeling of untruth in me. If I were to say the contrary, there would be a sense of the absurd in such a statement. I leave the reader to make what he can of these paragraphs.

3

Rather than be the scribe of ephemeral fact let me, O Lord, be the scribe of eternal vision. Let me write down word-for-word those divine messages which come to me out of the ether.

4

It is both my fate and my joy to labour to the last as a medium for this voice within me. I shall put down my pen only when I put down my life.

5

It did not occur to an unimaginative mind that I could always conquer a competence with my pen, whether I wrote highly paid publicity material for large commercial companies or lowly paid instructional and inspirational material for struggling spiritual seekers. A narrow mentality could not arrive at the understanding that my fortune lay within my head and underneath my pen-nib, not within the ashram of any individual yogi nor underneath the Indian sky. How could anyone with whom my personal intercourse was necessarily shrunken by my nomadic life to the fewest possible words adjudge either my character or my motives? And what reply but contemptuous silence could I make when such a one started a chorus of calumny about my having sat at the feet of Ramana Maharshi meanly and merely to earn a livelihood? For how could an ignorant man know at the time that I carried a standing invitation to become the editor of a journal in the West at a remuneration many times more than my modest earnings from books?

The truth is that I am not and never have been a journalist; I am not and never have been a professional author. Most of my time and much of my energy are pledged, as sacredly and as sincerely as any human being has ever pledged them, to the quest of the Overself and to the communication of the results of this quest for the helping of other seekers. I always felt that the term of life was too short merely to be devoted to earning a livelihood or collecting luxuries. No!—I wrote about these higher things because something higher than my petty self bade me do so, and when it tells me to desist I shall certainly do so and never write about them again. Meanwhile I regard my work to be no less holy than a priest's. Journalists and authors usually think—and quite rightly—of the fees they receive or the royalties they earn as being so much payment for so many words written or for so many copies sold. I however am constitutionally incapable of thinking like them and therefore I know well that I am neither a journalist nor an author. For I am never really alone when writing but every now and then there rises before my mind's eye the vision of some man or woman whose whole life may take a new and nobler course because of a few paragraphs which flow lightly from this old pen of mine, or of some broken creature whose self-destroying hand may be stayed and stayed forever from a suicidal act because of a fresh understanding got from some sentences which trip out of my typewriter. There can be no reasonable recompense for such services. They cannot be properly priced in any of this planet's currencies, so it would be better not to price them at all. Certainly it seems to me that I have nothing to sell and that so long as I listen for and obey the Voice deep within the heart, so long will the world's rewards or the world's sneers be but of secondary importance. And so long as my critics think that I have come into embodiment for the same petty little purposes as they, so long will they utterly fail to understand me. The abyss between us is too wide and too deep for that. It is indeed the abyss between two short words: the impassable chasm between *get* and *give*.

6

My work is a "prophetic" message to our times, a religious revelatory work. An academic seal would put it on an intellectual and consequently lower plane.(P)

7

He could not communicate such discoveries as a matter for doubt or for settlement by discussion. He can communicate them only with a tone of authority and in an atmosphere of surety, for this is how he himself received them.

8

Each oracular sentence carries a message for someone, somewhere. The writer does not need to know who it is.

9

I am but a messenger. I proffer no initiation, and propose to perform no miracles for you. All I can do is to say, with H.P. Blavatsky: I can tell you how to find Those who will show you the secret gateway that leads inward only, and closes fast behind the neophyte for evermore. For those who win onwards, there is reward past all telling: the power to bless and save humanity. For those who fail, there are other lives in which success may come.

10

It is not my fault if my style insists on sounding forth an authoritative and prophetic tone. I do not create it by any act of will. It is as if some ethereal presence stands behind the mind and bids me utter its message.

11

Everyone who writes a letter to praise my books and express grateful thanks for help derived from them puts me through a stringent test. Do I see clearly and acknowledge freely that I was merely used as a channel through which his own higher self passed a message or an inspiration to him? If I take the virtue all to myself I fall into a miserable self-conceit.

12

I am a messenger, not a master; an awakener, not a teacher; my external work ends with the deliverance of this message through writing and the arousal of those minds who can respond sympathetically to it.

13

The few who cherish these spiritual impulses will understand why we must await patiently the cyclic moment for such a message just as they will understand that it is something more than a mere fable.

14

It is a wisdom fed also by many other minds than my own, and in the end by the divine intelligence itself.

15

Whoever regards such writing as a professional activity in which I have engaged myself is the kind of fellow who is unable to look underneath appearances and is consequently the constant victim of illusion. I have testified before and must testify again that I write at the bidding of a higher call than the purely professional one. This is the only kind of writing that interests me and this is why I have often refused and shall continue to refuse much more lucrative literary and journalistic proposals.

16

I have tried to put into this book all that my mind can comprehend and my words can hold of these higher mysteries and their solution, but there is a chasm between thought and word which exists because of the transcendental nature of the subject itself. Nevertheless so far as human art can make the effort and so far as I have mastered such art, this chasm has been made markedly narrower, it is hoped, than earlier Western writers had left it.

17

Mine is not the only hand through which such spiritual messages are being indited.

18

Out of this wide orbit we have at last come to a point where the process of sifting the wheat from the chaff has sufficiently advanced to permit us to stand aside from all asserted teachers, to be indifferent to the utterances of all authoritative texts, and to devote no further time to researches in Oriental lands. Nevertheless, in the present book, owing to the personal progress which has been made since the completion of the previous volume (which is not nullified by the fact that the long path we have yet to tread reveals by contrast how little advanced we really are), we have been guided more than anything else by an inner guide in such cases where limited attainment made verification not possible. It taught us what to set down where we could not see and it told us what to give forth to others concerning regions where we could not walk.

Inside mystical experience

19

I did not merely observe and describe these experiences from outside, as an intellectual scientific researcher might do, but I penetrated into them and revealed what was found there to others who lacked the capacity to accompany me.

20

The concept of the Overself's presence among us originated with the ancients but is validated by modern experience. This experience of the Overself provides the best evidence of its existence and reality: no other is needed. It would be a failure in duty not to acknowledge that I have felt and known this existence hundreds of times. It is no longer a matter of mere faith to me, but of absolute knowledge. This is not to be put by anyone to my good credit for what I am and have done in this life, but to my good karma.

21

Unforgettable as the finding of secret wealth was the day when this Overself chose to make itself known to me. For I had reached a crisis in my life and could go no farther if this troubling of the air with harsh thoughts was not put right in the only way that it could be put right. Many are the adventures and manifold incidents that have befallen me since that time, both of woe and weal. But now they do not matter, nor do I deem them worth the trouble of recording. For the mists that lay about me began to die away, and I came to know that man does not walk alone. The Overself *is ever with him.* As the years unfolded the dark curtains of the future, a strange quiescence stole upon the heart when it placed its life upon the altar of obedience, and when it grew to accept each day as freely as the wandering nomad accepts the pitiless desert in which he was born. It then cast the shroud of care that enveloped it and turned from the tomb of unsatisfied desire. So I came to wrap myself round with the silken mantle of secret hidden Beauty and sought to let no bitter brooding, no storm of passion touch it.

22

It was the opening of summer in 1953. An internal tropical malady caught from eating deliberately poisoned food a few months earlier in the Far East had run its course and was about to end, as it so often did end, fatally. I suddenly and involuntarily fell across the writing desk and felt consciousness slumping into a coma. I dragged myself somehow to a couch and there the coma turned out to be the death swoon. After a couple of moments I was already almost entirely out of the physical body. The line was about to be drawn to close the past lifetime's account. . . . In that condition and at that moment my body was found by someone who happened to enter the room, someone so highly sensitive and intuitive as to recognize at once what the hidden situation was. My friend called me to come back, emphatically, pleadingly, and insistently by turns. At the same time I awoke to a dreamy consciousness, half in one world, where the astral figure of a Master, well-known and well-loved, appeared to me, and half in the physical world. The Master said, "I have come to take you away. But you still have the choice, whether to return or to come with me." I reflected rapidly. Personally I felt quite willing to accept the vast relief from the burden of P.B.'s earthly life now offered me. But at the same time, I felt pity for those who looked to me for help. The work with and for them was unfinished. My mission to them and to others was unfulfilled. How could I go? All this happened in a very few seconds. Regretfully, reluctantly, the decision formed itself within my heart. I asked to be allowed to return to the flesh so that I could continue the service and complete the record.

23

These experiences gradually became a pointing finger, a directive and predictive message from the Overself to continue and complete the work which, through destiny, it has imposed on him.

24

The evening comes on apace but still I am loath to light the room lamp. For this is my favoured hour to escape the world, its dusk my daily invitation to return to the heart's silent mysterious depth. More especially is this so in the long summer evenings.

25

I know honestly and must say at the beginning that it is not through any egotistical conceit that I have told this story here. Others have told me, and I have also come to see for myself, that there is a special value for all of us in the description of such personal experiences. I want to share this experience with others and especially with those who have heard about it, who have recognized its supreme worth, and have unsuccessfully sought it for years. I feel that they need it more than other people. I want to help them give it to themselves.

26

All memory of my worldly business fell away . . . whereupon Truth smiled and raised her hand as if to signify that she understood very well that I came from a lower world, where the getting of food and drink or the mating of bodies in love were profoundly important things, but that here, whence one could view the coming and going of time itself, they could well be disregarded. A great sense stole over me that I had indeed been deceived and that the detail of my personal life was less important than I had believed. Happiness stood not therein but was ever at the side, if we would but turn the head and acknowledge her presence. As I breathed that air which seemed to come from a land of immortal youth, I learned a few things. I do not know whether they can be spoken of, for there are things which the tongue is not fully equal to telling, and these seem to be some of them. Yet I must try. I must pause to pay homage to those glorious truths. . . . And then my vision fell away from me but the mood did not. I became aware of my physical surroundings.

27

Although I did not come so close as Quaker John Woolman did ("I was brought so near the gates of death that I forgot my name," he reported), it was close enough.

28

I was sitting on a bench under a tree just outside the extremely picturesque but noisily busy market square of a southern French town, halting there for what was intended to be just long enough a time—a mere two or three minutes—in which to capture on paper a perception which had come up out of nowhere and then proceed on my way. But instead, barely written down, the work ended in a pause, a stillness rose increasingly around my head, and then the Visitation came.

29

These paragraphs are written from the *inside* of the mystical experiences, not from the outside, and this may be mistaken for a kind of arrogance.

30

It is my long-sustained and well-tested belief that I have had certain revelations from a higher source. The revelations are mixed, some dealing with the world's fortunes and misfortunes but others dealing purely with the Overself's wisdom and workings. The source is beyond me and met only in the profundity of meditation. I cannot name it or describe it, so others may call it what they like, yet I am directly aware of it.

31

I have had forty years' experience of these techniques, forty years in which to test the truth of the principles behind them. I have so far found only verification. If I had found at any time falsification instead, I should have sought a different outlet for my interests.

32

Whatever I write down is not only to guide or teach others but also myself. I was warned to be observant, not to miss and leave out any of the little details of the inner life, for all are useful. The Overself is not to speak through my words alone, but also through my actions.

33

I sought for the Overself amid all the conditions of life. I found it first in a series of passing glimpses that were stretched out at intervals through years and later in a series of unique and powerful experiences whose results were *enduring*. Yes, that is the all-important word, for if it does not leave something in the consciousness that lasts the lifetime, it is not enough to have had a mystical experience. The prodigal has still not returned to his father's home, but only seen it through the haze for a few moments and from afar off.

34

I seek not to describe these experiences but to reproduce them as vividly, as immediately, as I can.

35

How many a glorious moment has found its way from the inner life to my outer notebook!

36

I believe that there is a soul in man. This is a frank if commonplace avowal. Yet as I look again at these words, I find a false modesty in them. It is a poor tribute to truth to hesitate timidly in making the open declaration that I *know* there is a soul because I daily commune with it as a real, living presence.(P)

37

I must go out of myself to comprehend the meaning of the words "I AM THAT I AM."

38

I saw that all things are in Mind, that Mind is not the physical brain, and that therefore they were all ideas. Metaphysically they were transient and unreal. Even the ego is unreal. Mind is the only Reality.

39

(My Initiations) It made me aware of my faults and weaknesses. The revelation was very painful. I suffered.

40

The world around him, the social and industrial life that environs him, has become a mummer's show. As a vacuum-pump withdraws the air from a glass vessel, so has some strange hand withdrawn the sense of Reality from his surroundings.

41

Although I believe that I have something worthwhile to say, I do not succumb to any special conceit about it. I read the critics or listen to them in the humble hope that among the exaggerations, the falsities, and the misunderstandings it will perhaps be possible to find one or two hints worth noting, one or two corrections of my own errors. I do not at all believe that I am infallible; but I know from all past experience that the mysterious Presence which makes certain things known, but whose message I may fail to report rightly, *is*.

42

I do not meditate formally, as I get the same experience at night before falling asleep and again in morning on awakening.

43

The hour of escape from grey bondage is at hand, and a soft stirring of the heart announces the inner visitant. I pick up my pen from the desk.

44

I offer no proofs, no documentation, no argument, when IT is there; it is enough to silence me. But when I do offer them and speak, you will do better to depart.

45

I am unable to separate Life from God or the secular from the sacred. I find a divine element in all that is brought forth by time. But this is because when I gaze deep within myself, I first see it there, feel it there, and commune with it there.

46

It is not through a haughty confidence in his own ideas or an egoistic disdain for those of others that he has this certitude about the Divine Being's reality. It comes not from audacity but from experience, from constant thought and profound meditation, and from ever-felt presence.

47

Where others find emptiness or futility in their own lives, and even more in those surrounding them, he finds meaning and purpose. There was a need to escape from nihilism, and he succeeded. Now his being and identity increase. He knows, with joy, that he shares in an inner reality which sponsors the universe.

48

When he felt that he could secure no help from anyone else, so that it was useless to depend on human beings, he decided to turn to God as his only friend. He was actually doing what his Soul wanted him to do all that time, and he actually reached a stage which the advanced mystic wished him to reach. His darkness was really light and the aloneness was the requisite condition in which the Soul can be found.

49

The description of the mystical experience on the last three pages of Chapter 14 of *The Wisdom of the Overself* refers to a rare event and one which is usually attained only after arduous struggles. If one has had this experience, he is far above the average seeker in this Quest. To such, nothing short of the highest philosophical attainment—as distinct from mystical or religious attainment—will really satisfy.

50

I gave my years and my energies to this quest, faithful to faith, yet regardful of reason.

51

In my younger days I might have said, "If you will not show me a sign, I cannot show any faith in you." Now I knew better.

52

Plunged amid the cares and frets of mundane existence as we are, most will read such statements with wistful or scornful scepticism. Whoever doubts these thoughts doubts them with me! Sometimes they seem too good to be true and I try to turn a sceptical face towards them, but lo!—a strange peace invades my room, a sudden stillness descends on my mind, a grave grandeur elevates my heart—and I am undone! Then nothing seems too glad to be true, for then I have found the infinite Goodness behind life. And then too the last and greatest of the deceivers that hold us to life suddenly loses all its power.

53

I was frequently brought into previously unknown experiences.

54

Having had a rich and exceptional experience in the departments of mysticism and yoga, my maturest conclusions are surely more valuable than my immature ones.

55

There were the days when meditation failed me but the Presence stayed, whether in crowded trains or busy streets, being felt more powerfully when alone. But during the fourth year It also had left. The world insisted on a confrontation; its hard lessons had to be learned, my own fears and weaknesses exposed, intellect and practicality developed, science revalued for what it was worth, and the understanding why industry and materialism were growing to ever-greater power gotten.

56

Travelling in a taxi down Rome's Via Veneto and remembering "*this is my hour,*" I had little difficulty in entering the silent place of the Mind—despite that celebrated thoroughfare's car-filled road and thronged sidewalks. I do not recommend such a place for such a purpose—there are better ones—but modern life being what it is, it is needful to learn *how* to defeat the world.

57

From the writings of illumined men; from close personal association, observation, discussion, study, friendship, and meditation with living illumined men; and from my own mystical experience, I have been able to get a fuller picture of what cosmic consciousness really is.

58

These teachings are not the result of conjecture nor the mirror of opinion. They are insights got by an opening of the inner eyes. This fact must be pointed out, in all humility, if they are to carry to any reader the revelatory understanding which they have already brought the writer.

59

(1) With the increasingly sensitive awareness induced by meditation, there developed a psychic weakness which troubled me. It was a knowing of other people's mental attitudes and emotional states, their personal characters and inner conditions. I read each man's mind as easily as if it were an extension of my own. Owing to my inexperience, ignorance, and unfamiliarity, I did not know how to bring this excessive empathy under control. I was too easily drawn out of myself, out of my own ego-centre, into that of the person I happened to be with at the time. This weakened or even dispersed my concentration on the Overself and made me too subject to the influence of others. The result was chaos and confusion. It was a long time before I was able to get rid of this unwanted faculty and clear up this undesirable condition.

(2) Then followed an interval of some years, when a dark night settled over me.

(3) The first result was a complete change in my attitudes to life itself, to other people and even to myself.

(4) For four years, when I walked through the city streets, I marvelled at the insensitivity of the crowds, at their eager pursuit of small aims and trivial hopes, at their utter blindness to the inner reality.

(5) In those earlier times about one year was spent in traversing the three degrees. The first was a year of initiation, the second of dedication, and the third of revelation.

60

My Initiations into the Overself

(1) A force welled up in the heart, rose to the head, then passed forwards into space. As it left the body, I knew I was *not* the body. I saw the mass of human beings struggling in the misery and strife because of their greed, desire, and selfishness. I saw hands holding the globe. They belonged to a figure whose face I could not see but whom I named "The Master." He said, "Free yourself." I moved on in space and saw on the horizon a coloured sunset glow of half-light which was my destination. I then knew I was not the personal self. But I did not continue and complete my journey. This was because fear entered me—perhaps fear of the unknown. So I returned to the body.

(2) A great love towards all things rises in me at times since the experience.

(3) Since the experience I have been so eager to return to it that I feel frustrated.

(4) The Consciousness first remained with me throughout every day and every night. Then it slowly remained for shorter and shorter periods—one hour less at a time. By the end of a few weeks it had totally disappeared.

(5) In that deep silence the ego was integrated with the Overself. The operation was almost wholly done through the power of Grace. It descended in overwhelming force and crushed out the ego's tyrannical rule.

(6) I found that I could fully enter this transcendental state at any time and at will simply by reorienting my attention upon the idea of turning inwards in the way that a hatha yogi who rolls up his eyeballs and crosses them detaches his attention from the remainder of his physical body. In order to bring about this change of awareness, a certain object of concentration had to be used. Generally it was a simple and short declarative phrase, either an affirmation or the pictorial memory of my most outstanding experience. When the change was effected I found myself at the centre of my being. It was the real "I." Time was then brought to a standstill.

(7) During the illumination there was no jubilant ecstasy, no emotional excitement, no unbalancing rapture. It was a happy peace, a calm abidance in beauty, love, wisdom.

(8) There was no desire to play the missionary and spread the knowledge of it far and wide. On the contrary, I told no one about it but kept it secret.

(9) I found I could go on thinking, or not thinking, while still remaining in the higher awareness.

(10) The period of elementary training was completed, its experience finished.

(11) As this presence held me, it gave me an invulnerable peace and a strange detachment from personal matters or outer happenings.

(12) A new insight of this kind cannot be got by those who refuse to enlarge their visionless academic learning, those whose experience of the world is in the end mostly an experience of pages in books.

(13) I was overpowered by a peculiar feeling of being unreal, and for once even unsure of my own identity.

(14) No psychic voice came into my hearing, no psychic vision unrolled before my eyes. The spiritual and mystical life may be fulfilled completely without entering such a dubious realm.

(15) There was no one whom I met who was unimportant. My interest in everyone, however short or transitory our meeting, was full and complete.

(16) To sit down every day at my writing table and put this experience into words on the paper that lies in front of me, is itself heartening and inspiring. But the fact that there are other people in the world, unknown to me, who feel the same spiritual need that I once felt and who might find some hope or stimulation in such a record of personal experience, also induces me to create this little heap of manuscript.

(17) Although there had been experiences in the past of what purported to be fragmentary visions of former reincarnations, I now saw that those experiences did not belong to any level beyond the higher psychic. From the present level the entire process of reincarnation now seemed to be illusory because it belonged to the realm of illusion itself. The true Self did not reincarnate at all.

(18) This technique of combined deep breathing and energy-raising was discovered quite accidentally—or so it seemed at the time. Certainly nobody taught it to me and no book revealed it to me. I was convinced then as a matter of faith, and today as a matter of knowledge, that it was picked up afresh out of the subconscious memory of former reincarnations.

(19) I saw that every little detail is predestined, even the fact that I am to write at this very moment, and to write just these particular words. All that has happened to me in the past has brought me to this point, which makes the act a fated one. I am not free to do anything else than write, nor to write anything different from what I am writing.

(20) I saw that everything which happens does so in conformity with the World-Idea. The entire planetary situation, which includes the situation of each being within it, is providentially arranged.

61

At the roofed shrine of the giant stone seated Buddha, approached by a long paved causeway, I squatted in front for a few minutes by the flag-stones in the middle of the causeway. I received an encouraging message to proceed farther, a clear premonition of coming contact with the Khmer adepts that day.

62

Angkor Wat: The chief sanctuary on the third (top) floor of the temple. I squatted several paces in front of the shrine where a standing gold lacquered Buddha was positioned with one hand raised in a world-bless-ing. At his feet reclined another statue, the dying Buddha (unpainted), with one hand under his head and behind him three small bodhisattvas paying respectful homage to their master. Very soon, lulled by the peace of the sanctuary and sensitive to its extraordinary subtle power, I unified myself with that Buddha. My gaze was fixed across the intervening paved floor and doorless doorway, unfaltering, upon the eyes of the standing Buddha, the others being shrouded in the darkness of that small room. We became ONE. A spiritual current passed perceptibly from the mysterious figure into my squatting cross-legged body. In those divine moments before sunfall, when a sublime inner detachment and peace had engulfed me, I knew that I had got from Angkor Wat that which I had travelled over many leagues to get.

63

As I sit at this oaken table and face my future, I can now do so without worry and with an almost complete calm. I realize now what I have but dimly realized before, that though the agonies which will yet come to me will be no less real than the agonies which have gone before, there remains a vast freedom of action to mold the man within me who has to *endure* those agonies. I know now that I can build up the figure and form of a great hero within the small space of my heart; that this hero can fight the darkest fate with bravery and with determination; but that if defeat is starred to come, he will smile and say, "This, too, will pass," and not be too bitter about it. I *can mold* this inner man; and I *will* do so.

This, then, is my future; the fortunes or misfortunes of fate are the lesser part; the soul that meets and fights that fate is the greater part; and that soul can be shaped by *my own* hands.

64

Mine is a religion which cannot be named, a God who cannot be discussed, a worship which cannot be seen or heard. All that I revere rests in secrecy and silence.

65

My cynical and solitary nature was flushed with mystical feelings. Noons would come when for a few glorious minutes I was suspended outside time. Evenings would fall when, unexpectedly, I was held by the divine soul. Such occasions were memorable and instructive for they taught that it is possible for man to transcend his terrestrial existence. They revealed more than whole volumes of mysticism. But they came too infrequently, they shone too briefly to eradicate the bitterness with which I viewed God, life, and my fellow men. I could not command them. They eluded my grasp, and while taking the cream off worldly pleasures, they provided no permanent substitute.

66

Men will come and tell you that the spirit is a delusive mirage. Do not believe them. If that were true these pages would never have come into existence, for there would have been nothing about which to write. Thousands of mystics' lives rise out of the past to silence the lie upon their lips. Thousands more will yet arise out of the veiled future.

67

Still within the web of memory lies the bright day when first it drew the dark veil aside and showed me its Holy Face. For the first time I felt free of frustrated desire for any new outer possessions, circumstances, or persons. I found my joy within and my satisfaction through the Overself at all times. If anything was lacking on the physical plane, I could have it manifested into existence simply by stating to the Higher Power mentally what I needed but saying at the same time that there would be no real difference to my peace of mind if the lack continued, for I would plainly pray that "not my will, but Thine, be done." By giving up mentally what *I* wanted, I became detached and freed myself from the desired thing. Yet it was always given to me! By depending upon the real source of Happiness, I was allowed a secondary happiness in worldly things. An unillumined person cannot perceive that God is the very Provider of all. He believes that by obtaining money, position, or power he will find security and happiness. The illumined person *knows* that they are found only in God.

68

I had the eerie feeling of the nearness of another world. It was something considerably beyond the feeling of falling asleep.

69

Throughout the darkest period of intense suffering, the Overself was all the time present, supporting and strengthening him to bear what there could be no escape from, what his higher destiny had irrevocably willed in order to detach him still further from egoism and personal ties. He was in its hands always, in joy and in sorrow alike.

70

What travel and study, thought and interviews could give anyone on these matters, I also had received. But what personal experience of these inner states could give was an entirely different matter, about which only a limited number could testify as I had testified. Mysticism could not remain a dubious medieval activity. It needed to be put on an accurate foundation, and presented for people with brains.

71

Never at any time in my research did I depend on mere texts alone. There have been other and fresher sources: the living voice of reputed experts, my own metaphysical reasoning, and my own mystical experience. Equipped with a readiness to learn from even the most obscure expositor, an utter absence of conscious colour or racial prejudice, many years of advanced meditation practice, and a modicum of cultural preparation, I turned from the dead worm-bored manuscripts themselves to living men, discussing all the knotty historical, textual, metaphysical, and yogic-practice problems arising out of these studies with Sanskrit pundits, learned pontiffs, grave ascetics, mountain-dwelling hermits, contemplative mystics, heads of monasteries, and even specialist university professors. I did not hesitate to ask them hundreds of questions with plaguey persistence or to keep my critical faculties alive, for I sought to bring Oriental truth and not Oriental superstitions to the West. I also accepted a few mystical initiations from among those which were offered. The third source which has informed this exposition of the hidden teaching was an internal one. Being a practising and not merely a theoretical mystic, I sought whenever possible and whenever within the scope of my restricted powers to test and verify our revelatory statements before publishing them. For example, I succeeded in confirming in this way the truth of mentalism, a doctrine which forms the very basis of the hidden teaching. This happened during mystical semi-trances wherein I found the source of the surrounding things to be deep below the threshold of the wakeful mind. This single experience out of several is mentioned to dispel the misconception that these pages are merely an indulgence in academic theory, as also to encourage fellow pilgrims plodding farther back on the same road.

Nevertheless my attainment is only a limited one. I am unable to achieve similar verifications of certain other tenets. In such cases I have tried to check my declarations by those of ancient sages who, it is believed, themselves possessed the requisite capacity. Be that as it may, the labour of correlating all these fragments, the toil of eliminating the puzzling contradictions was an exceedingly heavy one. Abnormal reflective ability was needed to understand this philosophy and abnormal introspective ability was needed to describe its ultramystic experiences. The theme was indeed so far beyond an ordinary capacity that at times I strongly felt like renouncing it. I have elsewhere acknowledged our indebtedness to that practical philosopher His Highness the late Maharajah of Mysore for his patient personal encouragement in this undertaking. The immense mass of material which gradually accumulated within my head and notebooks was so confusing in parts that I had to reduce it to systematic shape by a comparative study and careful analysis which required so prodigious an amount of work that the excessive labour involved doubtless cut several years off my earthly life. It was only an iron determination to try to master something of Asia's highest wisdom that enabled me to persevere in putting all the pieces of this mosaic pattern together until they finally fell into proper places and an intelligible pattern came into view at last. Although India has been the central scene of these studies, conversations, and experiences, its insufficiencies compelled my visits to a number of other Asiatic countries upon the same quest, unexpectedly earning myself from His Holiness the aged Supreme Monk of Siam a gift of one of his personal treasures in the form of an ancient bronze statue of the Buddha as well as a Certificate of Merit.

72

I wrote for the living and not for the dead. Therefore I suited matter and manner to the circumstances of the present day. And although I built upon the foundation laid by the ancients, nevertheless I took large liberties in the erection of the superstructure, based on my personal experience during a quarter-century of practical research into this subject. If the philosophical system which I have presented in *The Hidden Teaching Beyond Yoga* and *The Wisdom of the Overself* is regarded as derivative only, it will be regarded wrongly. I have not merely worked out its character from ancient materials alone but also created it from modern ones. For I have gone deep into my own innermost consciousness too. Some of the knowledge found there as well as some learned from contemporaries, has been penned into the words of these books. Thus I have really worked at the emergence of a contemporary philosophic culture.

The making of a messenger

73

I have embodied in these pages the matured wisdom and dearly bought experience of many many lifetimes.

74

I learned this wisdom not only in India but on the limitless sands of the Sahara Desert, on the canyon-sides of the mountain-girdled Yangtze River, in the steaming hot jungles of Siam and Malaya, and on the snowy heights of Tibet.

75

I am not deceived by all the beauty with which the hangings and paintings, the carved figures and the colourful rugs present me. The allotted years left to me will now pass more quickly than the earlier ones: and then they will finish and the beauty with them. But this is not to say I did not appreciate and enjoy it. Philosophy taught me that even when it warned me against the brevity. Best of all along with this balanced view came the knowledge of what I really was—essential silent ever-living infinitely calm MIND!

76

I have met men in all their fifty-seven varieties and know a little about the motives which actuate human nature.

77

From different causes I lacked worldly wisdom, worldly prudence, and worldly common sense. This was the origin of recurrent troubles but, on the other hand, I possessed their contraries—that is, I did have worldly uncommon sense and this fortunately brought me on the quest which had become supremely important to me.

78

This is the way my mind was formed. It would feel stifled if kept down to petty trivialities, unable to penetrate to what is most important and basically real.

79

I could have changed places 400 years ago with Emperor Akbar's prime minister, Abu Fazl, speaking of his youth: "My heart felt itself drawn to the sages of Mongolia, I longed for interviews with the lamas of Tibet, I became acquainted with the tenets of all creeds. It is Thou whom I search from temple to temple."

80

I do not know how much it is true, and how little, of other authors, but I do know that in some measure every book I wrote implied an auto-biographical self-portrait.

81

Because in the past I wandered through the world visiting holy or wise men, I could rightly call myself a pilgrim. Now my wanderings are more inward than outward.

82

I have ransacked the world for its wisdom.

83

In all my work and travel the discovery of my own soul and of men who had discovered theirs was my real aim. I put up a facade of literary purpose in front of this quest because that smoothed my path in a conventional world which knows only conventional aims.

84

(My Initiations) Those earlier years were exhilarating ones, dynamic with eager search and adventurous exploration, teeming with fresh discoveries and inspiring contacts.

85

The simple and the learned came to seek counsel or to ask questions. They lamented personal tragedies or confessed personal ignominies, queried metaphysical teaching or related mystical experience. What I learned from them paid for what they got from me.

86

I tried to find traces of this knowledge in musty libraries of the old traditional centres of learning at home [in England] and on the Continent—and succeeded. But where were its living representatives today? The answer came, mysteriously and in unexpected places. And then came the decision to turn to the ancient Orient, so long associated with the faiths and wisdom, the superstitions and culture, of Man.

87

I travelled the world, let alone India, in order to find the Word.

88

If any fragment of divine grace, however minute and however imperceptible, comes from these contacts with the masters, I must—merely by mathematical calculation—have received it.

89

My travels have given me Oriental connections of an unusual kind. My publications have brought me global correspondence of a multi-level kind.

90

All these experiences, interviews, trainings, studies, and teachings brought into being a fuller view of Truth and a balanced understanding of it. Such a global research enabled me to do what the novice tethered to a particular school or cult could not do. It put contradictory doctrines into their places and corrected their errors.

91

I am essentially pragmatic in my judgement and businesslike in my methods. I test a theory not only by its practical result, a technique not only by its rational quality but also by its definite success or failure when put to work. I examine an institution not only by its own public claims but also by its own precise conduct.

92

I have read far more widely than my critics suppose but by temperament I dislike to make a parade of learning. Yet, my esteem for broad scholarship is qualified by my contempt for narrow pedantry. This is why I do not care to fit my quotations to page-number references, why footnotes hardly ever appear in my books, and why I am often content to give an author's name without his book's title. The academic atmosphere is too dry for me to work in, too blind to the spirit and insistent on the letter for me to respect much. I feel that the faculty of vision which can see through and beyond the meaning of a hundred facts is immensely more important than the blind collection of those facts.

93

The changes of domicile which a nomadic destiny forced on me were helpful to important aspects of research with the few spiritually more advanced members of humanity as well as to service of less advanced ones—all carried on quietly and unobtrusively.

94

For over a generation I have studied the different forms of contemporary mysticism and seen the different effects.

95

I visited monasteries and ashrams, gurus and abbots, either as a friendly observer or as a student of comparative religion and mysticism.

96

Those were the days when I went among the gurus, tossing questions at them and noting down the answers or, much better, sitting in silence with them.

97

I have seen and associated with widely varied types of the human species, from the lowest of the lower classes to the uppermost of the upper classes, from pariah Indian outcastes to European kings and queens, from ragged peasants to sleekly dressed prime ministers. Thus, what this planet has to offer us, and what we can do with our lives and surroundings, is often within my purview.

98

One natural consequence of giving so many interviews in such widely assorted parts of the world was that I learnt much about human beings generally, and about spiritually questing human beings specifically.

99

These conversations with men who were mostly idolized by a few but ignored by the many gave me access to a world far off from the common everyday one.

100

To write more convincingly about so unconvincing a subject as mysticism, one must write out of his own experience. To do the same about meditation, he must write out of his own practice.

101

They are truths which I have gathered during forty years of intensive research. And because I believe them in my heart to be a saving knowledge, I have worked for twenty-five years to bring them before those who wanted it.

102

I have made it my business to ascertain, so far as my limitations allow, the plot behind the World-Drama in which each of us has his role to play.

103

It demanded no less than hundreds of interviews with different teachers and hermits, thousands of miles of travel to reach them, and at least a hundred thousand pages of the most abstruse reading in the world before I could bring my course of personal study in the hidden philosophy to a final close. Today I have not got the time to take others through such a long and arduous course and they have probably not got the patience to endure it.(P)

104

I am a researcher, that is my special job. Then I go on to convert the results of my researches into notes and reports, into analyses and reflections. Later I draw upon this material for my published writings.(P)

105

I lay no special claim to virtue and piety which most men do not possess. But I do lay claim to indefatigable research into mystical truth, theory, and practice.(P)

106

My final appeal is to truth itself. The inherent rationality of the statements made in the following paragraphs should alone suffice to justify them, but the famous authorities also quoted give a rock-like foundation to such statements and should help to remove the misgivings of timid students. Let them not be intimidated by wordy moralizings and emotional thunderings.

107

The truth is always there, on its own level and in its own place. If no one can find access to it today, someone will do so tomorrow. I have no illusion about my own relationship to it. No special importance is to be attached to my personality because I believe it to be present in my mind or feel it to be working in my heart.

108

These are the views of an old man who has experienced much that is normal and supernormal but has thought, read, and heard even more about it.

109

The struggling aspirant may recognize his own face in some of these descriptions and his own problems in some of these solutions.

110

The opportunity of observing many persons engaged in various forms and stages of mystical seeking and religious practice both in the Orient and in the Occident, over a period of half a century, put in my hands a large mass of informative data upon the subject.

111

Having observed at first hand the spiritual destiny of thousands of seekers, I have observed much needless struggle and needless suffering.

112

His writings are as they should be—a looking-glass showing several hints of his inner strength and illuminated mind.

113

I gave myself up to curious studies and unusual researches at a period of history when only a very small interest was shown in them.

114

Reading through the thousands of letters which I have received from these readers, talking over the experiences and discussing the questions of many others met in my travels, has enriched my own knowledge of mystical seeking in our times, broadened my own understanding of it, corrected errors, and revised estimates.

115

Fate has given one advanced mystic a wide opportunity to learn something positive, an opportunity which has been given only to a few others. So if a person really wants to accept the Quest as primary, this mystic can at least give him a few worthwhile ideas.

116

Whatever is fully realized and crystallized in the Self achieves its own necessity for being put into writing.

117

While recognizing the debt which we owe to the pioneer work of these scholars I am unable to accept all their conclusions.

118

Not only did I investigate the subject; I also contributed to it.

119

People all over the world wrote to me, some sought me out during my travels, and while noting their experiences I could not help accumulating a vast fund of observations about the difficulties and techniques, the dangers and methods, the theories and results, the delusions and realities which beset the Quest.

120

I must write sincerely and straightforwardly, or not at all. I must communicate what I find in my own heart, or remain silent. I must draw material out of my own experience, not out of hearsay at second hand, if it is to ring with utter conviction.

121

This story is so strange, so aside from our preconceived ideas, that I would not trouble to set it down and thereby incur certain ridicule did I not know in my heart that it was absolutely true.

122

I, being a man of some little activity and not a monk wrapped in prayer nor a metaphysician concocting his cobwebs in musty libraries, have had to devise ways and means for my own life, ways of seeking a profound inner life amid the pressure of practical affairs and endless work.

123

I have visited many ashrams, temples, monasteries and found that what I was seeking was not there. The monasteries made it hard to live, the temples were too mesmerized by outer forms, the ashrams were stages for little dictatorships. None of these institutions was really congenial to a free mind. Every sojourn in them taught me anew that peace must be sought and could be found only in my own heart.

124

I take up my pen once more and let its slow-flowing words tell of a time when life opened a crowded page for me.

125

Caught in the tentacles of this mammonistic time, I tried my utmost to make materialism a sufficient guide to the labyrinth of life, but merely succeeded in confirming my belief in mysticism. We may try to dodge the Heavenly Hunter but if he loses his prey in one birth, he will catch it in a later.

126

A perusal of the earlier part of this book, with its harsh criticisms and dark prophecies, is likely to lead to the incorrect conclusion that its author is a pessimist to the soles of his feet. He is not. He has written of things as he found them.

127

Reading and reflection have helped to endorse what experience has taught. Personal contacts with mystics of every kind and status have still further confirmed it. The knowledge gained at the initiation through invitation into a secret order instructed by perfected adepts who dwell on a superior plane, finally clinched it.

128

When I ventured into it, I found a partially unexplored jungle. When I left there was a trodden path through this jungle.

129

I am a merchant of words, it is true, but they are words which leap hot from my heart. I have not cut down the expression of my views to accord with conventional ideas.

130

Youth to me was a perpetual quest, but I find the maturing ones of today incurious of any higher adventures than are afforded by cocktail bars and tennis courts. I remember how I was attracted to the literary portrayals of certain characters whom I felt must exist in real life, and whom I longed to meet. Was Zanoni a mere creature of the quill of Bulwer Lytton? Did not his prototype exist somewhere in unrecorded history, if not in the author's own experience?

131

Meanwhile I amused myself with dipping my cup into differing streams. Now it was Hegel on the meaning of history, and then it was Bacon on the virtues of scientific method. Today I took in Sidney Webb's socialistic investigations, while tomorrow I listened to the simple wisdom of Jacob Boehme. Anon the paradoxes of Oscar Wilde brought champagne to my beaker; then the remote thoughts of James Hinton engaged my attention. And so I moved on, visiting such other varying rivers of thought as the scientific Huxley, the irritable Schopenhauer, the imperturbable Emerson, the deep *Upanishads*, the Persian poets, the inspiring *Bhagavad Gita*, the delightful Shelley, and the unforgettable novel *Zanoni* by Lord Lytton.

132

The dedication of my intellect and pen to the spreading of Light was the first act of my literary career. It certainly helped me, by preoccupying my working time with spiritual ideas; and perhaps it helped the world.

133

I fully and wholeheartedly acknowledge the need of professional background, the worth of professional preparation. Medicine, surgery, and law are not for amateurs. But my profession is quite unorthodox, nay it is unique. There is no recognized institution, no public organization which trains one for it. For its qualifications are created entirely from within oneself, not created from without. Hence my statements of mystical experience personally passed through carry more weight among my followers than any academic recognition through diploma or doctorate could carry.

134

But if I have retracted my steps, revised my estimates, and clarified my pictures, I have gone forward more determinedly than ever in the new path. The pursuit of truth remains the grandest passion I know.

135

If I fell into certain errors, it is not only my own defects that must be blamed, but also the confusion in which I found the subject itself; and if I sometimes lost my way in this subject, then it is only in part my own fault and in part the fact that it is still a veritable labyrinth.

136

Destiny determined that the years of my most critical awakening to the necessity of a complete and radical alteration of my world-view should coincide with the tragic years of the world war.

137

The P.B. of 1946 is not the same as the P.B. of 1926. They differ on several points, although, happily, not on the fundamental points that man's soul *is* and that his duty here and now is to realize it.

138

If the further development of my experience led to the exposure of my own past illusions for what they were, that was a result which I neither sought nor welcomed nor foresaw. It was indeed a bitter one.

139

I did not come to this truth by the accident of inspiration. It came to me at first by deep thought and wide research.

140

I have not troubled to document my books partly because I was always working under heavy pressure of time, but principally because I considered that the authority of my own modern, personal experience was more helpful to modern seekers than mere references to other books.

141

If, in my writing, I have quoted so often from Saint Paul, it may be because during boyhood I for a time nourished my soul, amid the prevailing wilderness of modern materialism, on devotional thoughts contained in his wonderful "Letters." Ibn Tufail's *Awakening of the Soul* fed me too, in those days; but the other man somehow kindled a greater awe and respect in me because in every letter I saw how he was spending himself to enlighten so many people over so wide an area—and perhaps also because he eventually spent out his life in the final dramatic experience of martyrdom.

142

I am not concerned with what some men have thought and taught about other men. Nor is it for me to wander in the grey valley where the mists of opinion have been settling while the centuries raced them by.

143

Some may take up this book deceived by the title and thinking to find in it the fancies of a wandering imagination or the lively records of a sensational life. I assure them it is a true book and is none the less true because some of the adventures and a few of the characters are not easily met.

144

Such is the prime consideration which has recently led me to refuse all worship of personalities, and which has lately made me put principles in the foreground of my own quest. I have bought this lesson in the open mart of bitter experience. I shall sell it to my readers for a mere fraction of what it has cost me. I beg of them therefore to remember it, and not to let themselves be led astray.

145

My happiest moments have been spent either in mental quiescence or in mental creation.

146

It is also a historic fact that even where the Sanskrit originals are still inaccessible or wholly lost everywhere in Asia, many are saved for posterity in their existing Tibetan or Chinese translations. The consequence of these discoveries was that I later perceived the fundamental necessity of completing these researches in a wider field, taking these other parts of Asia into my orbit. I therefore pursued my investigations in such countries as Japan, China, Cambodia, Sikkim, Siam, and was finally fortunate enough to receive personally from the hands of a high lama of the Mongolian Buddhist order, as well as from an initiate in the Tibetan order, the esoteric key which unlocked several of the contradictions which had heretofore puzzled me. The above explanation is essential to make clear to Indian readers that I am no follower of their Advaita Vedanta school alone; I have taken the hidden teaching in all its integral fullness and refused to limit myself to those fragments of it which are alone available in present-day India. All Asia and not merely a part of it is now the repository of this teaching.

147

I do not say that my researches have reached completeness. I say only that they have reached a point which is sufficient for my present needs.

148

I have for years been carrying on the work of spiritual exploration. Some of it has led through dusky twilit lands of metaphysics where the right direction was often in doubt, and some of it has led through dangerous jungles in the mind's hinterland.

149

I have written in these pages as simply and as directly as I could about something that is *real*, about experiences that are not less every human being's right because few have claimed that right.

150

I can hear some readers of the foregoing pages murmuring because they have permitted me to carry them up into the uncertain region of cloud-land. Since I intend to waft them even dangerously higher, it may be well to give a few pages' respite and take stock of certain mundane matters which have their affiliations hereunto.

151

The author is neither a professional scientist nor an academic philosopher nor a theoretical theologian. He does not claim to have had the highly specialized training which would really fit him to write authoritatively upon the subjects pertaining to such men. Therefore in entering their domains he feels himself to be an intruder, whom they will necessarily treat with scorn and contempt. He does claim, however, that what books and dons have not taught him, life has taught. Through intense and wide living and deep reflection thereon, he has come to the perception of a true science, to the recognition of a true philosophy, and to the realization of a true theology. No don and no book can go farther than that, farther than TRUTH. The fashionable theories of our time have their entrances and make their exits, but there is an enduring Truth which outlives all change. Hence what is set down here through inward vision and uncommon experience bears its own authority and will convey its own trustworthiness to whomsoever is ripe to receive it.

152
This little pastel-covered notebook accompanied me everywhere in those times of search, study, travel, and expectation.

153
If some men give life in wartime service of their country, this man gives it truth. If his message is not heeded, appreciated, or understood, that is no reason for belittling the service he has tried to render. Any man may give his life whereas only the man who has won to perception of truth can give it to his fellows.

154
While they argue about the truth of these writings from the outside, I experience it joyously from the inside.

155
During these sacred communions I receive philosophic revelations or take delivery of celestial messages. It is understood that they are not for my own benefit, and that in due course I will pass them on to others.

156
I may have a long way to go yet but I have at least found the right direction.

157
He reached a higher degree of proficiency than many "authorities" because he was constantly at pains to verify every doctrine over long periods of time before he incorporated it into his own written work. His pages were written from firsthand experience; they were not copied wholesale from other books. He was essentially an original thinker.

158
My experiments were performed on myself but my conclusions were not limited to them. I watched the results in many other persons. But whereas they experienced them blindly, I experienced them critically, with my analytic faculties alert.

159

I went both abroad on land and sea as well as within mind and heart. The higher Self, the soul, God—whatever name we like to call it by—was the object of my quest. My findings were shared in my books and interviews.

160

I endeavoured to bring the theoretical principles and inner experiences of mental quiet into a thoroughly scientific form. This could only be possible by approaching them with complete impartial objectivity, with an attitude of mind that was sternly critical and yet profoundly sympathetic wherever criticism or sympathy were called for.

161

I write out of no other authority than my own metaphysical reflections, my own mystical experiences, my own studies and observations of other people's spiritual quests—ancient, medieval, and modern—throughout the world. Much of what I have described, here or elsewhere, has been what I myself have experienced. If nothing else hinted it, surely the precision of my statements, the vividness of my phrases, and the reality of my descriptions hint at firsthand experience? If I did not know from personal knowledge the course which this quest usually takes, if I had not endured its crushing darknesses and sacrificial anguish, its perplexing distresses and tantalizing oscillations—as much as its dazzling illuminations and unforgettable ecstasies, its benedictory graces and healing serenity—surely I could not have written about it as I did?

162

The shadows were falling all around me but still I was reluctant to switch on the lamp and dispel the half-gloom. For the stilled mind kept me in a stilled body, fastened to the chair by invisible cords.

163

If this were merely an idealistic message it would hardly be worth its ink. In the result such a thing would be a fine but futile effort. But because it is based on the firmest of facts, because it is truly scientific, I have taken the trouble of writing it down.

164

I sought and gained knowledge to impart it to the world and deliberately enmeshed myself in experience to share it with the world.

165

One day it will be recognized even by the academic world how much pioneer spade-work I have done in this metaphysical field, even as I had already done in the mystical field.

166

There is need of more personal experience in religion during the coming era. The old beliefs are too faded and the object of their worship too remote. It is only the spiritual leaders capable of helping others to realize such an experience who can show mankind the way to a true external peace. But if mankind do not listen in sufficient numbers to the few leaders who are now available, then their sufferings will not abate but rather continue and worsen. People do not realize the importance of such work as we are doing, because they rely on external methods too much and on internal ones not enough. Wrong thoughts and false beliefs being at the root of their troubles, only correct thought and true beliefs will bring them out of such troubles. The philosopher's work is to make this remedy available to them. There he stops for he will not force it down their throats. Nor could he.

The message and the marketplace

167

It is not for me to play any spectacular part in the present epoch. I have not issued these books for any propagandist purpose. Mine is a specialist's task working in a special field. But despite all this, it will not be easy for anyone to run a measuring-rod over the amount of work done. I have set ripples going but how far they will spread is the concern of destiny. P.B.'s body will pass away but his ideas will go on working. For these ideas have taken hold in some minds, who in turn will transmit them to other minds and another generation. The legacy of ideas which he toiled over during his lifetime will be with them long after his passing from this earthly plane.

168

If these pages can but recall a few people to the paramount importance of philosophical culture, can sustain in them large hopes for their own future as for that of mankind, can keep before them a shining vision in the darkness, the effort will find justification.

169

Whoever thinks that these talks present him only with mere abstractions is greatly mistaken; they really deal in things that are vital to human beings because they are the foundation things of life. Properly understood, these "abstractions" will help people to more successful living. Whoever will endeavour to translate the ideas of this psychological technique into action will find his prize in equipoised existence, inner peace, and spiritual power.

170

If this message is false, you cannot know this until you have fully investigated it, for to come to conclusions before thorough examinations is unworthy of a thinking person. If this message is true, then it is of colossal importance to the world, and to you.

171

The teaching which is particularly expressed in my books is not, so far as I know, imparted by any individual who is accessible to the general public; nor is there any institution to develop the capacities of learners along these lines. This situation exists because the teaching traverses its own unique field. None other approaches life from quite the same standpoint.

172

Some of these ideas are too new, others too old. Some, in their impact upon the public mind, have not gone beyond rousing curiosity, whereas others have gained ardent sympathy.

173

Those who would put this account aside as a mere dream and who would lay this printed record down as purely fantastic will have their ideas compulsorily changed within the while of a decade or less. There is no dream here. Nothing is more substantial than the eternal truth of man's spiritual existence. Nothing could be more real than the experiences which come to him when he can unchain the mind from the dense vibrations of the fleshly body.

174

We have a message for this age and we shall descend into the marketplace and give it. Hitherto, few would listen to the mystic's message, for he was unable or unwilling to explain it in terms of a practical application to the need of the hour.

175

In the long run and after I have gone from this earth, it is my work which shall vindicate me, for a pioneer achievement like that cannot be hidden.

176

The thoughts phrased in this book may yet enlighten the world and bring about a stranger change than any history has hitherto witnessed.

177

The work of providing copies of P.B.'s books for local public libraries where they are not yet available is a constructive one. It is a more effective method of spiritual propagation than costlier methods. It breeds good karma.

178

To a large extent, I created my own audience for these books. This in turn was a pioneering work which induced others to emulate my journeys or copy my writings—not only literally as to subject, style, and even words, but in their own several ways. I know also, from the evidence which continually came up, that this work brought many in every part of the Occident to appreciate Oriental thought for the first time.

179

It is a fact, and an indisputable one, that my writings have set many people on the Quest for the first time.

180

We must press this message forward, and we must persist with our pressure; but whether the world wants to accept it now, or will perforce want to accept it after its crisis, is less our concern than the world's.

181

I shall tie myself to none of the tattered fragments of organized religions which exist today. The exposition of truth I shall attempt to give will be along absolute lines, not the relative and veiled presentations of the past. My impulsive pen holds out little promise of soothing readers into somnolence with dead thoughts; rather will I let it leap beyond the bounds of prudence and startle them every third page with new or vigorous ideas. Finally, the main task must ever remain to announce anew the old truth of man's in-dwelling God.

182

That so slight a cause as a few pages of printed matter should lead to so serious a result as giving a totally new direction to some people's lives, is one reason why writing has come to mean for me a ministry whose character is almost as sacred as any vocation could be.

183

They will need to study these pages repeatedly until the ideas expressed therein seem lucid and logical, rational and persuasive to them.

184

Those who imagine this book contains a mere set of vague and ineffective words, flung out for public notice for a time only, to die down and disappear before the next craze for a mystery novel, are doomed to sorry disillusionment. History itself will echo every warning made here, and prove every point.

185

We had aroused a few minds to the needs of considering such age-old questions about human and universal existence, and if we had initiated a few more into unfamiliar methods of meditation, then these efforts would have justified themselves. But evidence has accumulated that those who have been directly touched number not a mere few but scores of thousands, whilst those who have been indirectly touched must number hundreds of thousands.

186

I wish therefore to put before readers the fundamentals of this hidden philosophy in concise form and plain phrasing, to substitute a brief bird's-eye view of the whole matter, which—though it may leave some stony places of thought difficult to climb over—will nevertheless put them in possession of the basic principles and provide them with an Ariadne's thread to guide them through the maze of life and its problems of reflection and of experience. Nay, even if I fail to do this but succeed only in kindling within them something of that love of Truth, that passionate quest for the meaning of all life, of all experience, and of all this wonderful world, I shall have accomplished enough to justify our coming together in these pages.

187

However interesting these ideas may be to some people, they will probably ask, "Can we extract any personal meaning, if not value, from them?"

188

After all, if this teaching helps some readers penetrate the mystery of the higher power even just a little, it will really help them a lot.

189

In writing this book to tell what I know of God, I am simply trying to tell other people about the possibilities of their own spiritual growth and to emphasize what has been said before: that through cultivation of their intuitive feelings and obedience to the disciplinary higher laws, they too may know the Overself.

190

If yesterday we had to travel in a lonely wilderness, today we have the pardonable satisfaction of observing others gradually shaping their ideas along the lines we had previously laid down.

191

The shadows of slaughter have fallen everywhere. Of what is all this the result? Ignorance! Those who know what life means and why we are here are lamentably few. The millions perish in darkness. There is, therefore, no better service for him nowadays than to contribute the knowledge he has gained in the hope that it will alleviate the dark corners of the world of their distresses. I say "corners" deliberately, for the world at large will be too insensitive to him.

192

This book is the "gospel" and not the "grammar." It proposes to show direction, to give a stimulus, but it does not profess to go into many details and to explain a thousand minor values and methods. This is not to say that the "grammar" is not necessary or that it will not be written.

I have filled this book with generalizations and denuded it of details, and I have done this of set aim, because I believe it wants *Aspiration, Direction,* and *Purpose* more than it wants trivial targets at which to shoot its thoughts and exertions. So, if I be accused of excessive generalization, of giving little data and less details, I plead guilty! The absence of facts and figures is explained more by my candid confession that I write to reach the intuitions of a few people alone, and less by a dogmatic assertion that these proposals are prophetic, in that they reveal the inevitable trend of our times and will come into being whether we work for them or not. I am trying to fix in the minds of those readers who will try to think with me for a while a sense of the direction we need to take in thus restoring our spiritual fortunes.

4

REFLECTIONS ON TRUTH

Sharing truth

A mere contribution to the world's thought is not to be despised, but it cannot change the heavy materialism which overhangs us. Spiritual regeneration can only come from a greater source. The greatest I know is God. And He has His instruments; He can pick on any man in this wide world and turn him into a spiritual Tamerlane—the blessing, and not the scourge, of this planet.

2

If we do not become wistful, envious, or despairing, it is usually helpful to hear of the spiritual experiences of others, and especially of their highest experiences.

3

There are lots of biographies of men and women who became famous because they achieved something in the world, but few biographies of men and women whose achievements were outside the world, and inside themselves, particularly inside their consciousness. Very few have become aware of Awareness itself, which is the highest achievement possible to any human being. These memorials of those who got outside the herd of ignorant mankind give their advice and suggestions to the few who seek to know themselves.

4

Buddha himself foresaw that a new teacher would arise within a few thousand years after himself, and that this man would have a higher spiritual status than himself. But what is of special interest is his further prediction that a higher spiritual path would, through this medium, be opened to mankind. Everything points to the fact that the date when this teacher and his teaching will appear is within the century. Both the effect of science on man's intellect and the effect of science on his wars have brought him close to it.

5

Others will take up this work where we leave it unfinished. If my effort can do nothing more at least it will make easier for those who are destined to follow after me a jungle-road which I had to travel under great difficulties. I have roughly cleared an area of human culture which my successors may cultivate and on which they may perhaps produce a perfect crop one day. I did what I could but the fullness of results will be theirs alone. The effects of my thinking will not fully declare themselves in our own day. It is not pride that makes me say that the volume which follows *The Hidden Teaching Beyond Yoga* is the first methodical embodiment in a modern language of this tradition, as well as the first synthetic explanation of it in scientific terminology, for the book is called forth by its epoch and someone would sooner or later have written it. What is really interesting is not who writes it but the fact that it was written in our own time. For something there achieved marks a most important stage of human cultural history.

I have indeed undertaken what I believe to be a pioneer work. I cannot give my patronage to any particular system. I can bestow it only on Truth, which is unique and systemless. For enough of the sacred presence is at my side, enough of the disciplinary self-transformation has been achieved, and enough of the mental perception arrived at, to enable me to take up the external task of preparing others for illumination in their turn.(P)

6

Important messages have been given on varying levels of understanding to the human race from time to time. Some have been given in religion, others in science, some in metaphysics, others in mysticism, and still others in the inventions and arts.

7

It takes time for ideas to seep down from original thinkers to those among the masses who sincerely try to learn and understand them.

8

When a mystic like Brunton writes strongly in advocacy of a revolutionary doctrine like mentalism, it is only a negligible few who are likely to be convinced that it is a true doctrine. But when a first-class scientist like Sir James Jeans writes even mildly in advocacy of it in his authoritative books, many will begin to sit up and take notice. For the name of Brunton means little today whereas the name of Jeans must be regarded with respect.

9

Is it our business to enquire into every detail of the messenger's life, or ought we to be satisfied with the message alone? Is it a sign of vulgarity, this desire to learn all we can about his person, his history, his background, and his circumstances? Is it not a fact that such information may enable us to understand the message better? Curiosity and wonder about great men are natural and must be expected.

10

Carlyle tells us that history is just the biographies of great personalities. These great ones are usually of the inspirational type. They are geniuses who are the creators and the initiators of new enterprises.

11

Every man who comes into the public arena with a mystical message may take it for granted that he will be suspiciously watched for signs of insincerity, commercialism, or self-interest.

12

A man can best convince people of his own kind, status, and class. It would be far more sensible for a businessman, for instance, to attempt to teach other men in their own way than for a yellow-robed swami to do so—to take an extreme case.

13

The prophet who cannot sanction the materialism of his time need not fall into despairing inertia. He is obliged to criticize this spiritual deep sleep for the sake of those who may respond, however few they be.

14

So sure is the revelation that, like the Chinese mentalist Lu Hsiang-shan, "He is prepared to wait for the appearance of a sage a hundred epochs later, and has no misgivings."

15

Who are the real benefactors of the race? A properly balanced answer to this question must consider *both* the spiritual and physical factors, both the intellectual and aesthetic.

16

Take the message, if you care to, and absorb what is useful to you in it; but do not seek to detain the messenger.

17

Were the wise men of the ancients any wiser than those of our own time? It is not entirely unprofitable to ask such a question, nor is it wise to give the snap answer, "Certainly not!" only because science and its knowledge, industry and its achievement, seem to demonstrate a complete and unarguable superiority.

18

How many wise men have died in the past centuries—and their wisdom with them—who have failed to communicate with their fellows in some way!

19

We know so little of the infinity behind human nature that those who return with reports of it deserve a better hearing than those who inquire into its finite manifestations. Yet do they get it?

20

Some of the greatest historical names have been those of men who were secret disciples, famous figures working in an imperfect world with imperfect people to carry out a purpose higher than a merely personal one. This is also true of groups.

21

I shall have to lay down my pen one day, but the intuitions and experiences which flow through its ink shall find other hands and continue to publish themselves to the world.

22

There are other writers who can take my place to equal or better advantage. The same destiny which used me can use them.

23

My task is only to *inaugurate* such a movement of thought; other persons must lead it.

24

In spite of their defects my books have made a useful contribution to a development which is urgently needed in modern society. Others will doubtless come after me and do much better and more careful work in this line of thought.

25

To revive this ancient knowledge, to reactivate its study, and to bring it into a modern adaptation and application—this has been the aim of several scattered pioneers during the past hundred years.

26

That a man who lives so near me as to be almost a neighbour, that such a man should have become the recipient of a divine revelation, seems highly improbable. The far-off scene carries a suggestion of mystery. There are greater possibilities in the unknown. The prophet who finds honour will get a better hearing if he travels forthwith.

27

If the masters have been buried, cremated, or killed, their inspiration has not been buried with them.

28

Whoever has benefited by these ideas is under an obligation to make them available to whoever else may be ready to receive them. They should pool their best experiences and finest thoughts through the written or spoken word as noteworthy in their inner life. Let them write of what they know, not suppose, of what they have come to understand as true or what they have felt, witnessed, or experienced. Let them take care to keep within the range of their experience or knowledge, for most articles on these subjects are vitiated by the flights of imagination over fact. There is enough material in life and in thought with which they are familiar to render it unnecessary to touch the unknown.

Seeking the impersonal

29

The essence of this teaching is to be found only in that unlimited sphere where impersonality and universality reign. No better name than philosophy could be found for it, because no other is so impersonal and so universal. Although Brunton has written so many pages about it, he does not want it called by his name and turned into a cult. If Bruntonism should arise, he himself would be the first anti-Bruntonist! He is not at all interested in the triumph or fame of P.B. But he is deeply interested in the triumph and spread of that attitude which will best advance mankind's spiritual life. He does not ask for personal acceptance and honour to be bestowed upon what is true and helpful in his ideas. He does not want people to follow him but to follow the quest of truth. He does not call them to a declared creed but to a suggested way of approach, to the integral philosophical way which secures results no narrow sect could secure. Let people use the signposts he has erected, by all means, but let them not ignore the many other valuable ones which have also been erected for their benefit from the earliest times until today.

30

Sharing my ideas with others is not the same as claiming to be a personal guru: the latter is a responsibility which I could not accept, do not desire, and have not authority for.

31

Because the Quest is, and must be, an individual matter, I have sought to present the Truth-Expression in a way best suited to our times and needs—through my books—wherein each individual may find for himself the message he is ready for.

32

If such intense and intimate experiences are here given out publicly, there is good reason for doing so; only small minds may believe that the motives are those of egotism and vanity. Rather is it a sharing with others to help them.

33

I regret that I cannot conscientiously recommend any particular teaching, school, or society, for none of them teach exactly what I teach myself.

34

When I die I shall leave no disciples—only adherents to my views or followers of my ways.

35

I would rather stir people's minds into an activity of their own than have them follow unthinkingly behind me.

36

I have not only refused to organize a cult but have prevented others from doing so who wished it ardently.

37

It was my mission to launch many readers on this quest, but to travel no farther with them. It was their part to find their way to personal teachers, to congruent teachings, and continue the quest with them.

38

Let them remember that the Truth comes not from any person but from the Holy Spirit. It is from such a source that what is worthy in my writings has come; the errors however are mine. Let them therefore describe themselves as students of philosophy, not as followers of Brunton.(P)

39

P.B. as a private person does not count. There are hundreds of millions of such persons anyway. What is one man and his quest? P.B.'s personal experiences and views are not of any particular importance or special consequence. What happens to the individual man named P.B. is a matter of no account to anyone except himself. But what happens to the hundreds of thousands of spiritual seekers today who are following the same path that he pioneered is a serious matter and calls for prolonged consideration. Surely the hundreds of thousands of Western seekers who stand behind him and whom indeed, in one sense, he represents, do count. P.B. as a symbol of the scattered group of Western truth-seekers who, by following his writings so increasingly and so eagerly, virtually follow him also, does count. He personifies their aspirations, their repulsion from materialism and attraction toward mysticism, their interest in Oriental wisdom and their shepherdless state. As a symbol of this Western movement of thought, he is vastly greater than himself. In his mind and person the historic need for a new grasp of the contemporary spiritual problem found a plain-speaking voice.(P)

40

Too many writers on spiritual subjects make too great an attempt to appear omniscient. Perhaps they are emotionally carried away by the force of their convictions—as I once was. Perhaps it is one of the traps which beset the path of writing. Perhaps it is nothing else than puffed-up conceit. But the end result, in any case, is to delude the reader.

41

The writer rarely learns to what consequences his words have led, but he goes on planting them, like seeds, anyway.

42

I discovered with the years that the prayer I had made, so often and so earnestly, as a youngster near the threshold of adult manhood, was being adequately answered. It was a simple prayer, nothing more than to be used for the spiritual awakening of others through the written word. It did not go beyond that. Consequently, when those who became awakened, as well as those who were already awake but needed new inspiration, tried to make me their personal guide for the further path and the years beyond, I shrank back and refused. Only rarely did I make any exception; when affinity was too close and service too willing, I left my solitude and gave whatever I could. But in nearly all other cases there was no mandate to enter a teaching or helping relationship of the kind that they sought and needed, and so I firmly resisted importunity. How correct this attitude was revealed itself usually in a few years, for these people found their way by then to the particular cults or guides suited to them, or mixed their diet and took something from each of several sources, or preferred to wait and work alone rather than do any of these things. Anyway, they did not still want me and I was left in peace.

43

I have stated the truth as I saw it, not attempted to teach it to others— which is really a different activity.

44

To be regarded as a spiritual master, or as a holy man, would be embarrassing to me.

45

Others may join any sect they like but I have never joined, and do not intend to join, the Bruntonians!

46

I have done what I could to prevent the existence of a Brunton cult.

47

It is *their* problem, not mine, to find the particular teaching and teacher best suited to their personality and level. It is not my duty to go beyond the general teachings given in the books. Those who demand personal instruction must find their own affinity. I do not give names and addresses and recommendations, but stay within the area of my authorization. Too many fail to realize that their own higher self has already begun to work and that they must co-operate with it.

48

If this text can jolt a reader here and there into new experiments and newer thoughts, it will be for him to take off from that point and get others for whatever further help is needed.

49

Let him take from this literature what seems to apply to his own case, what seems to help his own need. It will not help to follow a path specifically intended for other cases and other needs.

50

I am sorry that I do not know any teacher who can be recommended to them. The references in my books to the characteristics and methods of true teachers represent my conception of the ideal teacher and are not necessarily a portrait of someone I have met in the flesh. However, if I do not know where they can find such a man, or if he does not exist, then I am his forerunner and foreteller. He is needed and he must come. Providence will see to it and knows when and where he will appear.

51

It is not my business to get involved in other people's problems. Is it not enough to attend to my own? Years of experience have imposed humility on me. How soon one's own fallible service becomes meddling! I carry enough burden—why emulate Atlas?

52

The best way to stop interviewees asking personal questions is to shrug them off with a laugh, as if it is a joke, saying: "I thought you came here about your own self, not me, or about the ideas in the books!" This, if done in a light-hearted smiling way, will force them to turn to other subjects than me without disconcerting them.

53

For myself I reject every honour bestowed on me by those who call themselves disciples, but for the idea and office of teacher I accept it.

54

He will reject the name of disciple because he rejects the title of guru. For his wish is to draw readers nearer to truth, not to himself. If, however, they persist in their self-styled discipleship then he insists on remaining a guru "at a distance," in an impersonal relationship, so that it makes him a non-guru.

55

There is no particular system of philosophy which can be called Paul Brunton's, no movement or group attached to his name. There are readers of his books, but no personal disciples.

56

He is not a Jesus to save others from themselves: in the end, he believes, all will be saved anyway.

57

He is not a guru, belongs to no disciples, binds none to himself. He makes no promises of guidance, help, grace. Whatever of these things come forth from him, come as a bounty, a gift without desire for a return.

58

In the beginning I did not know that the writer had any responsibility for his words. I learned this by degrees.

59

Do not deify man: nobody is guaranteed against the making of mistakes.

60

To the objection that since P.B.'s books contain teachings, he is therefore a guru whatever denials are made, his answer is: books are general, written for an anonymous mass-group whereas a guru is occupied with individual students, with named separate persons. An author's relationship with his reader is quite impersonal: the latter is quite unknown to the author, the former is never seen by the reader. But a guru meets, converses with, trains, and guides each disciple personally.

61

He will not seek to draw public attention to himself unless it is in his destiny to do so because he has some public work to perform. He will prefer to keep his holiness hidden from his fellows, and so it will be left for some among them to discover whether he is holy or not. This secrecy provides a wall of outward defense against the negative and evil forces which find plenty of vehicles among his fellow human beings.

62

I began with an audience but soon found myself with a following.

63

Many ask for a teacher. Mature experience has shown the inadvisability of taking such a course. It is better for each one in the end to be guided by the inner promptings of his own Overself which is always with him. Personal experience of teachers both in India and in the West makes it impossible to recommend them to others.

64

Should a philosophical journal be started sometime in the future, let it be clearly understood that there is nothing beyond that to be hoped for. There will be neither personal nor class instruction, other than the printed material contained in its pages. There will be no organization whatever. There is a possibility of receiving instruction in mysticism or philosophy through the pages of a semi-private journal, which is yet to be published. Even the idea of a fellowship of students is not acceptable, because it would still be some kind of organization.

65

The seeker must remember that his Real Guide is his own divine Soul, or Higher Self; that it is This which led him to his present stage of awareness, whilst my books were merely used as instruments. It is to this Self that he should address his prayers and petitions for Grace and Guidance.

66

I know that this free, uncommitted kind of approach is quite unsuited to most persons who feel and seek and expect to find some kind of definite structured course of training or guidance. Their way is proper and suited to them. I can help them but little; I cannot be a *personal* guide to anyone.

67

I would like to repudiate the mistaken impression that I can be coaxed or coerced into accepting the flattering proposals of certain people which would, in effect, give them permission to form groups using my name in some way.

68

If it be claimed that with the public appearance of my later books I became a teacher, whether I acknowledge it or not, I reply that if that be so I am one who seeks not to save his disciples but rather to be saved from them.

69

I soon began to get more letters from readers, utter strangers though they were, than I had the facilities to answer. Some asked for advice, others presumed to give it; but most expressed the keen desire to find a teacher and wanted me to recommend one.

70

It is not demanded that anyone approach these chapters in the spirit of unresisting discipleship, but it is demanded that he approach them with a certain degree of intellectual sympathy—for the time of reading the pages, at least.

71

I do not seek prominence in the limelight; I prefer a position of obscure, unfettered freedom. Because I have sunk all ambitions, want nothing from anyone, and can have nothing taken away from me, I enjoy the life of a literary man because it permits me to be freer, in contrast with the life of any other profession that I know. Fame curtails liberty and creates jealousy. Celebrity is also a form of bondage. Liberty is my need.

72

If he can read between and even behind the lines, he will get much more than is explicit in them.

73

I have made my readers collaborate on Truth's quest in all my writings so as to awaken them—not let them repeat parrot-like, like new theologians, in the jargon of cults.

74

There is no common meeting ground between the man who writes to arouse admiration and the man who writes to state truth.

75

I write for the few, and if the public wish to buy my books, they do so at their own peril of misunderstanding me!

76

The ideal of sainthood neither attracts my feelings nor appeals to my intelligence. I myself make no pretense to be a saint and it would be hypocritical to let any follower make it for me.

77

It will be a bitter irony of fate if the creed which I have dropped should become the creed of my students.

78

I refuse to let others regard me as a superior being and I will not meet them, either in person or by correspondence, on any other terms than those of equality. Since I make no pretensions on my own behalf, it would be inconsistent to let them do it for me. It is unfortunate that the reputation I enjoy is so exaggerated! And it is amazing how often people want you to be dishonest with them, just to satisfy their delusive preconceptions of you. How many have tried to induce me to become their personal master, or the head of an ashram, or the leader of a cultist following! How firmly have I had to detach myself from their pressures and become deaf to their importunities! No matter what I insisted to the contrary, they clothed me with qualities, powers, and knowledge I did not possess. I became very uneasy. It was of no avail that I denied the reputation fathered on me. Finally, I saw that I was lending myself to this false position by answering letters, granting interviews, and getting involved with friends who were seekers after help. All this was a kind of insincere posing, although it did not appear so on the surface. So I brought it to an end, cut off nearly all contacts with others, and made myself inaccessible. With that, many turned to the spiritual guides who were quite willing to collect a following, lost interest or faith in me, and left me in peace. If it be criticized that I have adopted a selfish attitude, I must defend myself by first recalling the Tibetan saying about a half-developed guide being like a half-blind man leading his credulous disciples into a ditch and falling in with them too and then pointing out that yielding to misconceived importunities is a weakness even when it takes on the semblance of compassionate service. To allow others to thrust upon me the role of personal teacher when no mandate for it has been received from within myself, my higher self, would be wrong. It is therefore my duty to resist their pleading.

79

It takes all my time and brains to teach myself, for my pupil is an intractable and forgetful fellow. How then could I be in a position to teach others? Hence, I have not given any encouragement to those who wanted to become disciples but have told them time and again to find their own individual road to attainment, to become the disciple only of their own higher self. I have asked them to look upon me as a fellow-student who is striving to perfect his knowledge rather than as a teacher who is seeking to impart it.

80

Although I have had a large correspondence from all parts of the world and given numerous interviews during my travels, I would never attempt to form a sect or a society for, with perhaps the single exception of the Quakers, the history of religious organizations and mystical communities is quite unedifying.

81

I cannot undertake the work of organized and systematic personal instruction but must, owing to the force of major circumstances, leave my books to make their own way, find their own students, and serve by stimulating interest and thought.

82

Organizations really exist to help the beginners. The advanced student cuts loose from the herd and makes his own path, or finds his personal teacher. And because my message is chiefly for the few who are advanced enough to appreciate it, I do not care to handicap myself with the formation of any organization.

83

It was never my desire to be the founder of a new school. If such a thing should develop after my death, it will be only because fate has shaped circumstances in such a way as to bring it about for her own purposes, not mine. For I have never been conscious of bringing any new truth to the world, although I have tried to find new ways of presenting the old truths.

84

It was entirely outside my purpose to encourage dubious cults and dangerous charlatans or to promote a Western emigration to Eastern ashrams. Yet it must regretfully be admitted that such institutions and persons have unfortunately benefited by my work, because there was nothing to prevent the unbalanced, the credulous, and the neurotic from reading it.

85

Those who were puzzled by the author's transition from writings which were praised to writings which were deplored were precisely those readers who most needed to make such a transition themselves.

86

No one is required to submit to any ruling made by me, but only to what his own intelligence can agree with or sanction.

87

I seek and possess no disciples, yet it would appear from reports that many somehow are being taught.

88

Because I try to share the results of my mystical philosophical researches with fellow students, nobody is entitled to sneer that I set myself up as a pretended little saviour. I have not yet so lost all sense of humour as to call my activity a redemptive one. On the contrary, I must confess to getting a little fun out of it. I leave to others the solemn illusion that they can change mankind overnight or even by next Wednesday. I have to do something on this planet, anyway, and writing being about the only activity I seem to be fit for at all, I might as well write about the things which interest me and a few like-minded people, as write about the places, the people, and the goods which so many publishers, governments, and advertising organizations have unsuccessfully tried with fat fees to cajole me into doing.

89

The books are a communication of ideas, not an invitation to disturb privacy. They formulate the results of various kinds of research, not the baby-food offerings of a guru to attract disciples.

90

I have stirred up their intellectual processes and, if I have exposed the prejudices of superstitions which unconsciously govern their attitudes, then I have truly helped them.

91

Thus I have unwittingly started the outer circle of a movement which I had no intention of starting, a movement which has no physical organization as its body and to which you will, therefore, be unable to find any reference in the usual directories. It is a movement which may be joined without fuss or trouble, without formality or fee. Membership depends on the applicant himself and not on me or other men.

92

If we have forced a few of them to think, they may end with clearer conceptions even if they do not end with our own conceptions.

93

In the postwar world where everybody overvalues political economic and materialistic panaceas, the philosopher may find a modest and humble duty of spiritual service to perform.

94

The mass of mankind, whether high or low in station, caste, status, needs identifiers, labels, titles, and uniforms—something which can be seen, heard, or read to separate one class of person from the others. If he is a minister of the church, he must wear appropriate robes so that he may be treated with the respect or reverence due to a titular symbol of the divine being. But who is to separate the philosopher if he refuses to show, wear, give, or use any outward signs of his inward condition? Who is to distinguish this man who is quite content to be inconspicuous, but independent, who takes his ideal from a Chinaman who lived 2,500 years ago, a certain Lao Tzu?

95

I wish no organized institution to be founded upon my name and writing. It is not the logical outcome of all my work.

96

I have a dislike, amounting almost to a horror, of being regarded as another cult-leader or as a professional yogi. I despise commercialized holiness and avoid its dupes. My only profession is writing and if I write on subjects connected with the inner rather than the outer life, that is only because they are vastly more interesting to my mind and stimulate my pen into activity where the others leave it motionless.

97

If these ideas are warmly taken up by people who are coldly indifferent to their source, I shall not be dissatisfied. It is the triumph of right principles, not of particular persons, that we should seek.

98

One principal aim in these writings is to enlarge their reader's self-reliance and to arouse his independent thinking.

99

Writing about these ideas, experiences, and practices does not entitle me to set up as a guru, does not provide me with any authority to involve myself in other people's personal lives. Although I have got myself personally involved in the teachings, I am still writing about them as a professional author.

100

I do not desire to create a school of thought; I do not want to solidify human thought into congealed dogmas; I do not wish anyone to worship a crusty organization.

101

Some reforming causes and occult cults and new religions tried to corral me into joining or supporting them, presumably because they thought my name as a celebrity would be an asset to them.

102

It may be mere conceit or else sheer stubbornness which makes a writer indifferent to other people's opinions of his work. Even if his indifference springs from a correct awareness that he is on the right road, still, he ought to be humble enough to believe that whatever he has done of worth could always be improved.

103

The books have for intention the awakening to certain ideas of minds that are at a point of readiness for them. The author of the books is not able to go farther than that; he is not a guru to guide the reader personally through all the successive stages.

104

My only serious significance as a writer does not lie in the quality of my work, about which I hold no illusions, but in the symbolic relation and representational capacity whereby I, as a Westerner, sought Eastern wisdom and I, as a mid-twentieth-century man, sought deliverance from the prevailing materialism.

My own personal quest is unimportant but Western man's quest is not. Something more than my personal life is involved. So far as my own character reflects certain characteristics and shares the trends of my generation, it is not arrogance to say that my personal search is also representative of one group within that generation's search. But so far as my character outsteps it, the search is a creative and pioneering one. The same struggle which enacts itself within my mind repeats itself in dozens of other minds. For it is representative of a development which must necessarily occur in this twentieth century above all other centuries to those who seek mysticism's true insights rather than its dangerous blindnesses.

I do not care to appeal to historicity and authority but rather to experience and intelligence. So I do not care to associate this teaching with P.B. as a person but rather with the research and seeking of his generation. It would be an error to regard P.B. as merely an individual airing his personal views. For a tremendous and momentous conflict between distinct ideologies is now going on in the world of thought. His attitude is representative of a particular one of these ideologies. The ideas at stake are immensely more significant than the ups and downs of one man's fame.

The challenge of formulation

105

Literature has a high mission to perform in these awful times. For it can bless us with mental peace amid the outward turmoil of alarms and chaotic situations. It can console us with philosophic reflections about the fundamental objectives of life amid the agonies of personal loss and illness, and it can keep alive the lofty ideals of goodwill and tolerance in an era when hatred and violence have bulked so largely before our eyes. It is through great writings that so many mystics and thinkers of bygone centuries have legated a golden record of their aspirations, a sublime catalogue of their dreams, a motley manifestation of their spiritual impulses, and a factual document of their celestial traffics. These bygone men and women passed the torch of knowledge and inspiration from one generation to another until we find it ready for our own hands today. It is our privilege and duty not only to look for the flaming torch but to bear it, and not only to bear it but so to cherish it that it shall burn ever more brightly still, when, in the days to come, a new generation will succeed to its possession.

106

Those alone who have descended from the sublime state of divine withdrawnness to be confronted by our world of intolerance and hatred and greed and jarring strife can appreciate the difficulty of this task, can perceive how hard it is to express the ineffable.

107

The greater task has been to formulate, and not to disseminate, this teaching.

108

Such public self-analysis may come uneasily and with difficulty out of a mystic's pen, but surely it will give a little light upon both quest and goal to the neophytes.

109

To find words that would fit, represent, and be worthy of these ideas and experiences, which would have scientific precision and poetic richness at the same time, requires time and talent beyond mine.

110

The most precious thing which anyone could find cannot be given to others. Spirit is incommunicable and impalpable. But words, which tell *about it*, can be given to them.

111

Because the very inwardness of philosophic truth makes it necessary that it must be understood by each person for himself, those who have found it know how hard, how insuperable, are the difficulties in the way of communicating it.

112

What anyone writes about Reality remains nothing more than a series of black marks on white paper unless he writes it out of his own direct living experience. Then his words become inspired in themselves and inspiring to others.

113

How can a poor mystic come to one of these and tell him of the simple mystery? Hence, the strange veilings in which his thoughts are wrapped, the writing—rifted with occult similes and mystical metaphors—that is the native language of the soul. The higher part of man shrinks from kissing his bestial mouth, and so veils her face seven times, that she may move through this world unharmed and recognized only by her own fit mates.

114

Any penman with experience can write of high matters, divine matters sometimes, but he is then called upon to live them. His words come back later, to praise or to accuse, according to the result.

115

It may be that too intimate memory of a remarkable mystical experience has afflicted me with the torments of literary Calvinism so that I always accuse each page of being born in the sin of spiritual ignorance.

116

Few are able to find the needed time to make the independent researches that a proper clarification of the subject requires, while fewer still have the ability to do so.

117

Thoughts, which seem to come glibly enough to the utterance of this pen, were usually found after long travail and sometimes after many tears.

118

A combination of analytical capacity with firsthand personal mystical experience is needed for such writing, quite apart from the intellectual talents which are needed for all serious writing.

119

We writers must find what words we can for those experiences, truths, moods, intuitions, and states which are called spiritual.

120

Everyone needs to read. He who has no time or taste for such an activity has no time or taste for learning truth, widening knowledge, removing error, and avoiding suffering. For reading, like reflection and travel, will enable him to compare his own little heap of experience with the experiences of other people all over the world. He may, if he chooses, benefit by their recorded experience and learn where he has been wrong, where right. He who travels widely, intelligently, and observantly, that is to say, with an active mind and not like a baggage trunk, will at least build a broader perspective on life. Literature records the results of mental travel and to read right literature is to start your mind on journeys from which much may be gained. But it is better not to read at all than to read rubbish. For good reading will enrich life whereas bad reading will deteriorate it. This book, then, will try to make its readers *think*—which means that it will probably make some quite angry but many others a little wiser. It is not possible to write a recipe for a dish which shall satisfy all tastes and it is not possible to write a book which shall satisfy all readers. I accept beforehand therefore the fact that many people will dislike these pages. Even the mystical aspirants amongst mankind are a mixed, complex lot with contradictory outlooks and conflicting aims. There is no doctrine that will appeal to all.

Obstacles to inspiration

121
A whole lifetime of constant quest for the Beauty and Truth that lie hidden in the heart of the universe will not be enough to find them.

122
How dismal to hear a cynic's exclamation: "A man cannot change himself." But how hopeful to hear Socrates' own experience that he had come into the world with many vices yet had rid himself of them with the help of reason. In the Bible it is written that man is made in the image of God. Would not that noun more likely be positive in attitude, uplifting in spirit?

123
Everyone is entitled to do what he can do for himself, but not everyone is wise enough to do what is good for himself.

124
Now and again I am compelled to stand aside and gaze at my fellows in awe and wonder, for their one aim seems to be the very reverse of "Excelsior!" With them it is ever downward—deeper and deeper into matter, mammon, and neurasthenia. Verily this is the Gethsemane of the Christself within them—that immortal spirit seeking to free them from the thick folds of illusion in which they have been entangled. I know that this is so, for I too have sinned with them, and gone down into the dark depths, and become entangled in those tempting folds; but never could I still the hunger of the heart to fulfil the most sacred and primal purpose of life.

125
He lets the five senses delude him into taking their world as the acme of reality. He lets the ego intoxicate him with its own passions, desires, ambitions, and attachments. Is it any wonder that the word "soul" becomes devoid of all meaning for him in the end?

126
The grand term "philosophy" has come to mean a system of speculative thought, that is, a series of logically stated guesses.

127
Complete impartiality is as impossible to achieve as complete detachment. Where are those who can look at a situation from all its sides, or take the loss of all possessions without any feeling of pain at all?

128

If I can enter into communion of the soul with a man, and not merely into communication of the intellect, each of us will come nearer to the other in understanding and friendliness.

129

They are experiencing the world in an upside-down fashion. Matter, which is illusory, is felt to be real. Spirit, which is real, is not even felt at all.

130

What is it that leads us into sympathy with another's painful suffering?

131

When contentment is pushed to extreme, it turns into irresponsibility and indolence. When it is replaced by discontent, the door opens to greed, ambition, and fleshly desires.

132

What formerly attracted him will now leave him listless or bored or even be seen as a source of anxiety in the end. No longer content to obey the urges of the physical senses or the curiosities of the mental ego, he may merely drift along or else repeat the rituals of worldly life more or less automatically.

133

It is at the sight of such a melancholy spectacle that we bless those earlier days which were spent in editorial work. For all editors tend to develop a touch of cynicism, to price everything but value nothing. Thus they are less easily fooled than most people, and less easily fool themselves. They will not so readily evade unpleasant facts nor avoid unpleasant deductions based on these facts. And they understand, too, that if we find in the world people of different mentalities, there are accordingly different views to suit them.

134

To scorn material values in the name of a spiritual faith, to denounce them as delusory in the name of a metaphysical reality is unwise. Ask famished refugees in Asiatic and African countries what they think about them.

135

It is not new. Cicero called the materialistic systems of thought "plebeian philosophies." Plato believed them suited only to the uneducated masses, unequal to the strain of mentalistic thought. On a somewhat higher level Cicero included the half-educated body-is-the-only-reality Epicureans.

136

He is torn between an intuitive idealism and an acquired materialism. In the end, his decisions are inconclusive, his actions wavering.

137

The path is hard to tread, but so is life itself.

138

Those who fall all-too-easily into the worldly lures of obsession by business success or social triumph, who mistake baubles and illusions for treasures and realities, cannot enter the Kingdom of Heaven.

139

The narrow-minded among religionists will mistake such views as blasphemies, the materialistically minded among educated people will scorn them as fantasies.

140

Write a para on five things which we have to do when confronted by a difficult or painful situation which we try to escape by indefinitely delaying. We may not even know we are delaying when shifting the doing to someone else or some organization. Most of us do not realize that the shift is itself an indirect way of doing it or that everything we do involves a decision or judgement.

141

The man who is always careless, who makes no effort and takes no thought to rid himself of this faulty trait, will find that it gradually gets worse until it expands into recklessness.

142

How often we have seen lofty ideals and deep inspirations dissolve in the trivialities of domesticity.

143

It is not less gracious to accept most gifts than it is to refuse them. Take for instance Bishop King's unexpected offer of *all* his valuable esoteric material. It must have hurt his feelings about their value to hear their unexpected rejection. Take also the Russian Church mystic's offer of the ancient icon which has been in the hands of so many practising mystics of high position. It must have been almost an insult when they too were refused. In both cases it is now revealed *why* they were inspired to make the offer, what higher purpose was behind it. The lesson is valuable.

144

The illusion of owing nothing to other embodied selves is at its strongest in men who hate, as it is at its weakest in men who pity.

145

Too much remembrance of the world leads to too much forgetfulness of the higher purpose of our life in the world.

146

He who starts with the supposition that he has only to present what he himself feels to be true and great for others to recognize it as such, will quickly be disillusioned.

147

What can be done for those persons—alas! so many in these times—whose minds are covered in midnight darkness where the Overself is concerned and whom no spiritual intimations seem to reach?

148

What did Jesus mean when he rebuked those who sought to enter the kingdom like thieves breaking in over a wall? He meant that they were trying to enter without giving up the ego, without denuding their consciousness of its rule. Who are these robbers? They are the seekers of occult power.

149

They prefer to wallow in the comfortable and warm bog of materialistic inertia rather than to take to the rough and stony road of creative spiritual achievement which winds painfully uphill. They have failed partly because they fear to attempt.

> In idle wishes fools supinely stay,
> Be there a WILL, and wisdom finds a way.

150

We vaccinate our children against smallpox, but do not trouble to vaccinate ourselves against small minds.

151

The problem has two faces. The first is how to preserve even a stunted inner life from vanishing when the outer life is drawing all our time thought energies and feelings. The second is how to create the beginnings of such an inner life for those who have never known it.

152

In a happier and halcyon time, when peace and personal hopes for the future were reasonably assured, people generally were satisfied with the religious pabulum they received, or the irreligious indifference they acquired, or the outright atheism they fell into. Few were able to create any interest in a mystical or philosophical teaching of this kind; it was indeed regarded as of no importance and of no value. The popular attitude was a comfortable one and, in its own estimation, a sensible one. Consequently, such teachings were left to the study of supposed cranks and neurotics as well as to the uneducated credulity.

153

Wholly immersed in the consciousness of the body and wholly engrossed in its activities, pleasures, or pains, as they are, what wonder that they become oblivious of the fact that the body itself is so transient a thing that it may be here today but gone tomorrow?

154

Those who question the usefulness of these ideas are always those who are still mesmerized by materialism. Because they persist in thinking materially, it is impossible for them to respond to the truth. They would be easier to deal with if they were merely unimaginative or simply unreflective.

155

So long as they confound error with truth, and remain infatuated with the result, so long will warnings be wasted and superstition thrive.

156

The fanatic or the neurotic who pounces on a piece of general counsel or warning and applies it egocentrically to his personal case, where it does not fit at all, is met with at times on this quest. His nerves begin to suffer as a result of this misconceived attempt. There is no cure for his avoidable and unnecessary misery save truth.

157

I look around at my neighbours and I see that they are covered with chains, the chains of slavery to their lower nature, but they seem to enjoy their handicaps. Aspiration is not a thing that agitates them, not a mood which they entertain. Their sight is limited to their immediate needs and their immediate family. What they are here for, where they are going is no concern of theirs; yet I believe that, living by this beautiful lake and the stupendous Alps, sometimes a blurred vision of a greater moment may flash past them.

158

What lies behind the faintly enigmatic but restful smile of a Buddha, the smugly complacent smile of an Emerson, the sardonic grin of a Voltaire? All were truth-seekers but each exposed his personal colouring of that *aspect* of truth which he had found. This, without any reference to its fullness and depth.

159

He who is unable to welcome truth because it falls from the lips of a man belonging to a disliked race or because it flows out of the pen of a man belonging to a despised one, will assuredly never find it.

160

Existentialism, which sees the Universe as absurd, without meaning, without purpose, produces a brood of fatigued despairing minds, or sloppy lazy ones, or sinister amoral delinquents; but on its higher levels it has also produced serious well-intentioned persons trying to "modernize" their interests or studies in theology.

161

What is desirable is one thing; what is attainable is another.

162

The aspirant who dreams but never does things will live continually in the unsatisfactory state of deferred fulfilment.

163

There are important lessons to be learned from questions like "Why did Sarira die so quickly when hearing the prediction of inability to attain the goal?"

164

The selfish man puts nothing back into life.

165

We may meet other people in society or live with them in a house, we may talk with them every day, and yet there may be no real communication between us if our hearts and minds are uncongenial.

166

The dreamer is unable to look upon urgent practicalities but can only look upon far-off possibilities.

167

We are forever unconsciously acknowledging our imperfection.

168

Whilst men can see no reality except in what lies all around them, they are sorry victims of illusion.

169

I came to mistrust those who claimed that their way, their view, their teaching, was the only true one. Each could probably make some useful contribution of knowledge, thought, experience, faith, or revelation; but one-sidedness was likely, a limited outlook.

170

There is a littleness of mind which is antipathetic towards originality whatever its form.

171

The ministers of religion who claimed to be doing God's will and the advocates of godless communism who claimed to be doing the work of historical necessity were both merely uttering personal opinion. What did God or history really have to do with it?

172

If he is not to keep the truth within a restricted circle of personal pupils alone but to open it to the reach of all, the many will have to be content with what they can understand, leaving the rest to the few who are better equipped.

The limits of yoga

173

I discovered in the end that the yogi is afraid of action and consequently indifferent to the troubles of the world and unconcerned about mankind's well-being; that his society and presence does not radically change human character for the better, as is claimed, but merely lulls its worst qualities into semi-quiescence to spring up again, however, at the first release from his immediate influence. I perceived how I had over-idealized mystics in the past and wrongly thought them to be sages, how I had mistaken their attainment of yogic peace for the true self-realization, and how inevitable was their preoccupation with themselves when the knowledge of universal truth alone could give the wider interest in the welfare of others.

174

I have returned from the tropics to the northern hemisphere not merely for another visit but, at the bidding of health, for a permanent settlement. This is of no importance to anyone except myself. What is important, however, is that I have returned from the East not merely physically but also spiritually. It may be that the striking coincidence of the two necessities was predetermined by the wise operations of fate. I do not know.

My modest attempts to explain the importance and point out the merits of Oriental mysticism were quite proper in their place and time. But I consider that the interpretative phase of my work has come to an end. In the prefaces to *The Hidden Teaching Beyond Yoga* and *The Wisdom of the Overself*, I hinted that wider experience and deeper knowledge, sharper reflection and significant episodes were forcing me out of the narrow groove of being an uncritical enthusiast for Indian yoga as it exists today. That movement continued to its inevitable end. This is why I consider my return to the West as being not just a further phase of my varied bodily travels but a grand climax to my equally varied spiritual seeking.

175

Let him learn by experience that the worship of human idols, or the segregated life of an ashram, with its sanctified selfishness, or the mere wandering around India, whose outward degeneration is an apt symbol of its inward ignorance, can lead only to temporary titillations of the emotions, whether ecstatic or otherwise, but never to that sublime knowledge which releases man forever from all quests and all hankering and alone confers the realization of what we are here for and alone bestows immortal benefit to himself and all creatures. If I were to put on a yellow robe and assume the outward forms of sanctity, found an ashram on top of a mountain in India and stay there for the rest of my days, I would get much more respect for my words than I do now from those who have to penetrate the veil of appearance and have to understand *why* I deliberately chose to assume the form of a man of the world, a scribbler and traveller.

176

When the editors of the popular Penguin series of paperback books asked me to write a manual on yoga, I declined but recommended my good friend Professor Ernest Wood. He was given the assignment. The reason for my refusal was that I had been too much identified with the exposition of yoga in the past and wanted to get a different, wider identity. Yoga was an essential preparation, but all too often it led to a self-conscious spirituality, a professional truth-seeking, that shut out other important facets of life as trivial. I felt, with Japanese Zen and Chinese Ch'an, that the ordinary everyday life, the world, the body, the arts, could not be ignored without loss, that a fuller vision included them all.

177

My exposure of the demerits and dangers of yoga brought, as expected, a storm of criticism and a shower of disapproval from Hindus who thought I had attacked their religion. These people confused truth with superstition, and mistook my scientific impartiality for the superiority complex of the average Westerner.

178

It is open to a philosopher to speak differently in different capacities and in the *Statesman* article I spoke as a critic of yoga, deliberately stressing its demerits, because I had written too much in its praise and people were apt to get a one-sided and therefore incorrect picture of it. I spoke also as a critic of the yogis because the reports of other people's experience and the confirmation of my own revealed that there was far too much disastrous exploitation of gullibility and far too much social parasitism among them. Many readers came to think wrongly that, because I supported the positive beneficial aspects of yoga and praised the concentrative powers of the few genuine yogis, I therefore also supported the negative, harmful, queer, and questionable aspects of yoga and endorsed the numerous exploiters, idlers, idiots, and fanatics in the ranks of yogis. Nevertheless, the *Statesman* article did not express my considered judgement nor did it represent my complete attitude.

179

The scientific proceeding is to test methods by their results. If we ask ourselves what practical results have been yielded by yoga in the hands of its twentieth-century followers, we shall be compelled to answer: very few.

180

In China years ago, the existence was discovered of an organization called the "Buddhist National Laymen's Association" which operated its own private radio station and every night disseminated the message of Chinese Buddhism to its listeners. What they did to spread their own religion, we of the West could no doubt do to spread philosophy.

181

They welcomed me as a supposed recruit to Hinduism as a religion. But the years taught them that they were wrong. Alas! the lesson brought bitterness in its train!

182

I wanted to lean-strip yoga, to divest it of all its obscurity, and to reveal the true secret of these men who crouch on their hams in contemplation.

183

Yoga is the ABC of Indian Wisdom: I am trying to unearth the XYZ. Do my critics want me to stay in the ABC stage forever or to continue my researches? If further knowledge has caused me to revise my former estimates, then they ought to be happy at the unveiling of this knowledge. Yoga is one of the most valuable practices in the world, but it is only a stage on the way to truth—not, as I formerly thought, the direct path to truth.

184

I practise yoga every day and regard it as a fundamental part of my daily life.

185

My earlier researches in yoga were a prelude to my maturer researches in philosophy. Had they done nothing more than to direct attention to a neglected line of enquiry they would have justified themselves; but in forming a stepping-stone to the immensely important philosophical discoveries of the ancient Asiatic sages, they have more than justified themselves.

186

Problems began to suggest themselves. I could of course have imitated mystics and dismissed them as unnecessary agitations of the mind, but I had entered into the practice of yoga in the hope and belief that it would lead to the discovery of Truth about all life and not merely that little part which was individually represented.

187

My faith in the value and utility of yoga stands unshaken. But I would be untrue to the quest I have undertaken if I did not make a fair appraisal of its disadvantages as well as advantages, and if I remained blind to the defects which yogis themselves frequently show. I am still an advocate of yoga as much as I ever was, but I am not an advocate of the unbalanced practice of yoga nor of the extravagant valuation of yoga.

188

I collected a number of extraordinary events and described a few almost fabulous personalities. My work as a memorialist of those Eastern men is finished: I have put away the pen so far as the yogis and mystics are concerned.

189

For months and years I sat in mosquito-ridden rooms and endured countless sharp stings with stolid stoic patience for the sake of studying the Indian wisdom and practising the Indian yoga. Hands, feet, and face were mercilessly attacked by numerous legions of these pestilential insects, which were often ably assisted by little brown biting ants. Yet to feel that I was absorbing the one and mastering the other was sufficient reward for my sufferings. If my body was spasmodically tortured, my mind was soothed with growing peace.

190

The reaction to all this youthful and naïve over-enthusiasm was a salutary disappointment, following a number of eye-opening experiences. For some years I practised a studied avoidance of ashrams and yogis. But such an extreme course was uncalled for, and I substituted a prudent discrimination for it.

191

My work in the East has come to a final close. My real work in the West will soon begin. What I had done there before was but an imperfect preparation for it.

192

The truth is that I am not an enthusiastic advocate for some Eastern cult. On the contrary, I hold that we in the West can work out our own salvation.

193

I am not sorry that I made this research into Eastern mysticism but only that I overdid it. Wisdom required that I use it as a contributory stream, but ignorance turned it into the great river itself.

194

It took a long time to disabuse me of this notion that the tropical jungles of Hindustan or the snowy wastes of Himalaya secreted this earth's wisest men.

195

My opponents cannot deny that the fact that yoga has begun to enjoy a new vogue in India—the land of its birth, and this time amongst the educated classes with whom it had formerly lost its prestige—as well as a new introduction in the West, is attributable to the success of Paul Brunton's books.

196

When I saw that yoga was being taken by most people as a sensation-seeking cult, I felt that they were going too far. And when I saw that a crowd of exploiters—both Western and Eastern—had begun to take advantage of the interest aroused by my works, I felt that it was time to call a halt.

Living with truth

197

While others pile up their documentation and run from book to book, he hears the divine voice, feels the divine presence, and surrenders to its stillness. The academic man does a useful service, but if it remains on the intellectual level only, it is not enough to provide what the heart needs.

198

The Divine Arms still enfold us and some have been fortunate enough to receive intimations of that fact. They will get even more than this later.

But those who have discovered the life beyond ego have incurred a duty. Perhaps destiny will give them the privilege to be of humble service in a way commensurate with the time's need.

199

I walked among the shady groves of the Philosophers. And I asked them, "What is truth?"

And some said: "It is thus."

But others declared: "It is not thus."

And yet again: "It is incomprehensible to man while he is yet mortal."

I pondered upon these answers, yet I was not satisfied. Therefore it was that I fared farther. And I came to one who sat upon the stump of a tree trunk. And I saw that he was an old man who had been cast out of the ranks of the Philosophers because he could evolve no system.

And I asked again: "What is truth?"

He made no reply, but instead fixed his gaze on me. We sat silently together. His eyes gleamed with a strange lustre. And in that hour I came to know the meaning of truth. For his answer came through SILENCE.

200

But is the task so barren, so thankless, and so fruitless as it seems? We do not think so.

201

He should pursue an even path, undisturbed by the malevolence of jealous enemies, unmoved by the criticisms of the thoughtless and ignorant. His mind is made up, his resolve to spend the remainder of his incarnation in quest of enlightenment of others is unalterable. He should surround himself only with those who have formed a like resolve and who are not likely to vacillate from loyalty to it, come what may.

202

Just as the aroused passion of sex absorbs all of an animal's or person's attention, so the awakened consciousness of the Overself absorbs the aspirant's whole attention in brief ecstasy.

203

There comes a time when all the advantages of an existence around a fixed centre far outweigh the disadvantages.

204

When a man's hope has been darkened or abandoned often enough, he may be ready to learn this old truth.

205

The infinite truth cannot be put into a limited formula without being crippled or caricatured thereby.

206

The Truth reconciles all opposites and relates the countless imperfect lives struggling in time and space to the ever-perfect Life-Power beyond both.

207

The depth of the illusion under which we are held is a shadow of the height of the reality which *is*.

208

The evenly adjusted scales have always been a symbol standing for justice. But justice depends on truth.

209

The very meaning of the term "movement" means some idea arrived at, a novelty and an innovation, whereas all the truest, most important ideas of life and living are as old as prehistory. Truth itself does not move, only man's thought about it does. Today, "movement" means a new form of lunacy, a fresh expression of perversion and distortion.

210

It is easier to know what you want than to get it. Thought is pliable and flexible; will is hard and stubborn.

211

The Quest is always interesting to talk about, even if it often is not practicable to follow!

212

What is the quality of your life, its worth measured on a just pair of scales, its value to yourself and society?

213

If so many men find it hard to believe that the soul is a reality, others find it equally hard not to believe. This is because the first ones are really as dead and only the others alive.

214

Life—so large in arousing early hopes, so small in final realization.

215

In the world of thought, one is very close to truth. It is here that one will eventually come face to face with the soul—and, thereafter, whatever one's afflictions may be, they will be of secondary importance. It is in this world, too, that one will find one's Master—and one's Master will reach him.

216

P.B.'s Answers to Professor Floriano's Questionnaire (Verona):

(1) God is Father of us all.
(2) Man's highest goal is to find his relationship to God.

(3) Man is a creature or babe of God.

(4) Man's duty toward God is to learn what is God's will and to obey it.

(5) Sin is the departure from the will of God.

(6) There was a historical descent of man from a state of innocence (not goodness) into one of pollution or sin.

(7) Man fell into it through his wanting experience, and thus came into physical and intellectual pollution.

(8) Suffering is God's will, partly to educate man and partly to punish him for his sin or downfall.

(9) But it is also God's will for man to enjoy. We do not see him only suffering.

(10) Man's greatest good is to learn God's will and obey it; his greatest evil is to remain in ignorance of it.

(11) There is a Providence which takes care of us all from the very beginning to the very end.

(12) Contemporary society's good is its claim to search for truth (through intellect) and its bad is its excessive extroversion.

(13) Man will get worse but then later he will get better than now.

(14) Nature is the visible world made by God, and supreme nature is the invisible world. Both work together as one. Both are in us.

(15) The evolved man like others has need of a religion and of a church according to the degree of his evolvement. Why? Because it is religion which begins to teach him his relationship to God, and it is through religious feeling that he begins to become aware of it.

(16) By religion I mean any system of worship and ideas which leads man to know his relationship to God. This relationship can be a revealed one.

(17) How can anyone know that a revealed religion is true? He cannot know; he can only accept or reject it. For if he knows enough to judge whether it be true or not, then he does not need a revealed religion.

(18) Each established church and each obscure sect can claim to give out religious revelation. Its members must accept it as such. Others who reject it can do so only from the point of view of human intellect; their judgement is only reasoned opinion, not revelation.

217

Even if their writings are not intelligible and their phrases fantastic, the final inspiration behind these writings is not thereby invalidated. Truth is still truth, even if it is uttered in pidgin-English, even if it is gestured in the most cryptic sign language.

218

To a certain individual it may be said: "I have faith in you—but the real You has yet to make an appearance. When it does you will then find your real work in life."

219

But now the words have gone forth, the sleeping eyes shall be opened, and the seven seals upon the Book of Truth be removed one by one.

220

Although I find my deepest interest in attempting to explore the dark mysteries of man, although this world is seemingly full of worry and woe, I still try to remember that there is another world—not so far off as most imagine—where ineffable bliss holds its inhabitants as permanent captives.

221

Every man carries his motto—sometimes in his face, sometimes out of sight in his heart. Choose your motto well.

222

When a man grows as unconsciously as a flower, it surprises him to discover how much larger is the area, how much deeper is the penetration, of his personal influence in the circle of people which he meets.

223

I do not believe there is much chance for a lasting human happiness. Sooner or later life besets a man with its problems, griefs, oppositions, and maladies.

224

He is on the right track who seeks to disengage himself from the cares and annoyances of everyday life. He is also wise in coming to understand that the service of humanity must be based on balanced judgement.

225

The motto, "And This Too Will Pass!" which helped Abraham Lincoln endure the darkest days of the Civil War, was an ancient one. It was devised by Sufi philosophers hundreds of years ago as one to help sorrowing men and discipline happy ones with philosophic remembrance.

226

To acquire knowledge and respect its facts is to lose superstitions: one cannot keep both.

227

This onward rolling Earth is but a small part of the vast Cosmos, yet man has begun to escape from its confines. What would happen if he begins to truly escape from his own mental confines?

228

So stick to this quest with the iron determination not to stop until you have realized the truth. Don't worry about the remoteness of the goal; leave all the results to fate and do the best you can. With proper guidance the goal can be brought infinitely nearer than it seems. Those who know truth want to share it; what else do they care for? Make up your mind and progress from can't to can!

5

THE LITERARY WORK

For kindred souls

I write for those who have felt the truth in intuitive flashes as well as for those who must be argued into it by intellectual reasonings.

2

My work has also been to open up new paths, both for those already interested in spiritual seeking and for those who in the past were not but are now ready to begin it.

3

It is not possible to estimate correctly the number of those who have ennobled their characters and exalted their purposes because of this reading experience. Small it must necessarily be, for people are too mesmerized by the prestige of old churchly institutions to listen to a new voice speaking to a new age struggling to be born.

4

The man whose mind has hardened around the dogmas of some sect will be unwilling to receive truth where it conflicts with those dogmas. I do not write for him. I write for those who, noting the bewildering confusion of contradictory doctrines offered to them, prefer to keep themselves free of any commitment and unjoined to any particular sect. In that way, they are open to receive additional truth and to correct previous errors.

5

Throughout this writing, I have tried to give one hand to the realist and the other to the idealist. Only so could I walk safely, and my readers with me. Therefore, these are positive techniques designed to fit real needs with something that yet stretches away to the ideal.

6

To attempt this book will be an adventure for the Warriors of Light, but the wanderers of night will put it down with much celerity. For these pages are enchanted with a white magic which can inflict no greater injury on adversaries than to permit them to resist the principles contained therein.(P)

7

Some of these lines are written for the few, for the few out of each million who have inborn attitudes toward spiritual development. Such people will rise to the right path once they are shown it. If I attempt to teach them the truths of directed aspiration, it is because I have myself wasted much time in misdirected aspiration, and now know the difference.

8

Since this is intended less for the casual reader or the academic student than for the aspirant whose earnest endeavour is to make something spiritually worthwhile out of his present life, it enters very seriously into regimes, training, self-denials, disciplines, and exercises.

9

We who write can only give the truth as we see it. That others have seen farther and deeper and better we must gladly proclaim, but we cannot remain in literary paralysis because of this fact. There are always readers who are not yet ready for, or do not yet seek, what is beyond their level. For them we may have some significance.

10

We address ourselves to those whose aim is to make themselves intelligent citizens of the world, not to those whose aim is to turn themselves into academic bookworms or whose view is bounded by the village in which they dwell.

11

I write for those who have to keep on working in cities, not for those who like to keep on idling in ashrams.

12

It is true that the limitations imposed by his own personal destiny, together with those imposed by the emotional prejudices of so many seekers, cause the number of those he is able to help to shrink to a small circle. Nevertheless, within that circle he will be continually active in self-giving endeavour to illumine its members.

13

In the past I tried to present a method, a technique, and an ideal that seemed suited to the generality of people. That is to say, the earlier books were works intended for such of the masses as were unable to find enlightenment elsewhere. That work has come to a natural close.

14

I was in the peculiar position of writing both for those who had no wish at all to become saints and for those who did have one. Most of those in the first group were intellectually curious or intellectually eager for the truth. Most of those in the second group felt a compulsive urge to achieve personal inspiration.

15

The casual and the curious will learn little from this book, but the thoughtful and earnest may gather a few spiritual fruits.

16

Spiritual dabblers are hereby warned off, but the sincere are always welcome. Those who flit from craze to craze, or seek to satisfy their flirtatious souls at the expense of our strictly limited time, will do better by turning their faces due north, and not in my direction. If I am often excessively kind to innocent kittens, I can nevertheless be excessively cruel to humbugs. In this respect I am like the moon, for I wax quickly with friendly warmth to those who use words to explain their heart, and do not hide it; but I wane rapidly into arctic frigidity when the insincere approach me with a smile on their lips and something quite different in their breast.

17

I write for those who are attracted towards reading about philosophy, as well as for those who have gone further still and practise it.

18

One method of teaching which the ancient rishees adopted was to lead the seeker gradually by way of well-defined, separate stages of enquiry. Thus the reality might first be taken to exist in Matter itself. When the disciple began to have doubts and ask questions later on, as he found this explanation insufficient, he was told that a higher reality existed and it was Life-Principle. In the course of time the limitations of this teaching were discovered by the student and the definition of nonduality was made clear to him. This is precisely the method which I have adopted in my books.

19

We do not expect the masses to feed on the caviar of philosophy.

20

I write for the individual of average intelligence and average power.

21

It was necessary to help all those numerous people who do not or can not take the trouble to think for themselves and who therefore have to accept the secondhand thought of other men. If I had to make these abstruse tenets more comprehensible to modern minds, I had also to make them more attractive to simple ones. Hence I have tried to transmit, in as easy and understandable a style as it was possible to achieve, these much needed philosophical ideas, mystical practices, and ethical ideals. Truth's message had to be formulated as explicitly and as clearly as possible. Such a vital presentation was not easy to create, for it had to avoid the forbidding rocks of technicality on the one hand and the deceptive shallows of super-ficiality on the other.

22

If I descended from the summits of philosophical truths to accommo-date those people, I ought not to be blamed, condemned, and sneered at for having apparently repudiated what I had previously taught.

23

I shall write about things seldom written of, hence this is not and cannot be a book for the ordinary religionist or the ordinary mystic or the ordi-nary scientist or the ordinary academic metaphysician who is satisfied with his religion, mysticism, science, or metaphysic, and who does not want to go beyond its limits.

A mixed reception

24

Some readers will have been consciously, even anxiously, waiting for some of these ideas. Others will have been waiting unconsciously for them. Still others will find nothing here that nourishes them, so we shall bid each other farewell—amicably, I hope.

25

The aim is to contribute a point of view, a way of thinking which will bring about far reaching changes in a person's life. But though this way is so uncommon that it will never suffer from the fate of popularization, yet it is so fundamentally iconoclastic that it must necessarily arouse bitter opposition. It is a challenge to the mental laziness of mankind.

26

These writings have created an intellectual unrest in some minds, which have been piqued by the unfamiliar ideas on the one hand and provoked by the desire to understand them on the other.

27

Those who are slaves to tradition will not welcome these writings. How can they since I am not a copyist? I believe like them that the eternal verities remain the same at all times, but I also believe that the formulation and presentation of them can be adapted to a particular time, with much advantage to those addressed.

28

I keep myself in silent obscurity and outward inactivity while waiting for the times which, out of desperate need, will accept me just as I am and on my own terms. Those times will not come until after Armageddon.

29

Belonging, as I do, to an old generation in a young world, there is no longer a line of communication, understanding, sympathy.

30

I would beg my readers not to decry these thoughts as worthless dreams until they have seriously investigated them and even more seriously practised them.

31

It is inevitable that such unfamiliar ideas can find their place in public thinking only with slowness.

32

Whether the reader accepts these thoughts as veridical or not is of no great importance to me; but whether he will think them over—presented here as they are upon no other authority than their own inherent truth—is a matter of great importance to himself.

33

The fact that the P.B. books have been translated into all the major European languages and a few Oriental ones not only recognizes that they establish an uncommon point of view but also that they make a contribution toward answering the greatest questions man can ask himself.

34

Why did the late Yuvaraja of Mysore keep a photograph of P.B. prominently displayed in a central position on his writing table at the Mysore Palace? Why did the Yuvaraja of Kasmanda keep a similar photograph on his own writing table at his Lucknow Palace? Why, when most of the yogis of India were at their command, did they take lessons in meditation from P.B. and honour him with their chelaship? Why did Yogi Ramiah, then esteemed one of the leading disciples of Ramana Maharshi and later head of his own monastery, declare on January 1, 1936 in the presence of some of his own Telegu disciples to P.B.: "You have learned all about yoga. There is nothing more for you to learn about this practice." Why did Captain Mohamed Rashid, A.D.C. to the late Yuvaraja of Mysore, say in 1939 when broadcasting from the Akash Vani Radio Station in India: "My learned and distinguished friend and European yogi, Dr. Paul Brunton, is now in our midst again. He has done more to clarify the subject of yoga than any other Westerner."

35

He is interested in the transmission of ideas to those who are ready for them, not in the dissemination of ideas among those who are hostile to them.

36

His message is for those who wish to listen to him or to read his words. Whether this means a small or a large number of persons, and whether anyone is willing to believe him or not, is not primarily his concern.

37

Any writer who seeks to find a home on paper for such far-out ideas must expect to find also that the unbalanced, and even the lunatic fringe, will claim them, too.

38

I would not be at all anxious if these strong ideas gained but a weak following at first. A roaring lion could be laid flat with your little finger when it was born.

39

I desire to form no spiritual "tea-circles" where the dilettanti of "other-worldism" may find a new craze with which to play across the cups.

40

I would rather be read than revered.

41

It is easy for a writer who sits comfortably at a desk to give voice to such truths. But it is hard for a reader, who is struggling with the cares and duties of everyday living, to apply them.

42

Are we to pay the intelligence of our times so mean a compliment as to hide such thoughts for fear that they will not be understood? I am often constrained to think so; but I am willing to make the experiment at least once. If the moment proves too inopportune and the age too ignoble to receive such a message, perhaps the effort will not be entirely wasted. Some other hand may pick up the remnant of these thoughts at some future time and utilize it for a more receptive people.

43

What an earlier century would have regarded as the barkings of a heretical dog of a mystic in the caverns of the ecclesiastical Avernus, a more tolerant twentieth century may now regard with mild amusement as an unimportant but well-meaning attempt to reshape the philosophers. Let them, then, look at this message in this superficial light; but Time, the Great Revealer, will prove conclusively how much of truth there is in what we assert.

44

All this will sound wild and foolish to the superficial mob or to those with such mechanical minds that they can grant existence only to the gross and material. Great truths and little minds cannot accompany each other.

45

So far as my eyes survey recorded history, it has never been a pleasant task to play the prophet to a scornful generation.

46

There are books which break chains, and books which bind them on tighter. May this one help someone to find a greater Freedom for himself.

47

Perhaps these unorthodox pages will shock those who prefer their philosophy unreadable. I am sorry. The cobbler must stick to his last, and I to my native outlook.

48

It is not to be expected that the busy and boisterous Western world will listen long to this spiritual voice which we would bring into its midst. We shall be content to catch the ears of the few, those elect souls who have fought their way through years of suffering and lives of heart-hunger to the silent certainty of God's existence.

49

No idea in this book is so very novel; but if each one is considered without prejudice and without misunderstanding, that will indeed be novel.

50

The world of readers may cast a complacent eye upon this book but is hardly likely to take its message seriously. Man is a creature of habit and prefers the stupid Sisyphean round to which he is accustomed rather than to any other saner way.

51

If my books have been widely read—instead of remaining on the shelves widely unread—the reason must chiefly be that they met an unfulfilled need.

52

My later writings are not likely to interest those who have been mesmerized into intellectual inactivity but only those who have felt misgivings aroused in them.

53

I contemplate with mixed satisfaction the results to which my books have led. Many individuals have been helped to attain a higher measure of interior peace and mental tranquillity, but others have foolishly confirmed their previous superstitions through a one-sided reading of what I have written. What has distressed me most, however, is a painful realization of the opportunity I have given to religious humbugs, commercially minded mystics, and half-baked teachers of yoga to exploit earnest but credulous people. I would not have my books exploited by mystic quackery and parasitic superstition. Still worse is the fact that an ashram which I had helped to make famous now no longer possesses the character which it had in the days I found it many years ago, so that complaints may justly be laid at my door for giving it regrettable publicity. It is my present duty therefore to warn all readers against the misunderstanding of my teaching on yoga, against the exploiters of questing ignorance, and against these ashrams which I had formerly praised so extravagantly.

54

If the ideas seem too bold, too controversial, too disturbing, remember that they are put forward not by a hostile critic but by a well-wishing friend, not unhealthily or destructively but healthily and constructively.

55

I feel out of tune, out of sympathy with the generation recently arrived. There is an intolerance in their attitude, a rudeness in their manners, a hardness in their tones, a spitefulness in their criticism—which is plentiful, widespread, and severe—and an arrogance in their judgements which repels me, even sends shivers up my spine sometimes. The abyss between me and these people is too deep and too wide.

56

Many of the good seeds have fallen on the stony ground of the general indifference to these matters, but here and there some found room for lodgement. The seedlings have multiplied as they sprouted and grew.

57

Only those who feel the premonitory force of these statements are likely to have the courage to bring their thinking to a logical conclusion.

58

In an age when men eat much and think little, the attempt to propound by ordinary means a spiritual message and prophetic warning of such profound import is hardly likely to be received with enthusiasm.

59

Indeed, how many Indians of the educated classes have confessed to me that they owed their intellectual recovery of yoga or their revived faith in religion to my writings!

60

It is not my task to convince people of the truth of these ideas, but it may be a task for others to do. What has been found after a lifetime's experience is not to be acquired in an hour or two's debate.

61

We shall sow seeds, diffuse ideas, transmit inspirations, and watch them take root in the minds of others; but it is a later generation which shall watch them grow into sturdy plants and bear good fruits in the lives of many more individuals. There is more hope for acceptance of worthwhile ideas from the younger people, for they stand at the door of life and fumble for the key.

62

Some who had never before heard of these teachings found them so reasonable, so inspiring, and so helpful that they instantly accepted them as true.

63

The medical profession, the educational profession, the church ministry and priesthood have not been sufficiently aroused to the importance of my observations, reports, and findings. This is understandable since I am technically only a layman in their eyes. So, appreciation has so far been left to the general public, to those who appreciate my independence and the consequent freedom from bias in my writings.

64

The pseudo-great men of our time, who live on the clamour of the crowd, who perform their pantomime antics for the sake of vulgar applause, will naturally not be pleased with the pages of this book and are little likely to heed its message.

65

If one wishes to gain a reputation and hold respect, one has merely to treat one's subject at arm's length, to be cold and distant about the warmest and most intimate topics, and to think no further than academic conventions permit.

66

In an age when the armies of materialism *appear* to be everywhere victorious, we must yet cheerfully carry a flag on which the single word *Truth* is boldly inscribed. For this Godless age will pass, this execrable God-denying epoch is doomed to disappear. Our flag stands as a rallying point for the few pioneers who perceive the inner worth of That for which it stands, and who hear the tramping of invisible armies which will later appear to worship it.

67

The thoughts in this book have been set down for the few, since they alone can receive and take my meaning; the latter is too simple and straightforward for the many, who will much prefer to misunderstand me. For instance, some among them will prefer to dub me a mystic, still more will regard me as an arrant atheist, while a few will find me too religious to satisfy everybody. I have attempted to satisfy nobody, but dug my sword into every dark corner that was near at hand. Truth has so many facets to it that it frightens most people away; they retire to their petty corners and contemplate the paltry glimpse of the single facet they have seen, usually spending the remainder of their lives over this simple process.

Responding to critics

68

It is not necessary to have a beard in order to have wisdom. Increase of years may also mean increase of foolishness. After all, age is not merely a chronological matter. When a man tries to live profoundly and travel widely, when his moments are tightly packed with the most diversified thoughts, episodes, and contacts, he will pick up sufficient experience to put him in the class of centenarians! He is then able to gaze out over the vast expanse of his fellow men with all the sense of superiority and all the smug authority of a unique old age! But he cannot expect to win such a temporal attitude and communicate its results to others without paying the cost both of the ascent and the communication with many an un-justified laceration and many a personal antagonism. Yet that which in-spired the ascent and prompted the communication will necessarily be developed enough to endure the laceration understandingly and even to smile at the antagonism compassionately.

69

One does not become a celebrity without becoming a public figure. This status opens him to everybody's watchful inspection—which is bad enough—and judgement, which is worse.

70

Whoever tries to put into words that which belongs to a totally different sphere should blame himself if he is misunderstood or, worse, reviled.

71

I must accept the blame with bowed head, grateful that it is not worse, as it could well have been. I must also accept criticism: it may instruct consciousness and educate conduct in matters where the ego is either ignorant or deficient. But I must also accept praise even though it leaves me somewhat embarrassed, for it may make clearer those positive qualities which the outside observer sees better. Both negative and positive self-regard and the outsider's view may help me to know what I am and what I am doing.

72

Instead of enquiring into the truth of his criticisms of their cherished dogmas or of confining their discussion to the subjects involved, they threw both reason and courtesy to the winds and degenerated into a howling mob thirsting for his blood. Any attempt to offer a calm and reasoned defense of his views brought down a fresh shower of highly emotional personal vituperation, but no real attempt to answer the points at issue. It would have been a waste of time and a completely futile endeavour to descend further into undignified controversy with such childish and malicious opponents. So he relapsed into Himalayan silence, shook the dust of debate off his feet. Why did such strong opposition to honest expression of matured reflection make its sudden appearance? Why did such intense resistance manifest itself against sincere statement of the results gained by profounder experience and more prolonged investigation? It is because they insist on taking their personal—that is, egotistical—feelings as proper criterions of truth. Such persons had followed him only because his doctrines *pleased* them. They had accustomed themselves to walk in fixed ruts.

73

Such people think a man who writes challengingly rather than colourlessly and appeals to reason as well as feeling is either not a mystic at all or one who has lost his mystical qualities.

74

Nevertheless, judging by my experience with the public, it is evident that so long as one writes what will please people he is celebrated, but as soon as he ventures to criticize their fallacies, he is execrated.

75

I know well enough what so many critics and friends have told me, that I repeat myself too often. I know also that sometimes I even contradict myself. These are admitted and regretted faults, but they cannot be helped. They arise partly out of the unsettlement of a wandering life and partly out of the unconventional methods of work which my temperament forces upon me.

76

Those who talk of my financial ambitions have the excuse of public ignorance—if not this, then the excuse of private malice.

77

The critics who have kept their worst venom for me do not belong to the materialist camp but to the mystic camp. Why is this? It is because I understand their defects to be defects.

78

That a man could devote himself to the study and dissemination of these tenets out of no financial incentive but out of pure love for the subject is something beyond their comprehension and, therefore, something to be regarded with suspicion.

79

They will—if past and present experience is any guide—unconsciously proceed to prove the imperfections of their outlook by the personal abuse which they will heap angrily on the writer of this statement, despite the fact that it is made quite impersonally and purely metaphysically. For it is one of the oldest tricks in the world to shift the point under examination when awkward questions will otherwise have to be faced and answered. It is so much easier to throw contumely on the character of an unconventional person than to discuss the character of an uncomprehended teaching.

80

The prime minister of an Indian state, whom I happened to be visiting several years ago, said to me during a conversation in his office: "Your book about the yogis has circulated too widely for my liking amongst the educated generation of Indians. People like myself, with a modern outlook, have been trying for years to uplift this particular generation from the superstitious, backward, inert, and medieval mental attitudes which are so responsible for the poverty, dirt, illiteracy, and misery of the masses whom they should lead. People like you are being quoted here both to sustain the faith in all those undesirable attitudes and to support the exploitation of religious impostures and mystical apathy which have harmed India for centuries. Thus you are helping to undo our good work and to retard the progressive movement in modern Indian life." This statement struck me at the time with the force of an abrupt shock. I had not dwelt in thought on this situation before. I am grateful to Sir Shanmukhan Chetty, then the prime minister of Cochin, for having given me this food for many month's thought and for having contributed towards my general awakening.

81

One rather expected, from men who professed to be so spiritual, criticism that was more gracious, with more comprehension and less redolent with ill will.

82

Candour was the one thing which was not wanted. Honesty was a crime and to be punished accordingly. Therefore the dual functioning of these two qualities in my public announcements that I had found feet of clay amongst the swamis and sadhus infuriated my critics.

83

I knew that if I committed truth to paper in such a personal form as a complete autobiography, the world would not believe me. Critics would rise up and remark: "This man is a complete egoist who suffers from the intolerable vanity of believing that he has solved what centuries of human history have not solved. His head is swollen, his conceit is inordinate."

84

Most reviewers tell us more about the state of their own mind than about a book itself and this is why I usually fail to get perturbed when a critic assails my books in the press.

85

So long as my views pleased those who read my earlier writings, the latter were admired and I was praised. Now that our views clash, my writings are criticized, and my character is vilified. Nevertheless, the experience has been a profitable one, for it has provided a further lesson in the fickleness of human nature when it has not undergone the philosophic training.

86

The well-informed do not need to waste their time over such nonsense as this criticism, but for the sake of others I deem it helpful to pen a timely answer.

87

I can afford to be patient and calm despite the barking of such critics, for a historical pioneering task for this generation has fallen on my shoulders. Such self-appreciation is not identical with self-conceit. The one is the unembellished knowledge of one's correct height, the other the emotional exaggeration of it to satisfy vanity.

88

In the next world, nothing can be hidden and everyone will be shown for what he really is. Here, in this world, a critic looks at my work and imagines that he has sounded the depths of my mind; an enemy looks at my body and imagines that she has seen me. My great comfort is that these opponents see only what they imagine to be P.B., whereas God sees the real P.B.

89

What critics like Douglas Ainslie call my "commercialization" of Hindu philosophy is really my *democratization* of it. For I have attempted to bring it down out of the rarefied atmosphere of academic circles into the common air of plain men and women, where alone it can help them. I have tried to make easily understandable what the academics and mystics have made ponderously incomprehensible. Moreover, it may be said that those who know well what they are talking about may have the temerity to simplify it, whereas those who do not know find it safer to mystify it! The first can really help truth-seekers, whereas the second can only hamper them. The reward of my efforts has been a larger circulation of my books than that achieved by writers like Ainslie himself—hence their envy and malice. I seek to serve the masses, not the classes, the many and not the few. I seek to make philosophy's message plain to the untutored mind of common people. At the same time, it will automatically be made plainer to the cultured intelligence of better educated people. If therefore my books are popular and those of the academics are not, that is not to be charged to my commercialistic spirit but to my democratic sympathy. Douglas Ainslie's article is not a genuine book review but a sorry exhibition of personal animus. The self-conceit from which Douglas Ainslie seems to think I suffer is simply the attempt to give a human feeling and personal value to ideas which have too often been ignored and neglected by non-mystical people because they seemed too inhuman and so impersonal. The deep conviction of my own importance, which he comments so sarcastically is his mistaken reading of the deep importance which I attach to the ideas which I have sought to describe intensely and put forward for the benefit of the few real seekers after truth among mystical people. If, in all these ways, I have succeeded in giving actuality to such ideas, if I have brought them to some life, then the results have adequately justified the means.

90

My critics argue in favour of a doctrine which I have never denied.

91

It was from the lips of my highly esteemed friend, Dr. A. Narasimhia— at the time principal of the Sanskrit College at Mysore, India—that I heard a sentence the truth of which became embedded in my mind with each unpleasant personal attack: "Your enemy is one of your best teachers; learn from him."

92

The fact that I have had practical experience of earning my livelihood as an editor has been made a subject of criticism. Were my critics not so narrow-minded they would have had the sense to see that exactly therein lies one of my merits. For this experience has purified me of the common mystical defects of writing whole pages that mean nothing, of recommending readers to attempt impossible tasks, of getting both thought and pen lost in the clouds to the neglect of the earth. It has taught me a robust realism and a healthy self-reliance—two qualities which are notoriously absent from the ordinary mystical make-up and for lack of which mystics commit many mistakes. My critics try to give the impression that earning my livelihood was a low act and that being a journalist was a kind of crime. These two facts are indeed held up against me as though they prove that I am both mercenary and materialistic, as though nobody with mystical aspirations would do the one or be the other. Such facts really pay me a compliment and do me no dishonour. But the blind unreflective followers of a dying tradition cannot be expected to perceive that. They cannot be expected to comprehend that I am endeavouring to bring mysticism into mundane life, to throw a bridge across the chasm which has so often separated them. And I know no better way than to have done so in my own personal life first before attempting to tell others how to do it.(P)

93

"Do not descend to the plane of malign critics and ignorant traducers," is the injunction I have constantly given myself when faced by the attacks of those who misunderstand my nature and mishandle my ideas.

94

How many have been talking or writing Brunton without knowing it, without acknowledging to themselves—and certainly never acknowledging to others—their debt to one they criticize or abuse so much! It may be that the debt is an unconscious one in most cases, but the influence is there.

95

He will study the writings or listen to the criticisms of those who reject his intellectual position, attack his philosophical world-view, and refute his mystical beliefs.

96

The actual and personal experience of all his friends and all those who have been allowed closer contact with him is his best defender. If they will remember only what they saw with their own eyes, heard with their own ears, and ignore gossip, they will know that he always behaved honourably.

97

An Indian mystic wrote me recently, criticizing what he called my "yearning to express" as being inconsistent with a true attainment of inward Peace. I do not make any claims about my personal attainments so I shall not discuss that point. But on the other point, I would like to ask him why should such a yearning be inconsistent with peace? Is not God ever seeking to express Himself through the universe? Did not Ramakrishna yearn for disciples? I seek (not yearn) to express myself primarily because some inner urge bids me to do so and secondarily because, however imperfectly and slightly, I follow an artist's profession. Neither inner urge nor untiring art denies anyone his peace. But men devoid of the aesthetic sense could not grasp this.

98

Sceptics who disparage these truths as dreams, who label our researches as endeavours to solve insoluble riddles, and who sneer at our ideals as attempts to attain unattainable states of mind, thereby display their own intolerance and superficiality. Converse with such unphilosophical mentalities and undeveloped hearts is unprofitable. It were better to keep a silent lip when they confront us.

99

The statement made by a Cornell professor reviewing one of P.B.'s books that "the author is always entertaining" is meant offensively, implying that those books are not to be taken seriously but only laughed at. That criticism was made long ago. Now, nearly forty years later, a hundred students from Cornell meet weekly in the same town to study P.B.'s and kindred authors' books, as well as to practise meditation, because they cannot get needed intellectual and spiritual help in depth from their dry professors.

100

The publication of a philosophical book is usually the signal for an attack by the dark forces through convenient human instruments, especially through so-called spiritual persons. Such attacks can only be met with dignified silence. It is also at such times that a student's loyalty to the Quest becomes evidenced.

101

I believe in the work of time, in the unseen power that uses it to weave wrong into right. In my own short life I have seen Hitler's false "thousand-year" kingdom hurtle to the ground. I have seen an Indian journalist, whose pen jabbed viciously at *A Search in Secret India* when he lived in

London, himself engaged in the same search a few years after his return to India. In his London review he denounced as superstition what in his later life he found essential to his mental peace.

102

The dignity of these truths which I have sought to present to the world is so grand, so stately, that I do not have to engage in their defense. But such is the common ignorance of these high matters that I do have to guard against the misunderstandings which, experience shows me, inevitably arise.

103

We must meet and answer these criticisms for the sake of weak minds or ignorant ones, but we must do so without rancour and without venom.

104

If we prefer to attack lies because we cannot accept them, we must prepare to put up with the consequences.

105

They may not agree with my conclusion but they cannot deny—considering my own past reputation as a mystic—its candour, its impartiality, and even its courage.

106

He is indeed glad and grateful that where little men and narrow minds doubt, scorn, criticize, or distrust him, great sages and lofty spiritual personages of the Orient, who read by inner reality rather than by outward appearance, confide in and trust in him.

107

Why do these impertinences come to birth? Why should it be thought that because a man has once been a journalist he cannot therefore be sincere? Have only those who follow other professions and trades the right to possess souls and not journalists? Have only doctors, butchers, lawyers, shopkeepers, and peasants a desire to understand the inner meaning of life? As a matter of fact, my old work was more editorial than journalistic and an editor is more finicky about his facts than most human beings. Cannot a man be in earnest even if he does wield a pen? No, these lightly made criticisms, so easy when you depend on appearances alone, are an indication of the arrant stupidity, the suffocating conventionality, the befogged outlook of the world at large. Whoever endeavours to break away from the old manner of presenting spiritual truth; whoever tries to sandwich the cheese of attractive anecdotes or interesting interviews between the dry crusts of philosophic doctrine; whoever seeks to stimulate individuals to new avenues of thought by showing that truth, religion, philosophy, and wisdom need not bore the average reader as they often have done hitherto; and, finally, whoever seeks to make as plain as day what has hitherto been as obscure as night, may expect to be termed insincere, superficial, liar, imposter, and perverter!

108

When I consulted my respected friend, Sir Vepa Ramesam, late chief justice of the Madras High Court, about these calumnies emanating from those who had repaid my services with ingratitude, his advice was: "Ignore them! Whoever *knows* you will immediately dismiss such attacks with the hearty contempt they deserve."

109

He who announces a truth discovered by revelation and confirmed by personal experience should accept the scepticism of those to whom neither has happened. But this ought not prevent them from playing with the truth as if it were a theory, a possibility, and watching whether it fits, helps, completes, or casts light on what he regards as verified.

110

These swamis and ashrams do not accord me the tolerance which they are so fond of preaching—to others. I, on the other hand, accord them gladly complete tolerance to teach and preach what they please. They criticize me as a perverter of Hinduism and a degrader of its ideals. They denounce me as a Western journalist who has picked up a smattering of yoga for mercenary reasons. Whereas they claim that the monkish state is the highest goal of humanity, I reply that the highest state has nothing whatever to do with monasticism. It is entirely invisible because it is an inner state, whilst monasticism is a matter of yellow robes, buildings called monasteries, non-participation in physical human activities like marriage, working for a livelihood, and so on. I further reply that I make no claim to teach or lead men to the highest state because I have not attained it myself; I have repeatedly pointed this out in various prefaces to my books. I claim only to tell a few others of ideas which have appealed to me and practices which have helped me. Whether they are the highest I do not know. I am interested only in what is practicable, not in what is beyond the reach of all human beings I have met and know. I am uninterested in what is attainable by theoretical human beings whom I have never met. Therefore I say that if the swamis criticize me, I criticize them back and call them materialists! For they are preoccupied with such a highly *material* matter as regulating the *material* body, whereas I am occupied with a purely mental matter, that is, with the discovery of truth!

111

He announces that we deny the existence of the external world. Such a man is not really criticizing our doctrine but only his own misconceptions of it. Therefore we are not called upon to answer him. If we do put pen to paper, it is an act of grace in recognition of the difficulty of comprehending this doctrine, not as an act of controversy in refutal of absurd ideas upon which we cannot waste our time.

112

He has to endure the pardonable sneers of the sceptical, the unpardonable hatred of those obsessed by the same dark powers which obsessed so many Nazis, the regrettable criticisms of the suspicious, and the unjust vilification of the envious. The attempt to introduce his ideas meets with hostility and opposition not only from the quarters of religious bigotry but also from those of scientific materialism. The hostile elements all select him as a target as soon as he takes up the unthankful task of lifting any of the delicate veils of Isis in an age when, in certain countries, the brute and the boor actually sit enthroned among them. He will have to suffer both from hard materialists and from fanatical mystics, who are either incompetent to understand the integrity of his motivation or instrumental for that adverse element in Nature which is the secret source of hostility towards such pioneer pathfinders. Ambitious preachers and teachers prompted plainly by envy and charlatanic cult-leaders attack the thinker himself even though they accept or use many of his ideas.

When anyone is incapable of fair and proper criticism of a man's ideas but capable only of vitriolic abuse of the man himself, there is usually some soundness in those ideas. Doctrinal opposition, which may always be proper and honourable, is one thing; but personal enmity, which is always improper and dishonourable, is another. It will be his special lot in life to attract critics who eagerly combine both.

But whether or not vilification gives way one day to vindication is a matter of indifference, for he will have lived in the present body long enough to have learned to look elsewhere for his own happiness. That a sincere effort to put forward ideas which are helpful in life's truth-quest should arouse so much personal antagonism is as amazing to those who do not comprehend the psychological factors involved as, with the ever-present vision before his eyes of the ever-approaching terminus of this little game called earthly life, it is amusing to him.

It is the spiteful business of those who have sought the soul but failed through their own weaknesses to find it, to speak evil, to spread slander, and to invent falsehoods about the man who does succeed in this enterprise. It is the noble business of this man to remain unmoved by their attacks, to refrain in silence from answering them, and to forgive their misdeeds in patience. These human spiritual failures strew the path's hinterland like wreckage. They persist blindly and obstinately in their acceptance of evil suggestion and are not to be confounded with those finer aspirants who fall, repent, and raise themselves again. A single reply to all their worthless criticism would be best taken from an Arab poet:

These are our works which prove what we have done,
Look therefore at our works when we have gone.

He has created something which has helped mankind. His critics have not. They have simply tried to tear it down. Having done nothing of worth themselves, they seek with their foul criticisms to destroy the work he has done; having given free reign to the dark, destructive, and negative qualities of their own characters, they assail his amid the safety of their private rooms. The help which, in sheer kindness of heart, he gives out is forgotten; the hatred which, in sheer envy, they carefully cultivate is remembered. He is paradoxically punished for the good that he has done to persons of evil character and mean mind. "It was when I began to love God that I got disfavour of men," sadly wrote the dying Hans Denck, the sixteenth-century German who was hunted from city to city because of his mystical preachings—which were eminently sane and truly Christian, but which menaced the vested interests of institutionalized religion. "I have loved justice and hated iniquity; therefore I die in exile," lamented the noble-charactered teacher Hildebrand. Each word, each hostile act, will become for them in later years a flail to beat their own shoulders. Such is the law. The harm done against anyone always reacts upon the wrongdoers eventually, but the harm done against a man who lives with head bent before the higher powers reacts more vigorously against the wrongdoer, for then they trouble not the man but the power which seeks to use him. These things happen with unfailing and clocklike regularity. But the backbiting, the thoughtless gossip, the envy and malice which prompts people to say untrue things about such a man cannot alter what he is. While they are busy concocting fresh treacheries, he will turn indifferently away from them and their world to find the divine peace which awaits everyone who has begun to commune with the higher powers. He is content to leave them to enjoy the fruits of the karma which they make. He is utterly helpless and cannot even raise his little finger in self-defense. He knows that even his enemy is not different in essence from his own inner being. Hence he has and can have nothing but goodwill towards each enemy; but the Law itself is not so kindly and will demand a hundredfold higher payment for every falsehood and every malicious word uttered against him. He has conscious knowledge of the forces that are working for him, of what they have done in the past, and of what they will do at the ripened hour.

He may not desert the broad work of human enlightenment which devolves upon him. That work has to be done and neither the malice of satanic human instruments nor the misunderstanding of the superficial and ignorant should deter him from carrying it out. He takes the advice of a wise old Tamil book of proverbs, the *Kural*, which says: "Patience is the first of virtues. It enables us to bear with those that revile us, even as the earth bears with those that dig it." So he sheds his shyness, continues his work, and offers malevolent enmity the silent indifference of one who knows in what sublime cause he is striving. He makes it a rule not to answer calumny, partly because he knows its true source lies in the promptings of evil entities who will continue their unseen activities whatever he says, and partly because God is his judge and he accepts no other. If enemies spit verbal venom openly at him or secretly behind him or in public print, he does not let it excite him or create bitterness against them. He remains serene and extends his goodwill to them, then comprehends that they cannot act otherwise, being what they are, and finally drops them out of his mind altogether. It is their business to plunge the daggers of malice and the stilettos of vilification into his side. It is his business immediately to assuage the pain by holding to the serenity of the Overself and to stop the bleeding by using philosophic insight.

113

If those books, despite all their admitted immaturity and error, rendered a modest service to mankind, then the intellect which produced them cannot be entirely unspiritual. The condemnation of the author by religio-mystical critics is therefore somewhat too sweeping.

114

Most critics and many readers have complained about what they called "the fault of wearisome repetition" in *The Hidden Teaching Beyond Yoga* and *The Wisdom of the Overself*. I am well aware that the modern mind dislikes it and prefers terseness, but this is one instance where I consider the ancient Oriental mind was a little wiser. Whether or not this is a fault depends upon the circumstances under which the repetition occurs. The recorded conversations and addresses of Buddha are chock-full of repetitions, for example. The *Yoga Vasistha* repeats scores of times most of its leading ideas. Why then did the ancient Orientals use this device—for so it really is? The answer may be partly given by one of them in his own words: "Repetition either of thought or language is no fault in this study. Repetition serves to bring out and give us mental practice in the great truths." These words were written by Suresvara, the personal and chief disciple of the illustrious Shankara. The second part of the answer is that the more important tenets of higher philosophy are intellectually extremely subtle, so subtle as not to be apparent at first contact with them, and extremely difficult to realize. The repeated contact with them, however, acts as a kind of indirect meditation and removes their unfamiliarity, renders them understandable, and causes them little by little to sink into the emotional consciousness. Alas! my scattered warnings in *The Hidden Teaching Beyond Yoga* did not prevent certain misconceptions from being quickly born. They arose out of the want of completeness in the part which was first made available. The separate publication of the two parts with some interval of time between them made it advisable to omit treatment of the most advanced elements in this teaching: they were based upon the mentalistic doctrine to which I had first to lead readers by dealing only with the more elementary topics. But in refusing to pluck the fruit of this teaching prematurely and in setting aside as not being ready for consideration such subjects as the genuine intuition, the higher or ultramystic experience, the nature of Deity, and the mystery of the Overself, I apparently laid myself open to the misconception that I now regard them as unimportant or unphilosophical. Consequently, some who had formerly complimented me now rained criticisms down upon my head— and wasted their time in asserting what I have never denied!

That such incompleteness inconvenienced several classes of readers must now be admitted. The proper place for *The Hidden Teaching Beyond Yoga* is alongside *The Wisdom of the Overself*, and in the supplementary appendix to that book I pleaded guilty of premature publication. I deeply regret the impatience and irritation which this act caused many readers, although it was done at the importunity of not a few readers themselves. An endeavour to anticipate and appease critics was made by writing an appendix to the book and distributing it in the form of a supplementary booklet, to be incorporated later at the end of any further editions that might be called for. This certainly helped a little to put right the principal misinterpretations, but it could not in so short a space either do so adequately enough or cover the less important ones which had to be omitted. No! The only way to mollify those who—making a quick judgement on what was after all only a preliminary work—wrongly thought that I had openly deserted mysticism and yoga, was to set down the actual teachings which supplement them and thus controvert these misconceptions. So, although I had formerly hoped to leave the task until after the war, I immediately took up work on the second span of this two-arched bridge and pushed ahead with it as quickly as possible under the unsettled circumstances which then prevailed.

The Wisdom of the Overself is the fruit of that labour, and those who have the patience to read it to the end will discover their reward in the doing of it.

Corrections, revisions, development

115

I am not the first writer who found his opinions changing, nor shall I be the last. Why must we be bound to an iron consistency when to be human is to be subject to change—outward and inward, experiential and mental, circumstantial and emotional? But what actually happened is rather that I shifted my standpoint a little higher. The resulting changes were merely the resulting larger horizon and better perspective. If I had written these same books later, I would have written them differently. But the difference in content would not have been so much one of inconsistency as of enlargement. The difference in style would perhaps have been greater. There would have been a loss of vehemence and impressionability in the descriptive travel works, but a gain in discrimination and knowledge. There would have been a loss of iconoclasm and superficiality in the philosophic expository works, but a gain of balance and depth and carefulness.

116

Although I could not help seeing how a higher power protected me against some of the results of my own mistakes and egoisms, it could not protect me against all of them.

117

Yes, my work is of pathetically unequal value. Some parts of it were written under the authentic guidance of the Overself and will consequently carry oasis-water to desert travellers. But alas! it is also true that other parts of it were written under the baneful illusions of the underself and may consequently bring them what is worse than nothing. The remembrance of this half-failure is one of the crosses I am doomed to carry until I can lay it down with my body in the ever receptive earth. It has brought me enduring humiliation and taught me a caution which makes me shrink from printing anything again. Humbled by the discovery of these errors, I did not take up the pen again for several years. Nevertheless, those who derived much help from the truths in which the errors were inlaid pressed and pressed me to do so. I had at last to put aside my reluctance, I had to yield and consent to write for them. However, if I made mistakes then there is the consolation that most pioneers inevitably make them. If I abandoned previously held positions, then there is the comfort that all search for truth is dynamic, not static. After all, so many years spent in teaching so many people such greater truths of life cannot be wasted ones. On the contrary, they are worthwhile and fruitful.

Saint Francis of Assisi felt that he was a great sinner, yet he did not allow that feeling to impede or prevent his work for the spiritual service of his fellows. Francis de Sales, who ranked high among the French mystics, remarked that it was precisely because the mystics felt they were so human and so simple that they turned towards the devotional life and tried the ascetic existence.

118

It is absurd to demand that what a man thought yesterday he shall continue to think tomorrow. Even stones, if given sufficient time, will crumble and alter: how much more ideas also? Those who find a discrepancy between my earlier writings and my later ones should, if they have enough sense, find it to be an evidence not of insincerity but of sincerity, a testimony to my own published declaration that those books represent an evolutionary movement towards truth and that they are the product of life not of its paralysis. For if riper thinking, wider and deeper experience, maturer balance, combine to bring a man to modify his former views, to revise his earlier estimates, and to correct his self-confessed mistakes, surely he has done what is laudable and not what is reprehensible? He who persists in an error, only because he is ashamed to acknowledge that he can ever be wrong, is to be blamed—not he who prefers to uphold truth rather than uphold his own vanity.

119

The paradoxes of my versatile profession have made me unite in a single personality something of the scholar and the explorer, the saint and the sinner, the reporter and the artist, without in fact being any one of these. The result has been that those readers who have been attracted by one particular aspect of my work are frequently confused when confronted by other elements for which they are unprepared, and sometimes in which they are uninterested. For instance, those who like to let their imagination accompany me upon the occult and psychic adventures which I narrated in *A Search in Secret Egypt* will probably show no great eagerness to pass through the door which is now open before them in these pages. The truth is that that former work appealed to those whom our conventional academic educationalists are likely to dismiss somewhat scornfully as the "under-brained," whilst this new book can only by its very nature appeal to those whom our conventional academic ministers of religion may dismiss as the "over-brained." This cannot be helped. If I have found that the carpet of life is not adorned with a mere medley of colours, but with a definite understandable pattern, it may be that others who are willing to make a similar investigation will discover the same kind of pattern.

120

If I look back to the man I was half a century ago, he seems naïve, narrow, immature, largely ignorant of the world, life, and himself. Not only have these deficiencies been made up since, but what is more I am at peace in myself. There is no need to search.

121

It need not be a surprise that, with the passage of one or two decades, I have shifted both emphases and proportions. But the fundamental bases remain: they were not abandoned, as some wrongly thought.

122

At no time did I choose the philosophic life: it chose me. If I follow mystical practices, it is because they seem a natural and necessary part of my being.

123

I have written on different topics as they occurred to me, but none so different as not to be connected with the quest in some way.

124

I have to bear the responsibility for words which, written in the half-light of thirty-five years ago, I would not write in the clearer light of today.

125

All the volumes that I have previously written belong to the formative stage. Only now, after thirty years of unceasing travail and fearless exploration, have I attained a satisfying fullness in my comprehension of this abstruse subject, a clear perspective of all its tangled ramifications, and a joyous new revelation from a higher source hitherto known only obscurely and distantly. All my further writings will bear the impress of this change and will show by their character how imperfect are my earlier ones. Nevertheless, on certain principal matters, what I then wrote has all along remained and still remains my settled view and indeed has been thoroughly confirmed by time. Such, for instance, are (1) the soul's real existence, (2) the necessity for and the great benefits arising from meditation, (3) the supreme value of the spiritual quest, and (4) the view that loyalty to mysticism need not entail disloyalty to reason.(P)

126

My earlier books were written too soon, too impulsively, and too immaturely. I ought to have waited several years. The time has come to put right the errors of past volumes.

127

It is a justifiable criticism of my earlier books that they make the Quest seem shorter and easier than it really is. They did that for obvious reasons yet I would not defend those reasons now.

128

There is too much prominence in my books for the benefits of meditation, too little for the possible dangers.

129

With the years I have become more careful about what I write, more aware of how small is the fragment of known truth.

130

One advanced mystic considers the quest of the Overself to be the most important and most exigent activity in which anyone can engage, and if he can help anyone he is happy to do so. Having made many mistakes in the past, burnt his fingers, and stubbed his toes several times, at least he can point out errors to be avoided, even if he can do nothing more.

131

When I wrote books about the extraordinary marvels I had seen in India and Egypt, people flocked to read them; now that I write books only about such ordinary things as mental quiet, inner stillness, truth, spiritual beauty, and the ruling of one's thoughts, few care to buy them. But I do not mind. I shall not sacrifice my art to pander to their curiosity.

132

Undignified and unfortunate though some of those prefatory pages were in *The Hidden Teaching Beyond Yoga*, they must be weighed against the very many more which rendered much service and gave great truths.

133

When at last I realized that my own experiences were important to no one but myself, and only the views distilled from them could have any value or interest for others, I resolved never again to write another of those personal prefatory chapters which mar several of my books.

134
Like Saint Augustine, "I am not one of those people who try to defend everything they have written." Like him, some of my views have been modified in the course of my literary career. But there are certain views which have not changed by a hair's breath and which remain basic to all the others. I have not wandered far from my original thought and intuitive knowledge.

135
The man who wrote that cycle of ten books is dead. The attitudes, the beliefs, and the standpoints out of which he wrote them have ceased to exist. None of these books has any relevance to his self, save as a milestone which has been passed and left behind.

136
Every writer who is worth his salt possesses at some time or another the ambition to create a single work, a *magnum opus* which shall be his literary testament to mankind. I, too, have possessed this ambition. The books which I have already written and published were really written to prepare the way and to introduce the present volume.

137
The psychical intensity of those years devoted to enthusiasm for meditation, the overconcentrative study of it, brought about a lack of perspective in my writings. It might have been better for myself and my public to have waited twenty years before submitting them to the printer's art; I do not know. But I do know that certain omissions—such as the moral and the devotional—make me dissatisfied with them. Something more is required of aspirants than the practice of meditation. If my books left the impression that it is enough to do only that, they have left a false impression. The time has now come to present my results as a better balanced and more coherent whole.

138
Whenever I grow introspective about my work, I perceive with regret its many deficiencies but with satisfaction its supreme service.

139
The reflections which I gave out to the world were imperfect but they were nevertheless important. They have already changed the whole outlook of some readers and have widened the thinking of many more.

140
I have so minutely described the technique and practice of yoga that there is nothing more for me to write on that point. Consequently, no further books on the subject will issue from my pen.

141

The rapidity with which I have worked my way upwards in this subtle world which I have chosen as my particular field of investigation, no less than the duty which I owed to the large flock of readers depending on my researches for their own guidance, renders the modification of earlier writings inescapable.

142

I overstressed certain points and thus disturbed the balance of the whole teaching. That is, I emphasized the intellectual and metaphysical aspects of this philosophy at the expense of the devotional and mystical aspects. That this was done partly because I had earlier emphasized the last two at the expense of the first two did not excuse the fault. A harmonious coordination is still lacking. Henceforth, I shall seek to provide it.

143

I have developed my previously held ideas and extended the results of my earlier researches. This has unfortunately led to unexpected modifications, to shifts of emphasis, and to revisions of values. These changes have led to a much broader outlook. People seem horrified when a man changes his views, but if it is sincerely done it is praiseworthy. That is what he is here on earth for—to change his views. They cannot be confined permanently in experience-proof and idea-tight compartments. With widening experience he should find his views widening, too. If he does not, then he is missing one of the purposes of incarnation. He is here to learn and he can not learn without modifying an old view. Each incarnation is a field of experience which he must plow, sow, and reap, not so much for immediate gains as for ultimate ones, not so much for material gains as for moral and mental ones.

144

There is a vast difference between growth based on the ripening of intellect and change based on the impulse of emotion. Those who do not perceive this difference accuse me of glaring personal inconsistency; those who do, know that is inevitable ideological development.

145

I am sometimes contradictory precisely because I am sometimes candid. I am not at all afraid if today's truth negates the maxim of yesterday. My purpose is not to present a case on behalf of any theory; it is rather to present a series of moods. If they hang together, all right; if not, they shall yet be published. I have never concerned myself to offer a thesis in the form of irrefutable syllogisms; there are plenty of clever men who can do that. I can but offer my erratic moods—do not expect more from an obscure scribbler like myself.

146

Re-reading these books after the lapse of several years, there is so much that I want to alter in them that they would have to be transformed into new creations in order to be in accord with my present views, impressions, knowledge, and feelings. And as my life is a continuous pressing forward to new discovery, I have neither the years nor the forces left to re-occupy myself with the outworn, old, and the faded past.

147

My advisors suggested that I should so construct my explanations of the revision of views as to save face and not openly contradict much of what I had previously published. But in my desperate sincerity and, as is now obvious, foolish indignation, unfortunately I did not heed them.

148

And yet, with all their errors and faults, which are now as deeply saddening to the blundering perpetrator as they must be deeply irritating to the perceptive reader, I have left enough sound stuff in my writings for posterity as to justify their creation. As for their continuation, that is a matter over which I exercise no legal control at all. Anyway my labours and sufferings have not been altogether in vain.

149

I have written many things in my earlier books which I now wish I had never written. Time has forced me to revise beliefs, impressions, estimates, and even principles. I was misled by others in some cases and went astray through my own defects in others. Again and again dark moods have come over me solely because of past mistakes. They have often caused me unhappy moments. Nevertheless, compensation creeps in now and then despite myself. For as a scientific friend at the University of Cambridge, who sees the white as well as black in them reminds me, the essence of these books is a true one, their general effect is a valuable one, and their contribution is a necessary one in these times. And, moreover, they are perhaps the most important contents, after all. If I have done nothing more than to affirm certain unalterable verities, such as the existence of man's divine soul, and to show a way to the discovery thereof, I have done something that has made many people happier and my writing has not been quite pointless. That is the credit which may balance my debits.

150

It is not the books which belong to my past that I have any esteem for or count important to humanity; it is the books which belong to my future. I feel intensely what Tolstoy felt in 1864: "I regard everything that I have published until today as no more than exercises."

151

Unfortunately I invested these men with a wisdom which I was to discover years later they did not possess; I assumed they had attained heights which I discovered later they had not climbed; I imagined their minds preoccupied with the service of humanity which I discovered later seldom existed.

152

The author of those earlier works is dead. He himself certainly, and perhaps many readers too, would not want to resuscitate him. The old P.B. had too many deficiencies, weaknesses, and faults for my liking. Time has turned and I with it. I have profited by past errors in dealing with individuals, but in any case larger issues will necessarily claim me henceforth.

153

The aim of carrying on to a new and better level the work begun so imperfectly by my earlier books is now close to my heart.

154

My present teachings seem to me to be on a higher level than my earlier ones.

155

I am not the first mystic who blundered in his quest nor shall I be the last. The very subtlety of its nature, the sad difficulty of getting expert guidance upon it, and the tests snares pitfalls and temptations that stage it, render this a common event. "I made many mistakes," confessed Madame Guyon, and perhaps it was out of these failures that she found her way to final success. In my own case the perils were greater than in most others, simply because I searched so widely and helped so many others so indiscriminately that I exposed myself to the attack of adverse forces almost incessantly. That I survived all this, that I did not lose bodily life or become a bodily wreck, that I have emerged mentally, morally, spiritually, and philosophically stronger out of all these trials was only to be attributed to the saving grace of my Guardian Angel and to nothing else. I have experienced the black depths of occult enmity and endured the harsh menaces of occult hatred. I do not refer here to their pitiful but feeble, their treacherous and vicious human echoes on our plane. They have only my silent contempt. If my nerves are today unshattered, it is because the power that has used my pen has also intervened at the last moment again and again to save my body and mind. All this need not frighten other aspirants on this quest, however, for most of them have not to play the pioneer role that I had to play and are therefore exempt from its special risks.

156

How much time I wasted in exploring a medley of foolish cults and a diversity of fantastic beliefs! But I did this so as to ensure intellectual integrity and emotional tolerance against any suspicion of partisanship or negligence in the search after truth. Truths do not stop being true because they are introduced into false systems. The contact is certainly unnatural. Nevertheless, it cannot alter their character or deprive them of their value. We may accept a part of these systems without having to accept all of them. We must disentangle what is worth such acceptance from what is not. Most of those which I investigated had more or less good in them but there was enough of the bad, the unsound, or the unworthy to render it undesirable to stay long with any of them.

157

He who sees inconsistencies in my work sees and reads it superficially.

158

But these errors, after all, make up not even a tenth part of my writings.

159

What is worthy in my work will bear consequences and be durable; the errors will be overcome by truth and time, and pass away. This is a result which I myself wish for it.

160

Am I a heretic to venture such criticisms? But even an ant possesses the right to its own judgement.

161

I do not denounce what I have taught in the past. Let this be perfectly clear. I do not reject the meditation methods which I have devised and given out in earlier books.

162

Those who expect me to go on repeatedly expounding the same teachings as though I were a gramophone have failed to understand me.

163

Whoever finds that further investigation puts at variance his earlier theories, and has the courage to expose the fallacies which led to them, is on the right road to truth. When misplaced fidelity to a wrong concept is praised in the name of honourable consistency, it bars the road to truth. A man who fears fundamentally to revise earlier conclusions, because he fears that his reputation for reliability will be damaged, may save his reputation but will forfeit more than he saves. Therefore, let us not pretend to be surprised when further effort is crowned with truer comprehension.

164

I am not responsible for the writings of the younger Brunton!

165

There are those who would accuse us of the crime of inconsistency. We plead guilty. Yet, though we have much to explain to them, we have little to retract and certainly nothing to repent. The search after truth is not a static thing. It drives the soul first here and then there, assaying and testing all the time, and if we pick up a nugget of genuine gold every now and then in the course of our quest, we may be forgiven for the jubilant whoop that accompanies each discovery.

166

Although those books were written at the bidding of a higher will than the merely personal, unfortunately I carried out that bidding in an imperfect and incomplete manner. In some cases this was because of the tremendously time-pressed circumstances under which they were composed, but in others because I myself was not then competent to do any better. Consequently, they appear as adolescent and immature efforts to my present-day sight. What is worse, however, is that their pages preserve what I now know to be traditional superstitions, factual errors and exaggerated estimates, wrongly placed emphases and disproportionate treatment. It might be said in a sense that their own defects usefully illustrate the general defectiveness of the mystical standpoint, which is, of course, the one from which they were written. These faults are indeed regrettable from the reader's standpoint besides being a source of personal chagrin from the writer's. Nevertheless, they must not be allowed to hide merits. The books are not useless for they still hold more of truth than of error, more of help than of hindrance, more of particularly worthwhile interest to our own generation than not.

167

Let me confess frankly that my books contain a number of errors, some unbalanced emphasis, and premature therefore inaccurate conclusions. For they were written at a time when I was very much on the move, both mentally and bodily. Virgil was so ashamed of its imperfections that he hoped his *Aeneid* would be burned. I, too, have suffered and continue to suffer still the same excruciating remorse as he. To the certain horror of my publishers (who own the copyrights), but to the certain satisfaction of my conscience, let me say that I would like them all suddenly to, in Shakespeare's phrase, "dissolve and leave not a wrack behind." But alas! there is nothing to be done in the matter now, for I can find neither the time nor energy nor interest to go over the same old ground again and rewrite them as they should have been written. The task of translating the subtlest truths and most metaphysical tenets accessible to mankind into understandable contemporary language is such a tremendous one that only a sage could have carried it out without fault and without error. Consequently, I warned readers in the prefatory chapter of *The Wisdom of the Overself* to expect mistakes when I warned them that I was only "a blundering student." The best that can be done is to resolve on the one hand that all future productions of my pen shall be as faultless in matter, as free from these particular defects, as they can be made, and on the other, to publish a little journal wherein readers of those older books can have their misconceptions continually pointed out and corrected.

168

I may have to unsay a few passages here and there and to retract a few statements which seemed factual descriptions at the time, but which were really interpretational, and perhaps expunge a few credulities; nevertheless, these earlier books are, taken generally, sound enough as guides for those who are still passing through the yogic-mystic stage of this quest.

169

The reflections and impressions which follow emerge out of maturer experience than those earlier and now so distant books. One learned through the years to glorify men less, but also learned to criticize them less. The insight into what is behind them, that which psychiatrists and psychoanalysts call the subconscious and unconscious mind, has penetrated deeper and magnified tolerance.

170

I know better than the reader the shortcomings of those books written alas! so long ago, and I do not refer to the technical blemishes, the language ones only, but also to the immaturities of knowledge.

171

In those early days of his quest, when he was groping like a half-blind man, some things were grossly exaggerated by his ignorance while other things were ludicrously minimized.

172

I have to confess that I have made my quota of errors in the past. No doubt many other human beings could make the same confession. But I do not accept such excuses from myself. My grief over the mistakes is very real. For they not only involve myself but also those who have been influenced by me.

173

The contradictory nature of these teachings and their visible results in action created new questions and finally turned my investigation into broader channels.

174

The experiences, the situations, the events which had formerly shaken his emotions and shattered his peace were now reduced to tiny proportions, leaving him unmoved and unaffected in any way. Such was the work of time. They were now like dreams, mere memories, mental pictures inspected from afar.

175

Philosophy itself is the unchanging verity of life but my understanding and interpretation of it, like that of most students, are neither infallible nor final. Hence my blunders. Hence the shortcomings and imperfections of my books. If I were anything more than mere student, if I were a master, these errors and defects would not have been able to insinuate themselves into my writing. But unfortunately I am not. Would it not have been better then to have remained silent, some will ask? I thought so myself for many years and, although a whole series of occult and spiritual experiences happened during my adolescence, I waited for a decade and a half before venturing to write my first book of a mystical character. Even then, I broke this silence at a bidding which was not my own and which I accepted as higher then my own. Even now, despite the poignant perception of all their faults and mistakes, I feel that my books contain much that was worth recording and was indeed too important not to record. It was enough to redeem them. Nevertheless, those faults and mistakes are there, so I thought it better to fall silent again for a while and see whether I could not do better next time.

176

Now comes the crux of the whole matter. So far as I can follow the teachings of the ancient sages, the path which stretches before mankind appears to have four gates set at intervals along its course. The first is open to the great majority of mankind and might be named "religion, theology, and scholasticism." The second is open to a much smaller number of persons and could conveniently be named Mysticism. The third which is rarely opened (for it is heavy and hard to move) is "the philosophy of truth," whilst the final gate has been entered only by the supermen of our species; it may be titled "Realization." Few readers would care to wander with me into the wilderness whither it leads. I refuse to tarry in the limited phases of development and have gone forward in further quest of the sublime verity which is presented to us as life's goal by the sages. I value tolerance. Let others believe or follow what suits or pleases them most; I trust they will allow me the same freedom to continue my own quest.(P)

A warning shared

177

If my work is to represent philosophy in practice, my critical treatment of certain subjects must be constructive, dignified, and restrained.

178

I have read from preface to end-page the wretched book of *maya*, and I know only too well what I am writing about when I indict it. If I refuse to dip my pen in the rose-water of our sentimental novelists, I have good reason.

179

With the end of the war, the personal karma which kept me tied for some years to the Orient's own karma, also came to an end. My limbs were liberated for wider travel once again and my energies set free for more constructive work. For many years I had foreseen that a gigantic war had first to enable mankind to put to the test all the existing theories and practices not only of a materialist character but also of a religious and mystical character. My own drift away from a self-centered and unscientific mysticism had been proceeding fitfully for some years, in consequence of reflection upon its theory and observation of its practice. With the war, however, all this came to a climax, for both the attitude of mystics towards that cataclysmic event and a series of explosive personal experiences in India, the largest stronghold of such a doctrine today, brought me to a parting of the ways.

Is there any justification for the conviction, which is held by quite a number of people, that a large section of humanity, aroused by the devastating agony of the war, wise with the tragic lessons of the terrible crises which foreshadowed and followed it, can at last come to accept a more spiritual world view? The vivid horrors of this decade, the terrible ordeal through which so many millions have passed, and the tremendous changes of environment, custom, and social contact would seem to have made a more spiritual outlook not only necessary but almost inevitable. The sufferings and upheavals of nations and individuals have brought about changes, re-alignments, and movements in the attitudes and consciousness of so many people that this is certain to result in a widespread demand for philosophic teaching and mystical inspiration. The prospects of a spiritual movement are brighter today than even a few years ago. The educated classes who led the trek towards materialism last century are indeed the very people who are now leading the trek away from it.

The beginning of the postwar period has consequently a peculiar importance. The mistakes of the years which immediately followed the First World War planted the seeds which grew not only into the miseries of the two subsequent decades but also into the struggles of the Second World War. The wisdom or foolishness which shape the next few years will likewise decide the characteristics of the experience which our own generation will enjoy or endure. For the early postwar period of dissolution, confusion, ferment, and search provides the proper atmosphere for such a venture as the "Quest." It is at such a time that a special effort is demanded of those who know a little about the laws of life to teach the true perspective of life to those bewildered minds who know even less. We can thus release constructive forces when they are most needed and, therefore, likely to be most appreciated.

180

Let nobody make the mistake of believing that I write such critical statements in a mood of bitter recrimination. That would be a great error, a complete misunderstanding of my attitude. The malicious tone and vicious temper of the partisan find no echo in my heart.

181

Preach the gospel—that is, good news—to a world which dreads that all-too-soon it may become joyless.

182

The world has fallen into the pit of pessimism. So, I shall write a new Jeremiah for it, though I hope the final notes will be higher and happier than one expects.

183

Is all our writing but a coloured veil thrown over the gaunt grey face of life? Those who can only see its hard, unsmiling features declare it to be so. They find its eyes bitter wells of tears wherein heavy shadows brood. Was it for this that they flung away so recklessly the breath that returned again and again to their bodies? If they were right, then indeed we are but decorators who paint an orange sun in a darkened room.

184

We are compelled to wither the preachers of a mad materialism with scathing scorn. Gentle words fall off their ears like water off a duck's back.

185

We must not stint our condemnation of such things as merit it. Yet it is not necessary to descend into the sewer of vulgarity in order to do this.

186

I will not attempt to write a learned treatise on the history of Mysticism, and so on; I must leave that for those who like to live in the past. The present and future are too ominous for me not to answer their irresistible call.

187

Why should we write of life in a mournful manner? Why should we take this temporary shadow-show of things, and treat it tragically?

188

I have jabbed my pen viciously into none; where I have covered effete and unworthy institutions with caustic comment, this has been done merely as a slight assistance to the natural process of dying which is already in full operation.

189

For the clairvoyant few to predict approaching disasters was to predict in vain. Wealth and Poverty hurried alike into the vortex of transient superficial pleasures; millionaire and mob gaily lived for the moment, reminiscent of that eighteenth-century person who flung the flippant remark "Après moi le deluge!" at the approaching French Revolution. Once we set to work several years before the war intending to write a small book to show the world quite ruthlessly its own subconscious, to lay bare the laws of destiny under which it was inevitably moving towards the edge of a precipice, and to pass on a message from a higher source which was at once a piece of practical advice and a tocsin of stern warning. But after the penning of the first few paragraphs, a dismal feeling of futility crept into the writer's heart, stole up to his brain in the form of clearcut deeply pessimistic thoughts, and finally passed down the appropriate nerves and muscles into the right arm and hand, which became stiff and paralytic. The task brought such a sense of vain labour, of a rolling upward of the fabled stone of Sisyphus, that the pen unresistingly fell from his fingers. He visualized the dread horror which lay in ambush for mankind if they did not turn back to insert some ethical ideals and spiritual wisdom into their social arrangements, but he visualized also the hopeless situation into which their own thoughts and deeds had forced them. For their chaos was such that they could neither draw back nor go forward nor stand still. He saw clearly that the many who needed the accompanying knowledge were too entangled in the net which their karma had woven around themselves to find any immediate profit in his words. Why then continue to waste valued time and spoil virginal paper? Why should he torment himself and others by writing such a book of bitter prophecy? The practical result could be but—nil! He put the book aside and busied himself with other matters, with philosophic researches into ultimate truths which brought him to sup with the Gods.

190

To put these dark forebodings between the covers of a book might help only a few readers but would thread despondency into the minds of all readers. At first this decided the question for me and I turned away from its further consideration. But six months later it suddenly intruded itself again and with it the idea that even despondency has a useful role to play in the evolution of human character and that I was merely being soft where I believed I was being compassionate. If ignorance and self-deception had contributed to creating this dark future for my fellows, not the perpetuation of these errors but their disintegration would contribute to the true welfare of my fellows. And if despondency forced reflection and this in turn exposed error, it ought to be welcomed, not evaded. Yes, it would not be wrong to persuade my reluctant pen to visit eager paper and work for humanity's best interest. For we need these great truths to steady our hearts in an unsteady and unsure time. We need to be reminded that beneath its menace and its doom, there still are eternal life, eternal peace, and eternal hope for us. We need to remember that the evil always passes, the Good alone endures. Yes, no one can really be hurt by the retelling of these truths, and someone will surely be helped by it.

191

Such a message, diagnosing the hidden sickness of our times and indicating the correct therapy, is too valuable, too important, to be held back because of doubts about its reception, doubts caused by its loftiness. Some part of it may still be accepted even if more of it may not.

192

Since the time between now and Armageddon is so short, we ought to hold nothing back but give people the chance to obtain full Truth.

193

The last war marked a turning point in mankind's history. Out of its pain and horror something better both materially and spiritually is going to be born, and it is our task to help this coming age as pioneers who can see a little farther ahead than others.

Book notes

194

The Wisdom of the Overself was a most difficult book to write and must be equally difficult to read. To start one's studies with it is like starting on advanced theorems in mathematics before having mastered the simplest ones. It is better to start first with *The Secret Path*, go on to *The Quest of the Overself*, and then to read *Discover Yourself*. (It may be in some instances that the best book to read first is *Discover Yourself*.) However, there are statements in these three books which the author would now withdraw or modify.

195

A Search in Secret India and *The Spiritual Crisis of Man* were the only books written at a leisurely pace. All the others were thrown together at a somewhat fast speed, owing to the pressure and travel that accompanied the period of their composition.

196

Alas! *The Secret Path* was somewhat too encouraging to its readers. The Path asks more from its treaders than those pages seem to indicate.

197

In *A Search in Secret India*, I described the case of a hatha yogi whose heart appeared to stop at will. Several years later a French physician travelled to India, bringing with him certain scientific instruments with which to investigate yogic powers. Another yogi known to me was examined by the doctor and the electric cardiograph was applied to the yogi's heart after it had apparently ceased to function. The result on the instrument showed that the heartbeat was extremely slow, but quite perceptible beating still continued. Thus, the evidence of unaided sight and touch on the part of the observer was actually refuted by the accurate findings of a delicate instrument.

198

What the book contains is of unequal value, and parts of it are mere journalese intended to attract readers to the more serious portions. It would be a mistake for anyone to attach to any chapter, such as the one dealing with Mahmoud Bey, an importance which does not really belong to it. In his case, I merely reported what happened and gave his own explanation of it, neither defending nor denying this explanation. I strongly disapprove of Mahmoud Bey's using my name to advertise himself. Is there any quite tactful step to put a stop to his exploitation of my name and book? I should have written about him in the same way in which I wrote about Meher Baba, as a warning against credulity. He is a clever charlatan.

199

In *Discover Yourself,* I have used the words of Jesus as mere pegs on which to hang my own teaching. This follows the example of the ancient religion makers. It has thus helped thousands of Christians, who might otherwise not have been reached by my words, to a higher concept of Truth. Therefore, it does not really matter whether Jesus was a full philosopher or only a simple mystic.

200

The basic reason why I must revise *A Message from Arunachala* is that it has so much negative thought.

201

It is not correct to regard *The Hidden Teaching Beyond Yoga* as the continuation of *The Quest of the Overself.* It continues only the metaphysical part of that book. The mystical part is to some extent continued in *The Wisdom of the Overself.* The religious devotional and moral re-educatory parts have not yet been written about in any of my books, nor have I described the various stages and experiences of the aspirant on the Quest.

202

It was expected that *The Hidden Teaching Beyond Yoga* would give its readers a few headaches at least, since it gave its writer many more than a few! Mystical trance is not everyone's line of progress and it is not an essential stage through which every aspirant has to pass but only one through which the majority usually do pass. Krishna states in the *Bhagavad Gita*: "By whatsoever path a man cometh unto me, O Arjuna, by that path also shall I receive him." A religious faith which is deeply felt and absolutely sincere, which affects the practical life and exalts character, is just as good as, if not superior to, the ecstasies and trances of many mystics. The sense in which the term religion was used in this book was the conventional half-faith reserved only for Sundays and kept in a watertight compartment from daily practice and ethical character, which passes so widely for religious life. But the subject of religion and God has been dealt with at length in *The Wisdom of the Overself.* Readers may find therein helpful and interesting explanations.

203

The Hidden Teaching Beyond Yoga gave the impression that the spiritual had been set aside and a mental plane adopted; but, as the opening chapters explained, this was done deliberately in order to interest a large body of intellectual people in the West who did not accept mysticism but who might be led gradually into it if the approach were made through the reasoning faculty and they were thus convinced. This book started from their standpoint and the second volume tried to lead them right into the spiritual camp. It is not enough merely to preach to the converted. The simple spiritual teaching will help a certain number of people and no more. Owing to the advance of science there are lots of people with intellectually tangled minds who also need help.

204

The Hidden Teaching Beyond Yoga has stated the reasons for this "Beyond." That Reality lies close to the terminus of yoga practice is granted; that the wall between them is very thin is also granted. But the wall is also diamond-hard: it can be penetrated only by those who have been instructed in the nature of Reality or, more easily, in what it is not; who can discriminate between it and appearances which seem like it. (Grace plays its part but it is beside the point to raise this question here.) Those without such knowledge are handicapped. For instance, the Sufi mystic who repeats the mantric phrase "Allahu Akbar"—"God is most great"—dozens of times has had the work of gathering in his thoughts made easier; they are repulsed with each repetition, and thus concentration is eventually achieved. The Indian yogi follows the same process and gets the same result with his mantram, "Jai Ram, jai jai Ram"—"Victory to the Lord"— repeated 108 times. (Beads may be pushed along a string for counting purposes.) Both Sufi and yogi may pass into ecstasy. But is this Reality or is it self-hypnotism?

205

The quotation in the last chapter of *The Hidden Teaching Beyond Yoga* about General Simha and war was taken from Paul Carus' book, *Gospel of Buddha*, Chapter 51, paragraph 17. Since then I have ascertained that it does not appear in any known Pali text and must consequently be an interpolation by Carus himself.

206

It is significant that two contemporary Indians have included in their teachings the very same critique of meditation which was made in *The Hidden Teaching Beyond Yoga*: I refer to Krishnamurti and Atmananda.

207

The criticisms of mystics in *The Hidden Teaching Beyond Yoga* were deliberately overstressed in order to give them a shock and wake them up. They are wedded to the *forms* of experience, such as mystical visions, to the *duality* of existence, such as spirit and matter, to the personal self, which makes them desire and gloat over meditational ecstasies. They do not see that these represent an intermediate stage towards the Real but are not the Real. This does not mean that mysticism is to be given up; on the contrary it is essential, but its limitations must be understood.

208

Did I overpraise action in *The Hidden Teaching Beyond Yoga*? The answer is given by Emerson: "Action is with the scholar subordinate, but it is essential. Without it he is not yet man."

209

Because in the second chapter of *The Hidden Teaching Beyond Yoga* I mentioned three ancient texts—*Bhagavad Gita*, *Ashtavakra Samhita* and Gaudapada's *Mandukya Karika*—it was supposed that my exposition of the hidden philosophy was entirely drawn from them alone. A wholly exaggerated importance was thus given them by several readers. Indeed, in the case of the third title, the teaching there given is as much opposed to my own on some points as it is in agreement on others. These three titles were mentioned only in passing just to show how I was introduced to the *literature* of the hidden philosophy, to illustrate a single phase out of several in my mental development, and for no other purpose. They represented only a *beginning* of my delving into those mysterious ancient texts which were written with sharp style-point on palm leaves now time-browned. From this first start, I went on to explore a wide range until I discovered and studiously plodded through, either alone or with learned pundits, a hundred others which were equally or more important—some, like the *Yoga Vasistha Maharamayana* (a huge work of several thousand pages), were lying half neglected because of their forbidding bulk, whereas others like the little *Ratnavali* were no longer extant in modern India but had become treasured classics in cold Tibet. The bulk of my exposition consists of important material that is not mentioned by these three books. My knowledge has been derived from several other Asiatic sources besides the Indian ones. Secondly, because I prominently mentioned my interest in the palm-leaf philosophical texts, it was wrongly believed that the entire teaching presented here is only a theoretical elaboration of such musty old writings. The texts were named in the reference partly for the benefit of Indian readers, who form a noticeable proportion of my audience, and partly for the benefit of those who like to lean upon the authority of antiquity.

210

Another reason why I introduced these three titles into the prefatory chapter was that they were also symbolic and representative of major tenets of our philosophy. Thus, the *Bhagavad Gita* stood for inspired action, Gaudapada's commentary on the *Mandukya Upanishad* for Mentalism, and *Ashtavakra's Song* for the concentration on Pure Thought.

211

A related misconception, which must now be cleared up, prevails chiefly among Indian readers. It arises out of the statement in the final paragraph of the final page of *The Hidden Teaching Beyond Yoga*, wherein it is asserted that every tenet of my exposition found its parallel somewhere in the old Sanksrit writings and could therefore be fitly declared Indian in origin. Here again I must remind readers of the aforementioned fact that I have refused to expound these tenets in the archaic fashion with its terse undetailed dogmatic and dry form, but have entirely reshaped them with the help of modern Western thought, adding numerous details lacking in the old texts. This reworking and renovation of the old tenets naturally tends to make them somewhat unrecognizable by Indians accustomed only to the somewhat dreary and highly condensed material in their own texts. To Hindus who criticize *The Hidden Teaching Beyond Yoga* as being unauthentic, I reply that the last chapter of *Aitareya Upanishad* plainly says that everything that is, is Mind. But the point I wish to explain here is that I soon ascertained the undoubted historical fact that several of the most important texts of the hidden teaching had been lost to India since at least seven hundred years ago. This was because they were the work of Buddhist sages, and they disappeared in the general stamping-out of everything Buddhist from India—a persecution practised partly by the Brahmin priests fearful for their own selfish power and financial profit and partly by the Muhammedan invaders antipathetic to what they wrongly regarded as atheism. It must here be pointed out what is not realized by most Indians today, that Buddhism and Brahminism dwelt as sister religions for several hundred years after Buddha appeared, their esoteric doctrines merely complementing each other, and their esoteric teachers friendly to each other. The philosophers of one faith showed no hostility to the philosophers of the other. It was—and ever shall be—only among the unphilosophical priests and uninitiated mystics and their followers, the masses, that mutual antagonism later reared its ugly head.

Unfortunately, in their craze for eliminating everything that seemed of Buddhist origin these persecutors—both Brahmin and Moslem—even eliminated many of their own pre-Buddhist texts because they seemed to teach similar "atheistical" doctrines. The present-day consequences of these destructive activities is that it is now so difficult to ascertain what precisely was the *complete* hidden teaching (as opposed to the mere fragments which are available) that whoever attempts the task alone and unaided will soon lose himself in a labyrinth of puzzling contradictions and tantalizing obscurities. The only way whereby the numerous tenets into which the general teaching ramifies can be collected in all their completeness is to enlarge one's research beyond the frontier of India itself. For thousands of Buddhist monks and scholars fled from the bitter persecutions and cruel massacres to the remote mountains of Nepal, Sikkim, Bhutan, and the interior of the Himalaya range, *taking such of their texts with them as they could carry*. In addition to them, there had been earlier propagandist journeys of Indian sages and philosophers to other parts of Asia, such as Tibet, China, and Cambodia, as well as the vast territory now called Sinkiang, and these ambassadors had already introduced and translated several important texts.

212

The Hidden Teaching Beyond Yoga was disruptive to the unripe mystic's self-centered emotions. With the coming of the Second World War, the time had come for mysticism to arouse itself and make a worthwhile contribution to the betterment of mankind. However, these disrupted emotions were somewhat soothed by the material in *The Wisdom of the Overself*, which is part of the higher revelation needed by our age. The first volume represented an attempt to engage the interest of the intellectual and sceptical class who with the second volume were led right into the mystical camp. The two volumes were designed to lead their readers onward towards an understanding through reason of truths which have usually been felt through intuition or experienced through trance. In this way, they could be of service in a wider field.

213

The Wisdom of the Overself took up again the heavy task which was left unfinished in *The Hidden Teaching Beyond Yoga*, whose pages carried its reader into the strange difficult territory of mentalism and left him there as in a flinty wilderness, for the promised land of the sublime Overself still lay too far off to be discerned with the naked eye. Now, if he wished, it became possible for him to resume the mental journey and even carry it through to completion. The trail which others had cut for him would give right direction—no small gain in an enterprise which is indeed the protracted labour of a lifetime. This said, he is still likely to have hard going. The kingdom of heaven is not so easy to find as old creeds and modern cults imply by their glib tones of familiarity. Oh yes, they can lead him into their particular conception of it, their imaginary construction of it, but not into the reality itself.

214

The Wisdom of the Overself shows in what relation the planetary Overmind and the individual ego-mind stand to each other, and the nature and extent of the "interference" set up by the individual. The contact cannot be established by the limited operations of intellect or by the emotional ecstasies of the mystic, as an entirely new faculty has to be brought into play. This has been called "insight" (following the terminology of the Mongolian Yaka-kulgan school). It is a transcendental fusion of thought, feeling, being, and act which yields an "isolation," as it were, of the principle of awareness. When this is done one, realizes how the electrical field operating in the colloidal structure of nerve cells can only provide conditions for the expressions of this principle—that is to say, for setting up a limited representation of it. In realizing this awareness principle as it is in itself, the whole system of memories, energies, and tendencies which compose the dual, individual, world picture becomes detached and the neurological mechanism with it. One then perceives that the scientific procedure which would set the physical apart from the mental must finally fail because of its dualism, even as the materialistic procedure which would immerse the mental in the physical must fail because the five senses can be banished in yoga trance while consciousness is kept.

215

The basic lesson of *The Wisdom of the Overself* is that space, which provides a stage for things, time, which provides an order for events, and matter, which supplies the stuff of both, are all three really experiences of the mind, inseparable from the mind, constructed out of the mind, and nothing else. In other words, Mind is the essence of all existence, all life, all form, and this Mind is non-material. Pure Mind is nothing other than God and its reflection in the individual is nothing other than the divine soul. The book is admittedly difficult—mostly because of its metaphysical character and its compulsion on the reader to do much close thinking. However, it would be enough, after the first general reading, to reread only those portions which are the easiest to understand or which make the most appeal. The ground it covers can be only gradually trodden. In any case, it was written mainly to reach those who want to work their way up from the scientific standpoint to the spiritual one.

216

Misunderstandings among readers led to the queer notion that I esteemed reason to be capable of providing the sole key to the mysteries of man, life, and the universe—"queer" because a more careful study of the book would have revealed hints here and there of a tenet in this teaching that there exists the supramystic faculty of *insight*, which was stated to transcend rational thinking. Admittedly no further explanation of it was given, but this was because the subject was too advanced for treatment there and had to fall into its proper place. Critics fell into such a misunderstanding of this doctrine by abstracting the part of it contained in the first volume from the rest and by ignoring the precautionary sentences sprinkled in that volume. Their error would have been impossible if they had been able to take the two volumes as a whole, which they were not able to do until now.

217

Some people get frightened at the mental toughness of those books. I had to write in such a tough way in order to appeal to the dominant authority of this particular age in which I happened to be born—the said authority being science, intellect, high-browism, and so on, which are worshipped as though they were God. The whole subject is really much simpler than it will appear to be from the books and not at all difficult to grasp.

218

The Hidden Teaching Beyond Yoga makes stiff reading because it was intended for the critical scientific and philosophic minds who are drawing nearer to this line of thought, but there are a number of paragraphs throughout the book which will be helpful to the student of mysticism also. He should study the portions that appeal most to him. This book tells something of the Ultimate Path, although the actual practices are reserved for *The Wisdom of the Overself*. The ultimate aim is to build a balanced personality, where reason and feeling will both be well-developed and harmonized. In the advanced stages of the final path, the faculty of true insight will be born, and it is this which acts as the harmonizing agent. The last chapter of the book indicates a desire to serve mankind. This may be done by contributing to the reconstruction which must come later.

This is the justification of the Quest, that it can and shall not only give the individual inner peace, intelligent understanding, and a perfect world-explanation, but that it also can and shall give society guidance in solving the great problems which face it.

219

Whoever will attend to what is most plainly said in *The Hidden Teaching Beyond Yoga* and *The Wisdom of the Overself* will then know that philosophy accepts, includes, and preserves everything that is worthwhile in religion and yoga and that it does not give up the attitude of prayerful worship or cease from the exercise of daily meditation. This being so, only those who misconceive what it is can allege that I have faltered in my spiritual quest and retracted my advocacy of yoga. But such misconceptions still thrive powerfully and even naturally amongst those whose approach to mysticism is solely on the emotional, personal side, and it seems we must endure them always as part of the penalty for attempting to point out a wider horizon to such people.

220

There are parts of *The Hidden Teaching Beyond Yoga* which are discouraging to those who have hitherto held the mystical ideal alone, but from the second volume, *The Wisdom of the Overself*, they will realize that this discouragement was unjustified. There is a great deal of absolutely new material in this book—dealing with higher mysticism, meditation, religion, and God—which should be a practical help not only to advanced students but even to beginners on the Quest. No doubt a first reading of the first volume was destructive to the emotions of many people; but the rational, intellectual, and practical side of philosophy was deliberately overstressed to help readers become better balanced human beings.

221

The Wisdom of the Overself represents the results of long arduous research conducted in several ways, a research which has shattered health and shortened life but which has not been without some success.

222

In these two volumes there was an endeavour to bring together in a unity the elements of a scattered doctrine.

223

So began a line of research which in the months and years to come finished up as a two-volume affair: *The Hidden Teaching Beyond Yoga* and *The Wisdom of the Overself*. They were the eventual and first results of that day's reflection. Now, half a lifetime later, something properly may be deleted from the pages, and new material added to them. Furthermore, a brief summing up should not be unwelcome.

224

The Spiritual Crisis of Man was indifferently received. It got neither attention nor circulation of any account. This was regrettable, for I had been allowed a peep behind the curtain of world events, behind the present pattern of the human scene on this planet, and there was a real necessity for knowledge of it if all of us were not to go down into the gravest catastrophe.

225

The Spiritual Crisis of Man was addressed to the man in the street bewildered by the world's fateful crisis. It was written out of compassion for his need of guidance and hence in general, nontechnical, simple terms. It had deep feeling, yet it was not an emotional book. It spoke of the soul that each may find in his own heart. It told him and his fellows that they cannot build their new and better world aright until they have looked within, found the soul's light to guide them, and made certain inner changes. These cannot be avoided. Man may consciously co-operate with the inner purpose of this crisis and intelligently participate in it to his own benefit. If, however, he blindly resists or lazily delays, he will suffer the consequences.

226

It was not easy for me to write the chapter on suffering in *The Spiritual Crisis of Man*, but it was immensely harder for others to read it and bear what was said.

227

Although I deny the criticism that *The Spiritual Crisis of Man* was a negative and pessimistic book, still some people thought that it was a dirge for a decaying civilization. They objected to being reminded of their grave peril and thereby made miserable.

228

In writing the book, *The Spiritual Crisis of Man*, I used all possible discretion in my references to the future course of events. I took every care to avoid giving grounds for possible accusations like war-mongering and depressing the public morale.

229

I wrote *The Spiritual Crisis of Man* as Jeremiah wrote in his own times. It was partly intended to be a warning of grave calamity which I knew positively was due to come if no new attitudes were adopted in public policies. I was not permitted to utter this warning plainly, nor in detail, but only to sound a vague hint.

230

I also wrote my book as a humble contribution to "other-mindedness" in a fear-and-money-ridden world, when all the basic values of life seem to be in the melting pot. I am told that life here in Europe is so difficult and the speed of it so rapid that one has no time to study the beautiful around one, but my point is just that it is we ourselves who make it so rapid and so difficult. If only we were content to search for less material wealth, we should have more time to devote to the search for "the beauty of life," and it is only, in my view, an appreciation of this "beauty of life" so absorbed by the hearts and minds of a truly religious art-loving people as to appear in our daily lives, that can save this present civilization from destruction. I feel I must unburden myself of this profound conviction and give the message which I feel it is my duty to give. If it passes unheeded, at least I am free from the accusation of not having had the moral courage to fulfil this duty.

231

If a new term is helpful, why not use it? It need not and does not displace the existing ones. The "Overself" was chosen just because it lacked precision but served an idea.

232

The term "Overself" was used in one sense in some passages of the books and in another sense in other passages. This is confusing to the philosophically minded. However, these books were written primarily to extend the doctrine of mysticism or meditation. From this standpoint, the inner self of man is the goal; from the philosophic standpoint, the Universal Self is the goal. The latter, of course, includes the former.

233

The Overself has not expressed itself in matter simply because there is no matter! It has not improved itself by evolution, but finite, individual minds have done so. The universal gods are the Overminds, the sum totals of each system—that is, concepts of the human mind which are dropped by the adept when they have served their purpose in bringing him to That which is unlimited. Seek the kingdom first, and all these occult powers will be added unto you.

234

The planetary Overmind is the active aspect of the Overself but still only an aspect. It works with space and time, although the latter assumes dimensions far beyond that with which waking human capacity can cope. The Overself in its passive purity is timeless and spaceless.

235

The word Overmind should never have been introduced, but now that it is here it must be explained. There is only one Reality. The nearest notion we can form of it is that it is something mental. If we think of it as being the sum total of all individual minds, then it is Overmind; if we can rise higher and know that it cannot be totalized, it is Overself. The first explanation was originally introduced to explain why abnormal phenomena can happen but not as a final explanation of what Mind and Reality are. People have confused the two aims. Actually there is only One thing, whatever you call it, but it can be studied from different standpoints and thus we get different results. That thing is Mind—unindividuated, infinite.

236

It is needful to define here what is meant by the word "spiritual." *The Hidden Teaching Beyond Yoga* points out how ambiguous it has become, how wide a range of connotations it now possesses. To simplify, it can be used generically to cover any or all of the three aspects of human culture which oppose themselves to a materialistic interpretation of life, aspects which may conveniently be named the religious, the mystical, and the philosophic.

237

The word "philosophy" is really insufficient for my purposes. I have always considered its unsatisfactory usage to be tentative and temporary, but it will have to be continued until an alternative can be found.

238

Shall I connect with Interior Word the "breaking of silence," the Logos or Word, Kabir's *Shabda*, Divine Word?

239

The word "lifeless" as used in the book *Discover Yourself* is not quite correctly interpreted as "impersonal." It is an ambiguous word as used there. It really refers to that condition wherein everything is latent, potential, unexpressed, unindividuated, unmoving. The best way to understand it is to think of the mind during deep sleep. It is not functioning then and is apparently without life. Yet the potentialities are all there.

240

Dear X:

Theosophy, esoteric Buddhism, and Hindu sects like the Vedantists come at several points of contact quite close to the Hidden Teaching, but diverge at others. The septenary constitution of man is somewhat theoretical—as actually there are only two entities, the ego and the Overself—but it may be useful for analytic purposes.

Your understanding of different ways in which I use the word ego, and in which Theosophy uses it, is correct. What happens metaphysically to the further existence of the being resulting from the conscious union of the ego with the Overself is guarded as a mystery, and may not be discussed.

Those who call Madame Blavatsky an unmitigated quack are talking nonsense. Although her teachings were partly unreliable, there was nevertheless a great deal of truth in them; and although she herself was imperfect, and occasionally unreliable, she was mostly sincere.

241

I do not perceive any fundamental difference between the Buddhistic teachings and the philosophic teachings expressed in my books, although it may be that I have written about some matters which Buddhism does not deal with. Much in Mahayana Buddhism is acceptable to me, even though I do not care to put any labels on what I have written.

242

I read my own books as if they were those written by a stranger.

243

The words which had flown out of my pen were now bubbling and boiling in the linotype machine and would soon settle into cold leaden slugs.

244

The responsibility for such statements which have appeared on the paper jackets of my books does not rest with me but with my publishers. Had those statements been submitted to me prior to publication, I would certainly have corrected all the errors they contain.

245

My publisher, with motives laudable enough from a commercial viewpoint but reprehensible from a spiritual one, has done me a serious disservice in glaringly stressing the sensational elements of my books.

246

A shrewd reader will observe, as he courageously travels through these pages, that in dealing with the remarkable personalities selected for mention, I have offered little of comment and less of criticism. So far as my pen permits me, I would play the part of a descriptive reporter. Very likely, in some later books whose date I know not, I shall don the philosophic mantle and ascend the rostrum.

The aforementioned shrewd reader, if he is inclined to be somewhat critical, may easily retort that in that event it is as well that I do not philosophize excessively now, since by that time I shall be older and therefore wiser. But of this I am not so certain as formerly.

247

The subject of this work is no less than the total regeneration of man. No more practical subject could be written about, yet it is too often deemed interesting only to dreamers or fanatics. No more important one could be brought to our attention, for it is the very purpose for which the infinite power has put us into existence on this earth today. Jesus proclaimed it when he said, "Ye shall be born again." It is the process which plants, grows, and ripens all those attributes of the true human being that distinguish him from the merely animal being.

Seed thoughts

248

The time came to give public expression and coordinated form to doctrines which I had hitherto either not received at all or else received in disjointed fragments and torn scraps. I not only tried to simplify these metaphysical ideas for ordinary readers, but also to systematize them for intellectual ones, and to expound the whole teaching in a clear and continuous manner. Indeed, some readers have been kind enough to say that they find that these two books (*The Hidden Teaching Beyond Yoga* and *The Wisdom of the Overself*) possess a logical development of their argument which helps to clarify the difficult subjects they deal with. Whether this be true or not, the fact is that it is normal for me to write merely disjointed fragments, but abnormal to write a sustained thesis; easy to throw off a short article for a periodical journal but hard to elaborate patiently a complete book. I like to announce in short staccato jerky sentences the truths I intuit, but self-discipline has made me argue them out in long flowing ones. All that smooth transition from paragraph to paragraph which is rightly held to be one of the prominent features of literary artistry, is absent from my natural capacity. What little I may have gained has been gained with great labour. Like Beethoven I have a habit of working at three or four compositions at the same time. And like him I often transfer a short fragment or even a complete piece from one composition to another. But the method of composition which is most predominant of all in my make-up is the peculiar one of jotting down my ideas about a theme without any order whatsoever, so that its end middle and beginning are jumbled together anyhow. Only after a certain period has elapsed do I undertake the task of arranging it in proper sequence.

249

My fashion of approaching the same topic from a number of sides, as well as of emphasizing the importance of certain neglected or ignored sides, led to frequent repetition which bored, irritated, or disappointed a section of my readers. But it was deliberate, and it helped other readers. It was an ancient Oriental style which was really a special method of illuminative teaching and a tested means of assisting the mind to open tight-fitting or obdurate closed doors, and of becoming aware of hitherto unperceived truths or getting to understand more easily what was before hard to understand. It was much used by the Buddha. I felt that my explorations of the spiritual realm had to be made as explicit as my pen could make them, and this was one way of doing so.

250

After so many years the endeavour to reconstruct from memory alone a conversation correctly would be a vain one, giving either a distorting caricature of truth or a misleading shift of emphasis. It would be better to make the report quite a short one if scraps of notes written at the time, however hurriedly, are available. This is why so many of the accounts are so brief. Where no notes at all are available, no mention of the meeting has been published, except in certain cases where a high degree of importance warrants the recording of impressions, atmosphere, trend, and general attitude.

251

They started as disorganized notes written at odd times. They grew into a compact bungle and remained so for quite a while until I sensed one day that they were pleading to be united into a properly embodied form—so they were born as a book.

252

My books have grown up—where they were not travel reports—somehow. They were not made up in orderly sequence from beginning to end. I cannot work that way although it is the usual one, and certainly the one most suitable for most writers. My ideas come separately, unjoined to other ones: each is independent and they are not attached to a single theme.

253

A strict coherence of paragraphs and sentences is something I manage somehow sometimes to achieve, but only with great difficulty and by some kind of underground travel.

254

I went into myself first, and what I found there I put down on paper.

255

The egoism and conceit which appeared in some of my pages were a pretense, the traits of a literary figure whom I had to set up to give thought-provoking individuality and stronger emphasis to certain ideas.

256

If a book is to be given scholarly academic form, if documents are to be cited continuously in support of the statements made, that is as good a presentation as could be expected. But it is not mine.

257

A scrupulous author will substantiate his assertions by documentary references and abundant footnotes; he will give source and date for each one. I alas! do not come into this admirable category.

258

Poetry is at its best when it leads man towards spiritual beauty. This indeed is the mission of all the other arts also. To write a book that will sustain a single theme through three hundred pages is an admirable intellectual achievement, but it is not really my way; I have done with it since long ago. A man must express himself in his own way, the way which follows the nature he is born with. I prefer to write down a single idea without any reference to those which went before or which are to follow later, and to write it down in a concentrated way. The only book I could prepare now would be a book of maxims of suggestive ideas. I have not the patience to go on and on and on, telling someone in a hundred pages what I could put into a single page.(P)

259

If a conversation helps to illuminate this dark subject, it is worth recording.

260

The writing I have done is in fragmentary form; there is no whole completed record of what philosophy means to me.

261

These disconnected sentences of mine are like beads waiting to be properly matched and strung together on a string.

262

Much of my unpublished writing consists of disconnected paragraphs standing by themselves, isolated from each other. I call them my seed thoughts. They are ideas which come to me at odd moments, almost every day, and I have not the time, when they arise, to develop them; but I do not want to lose them, and hence jot them down. Since they are incomplete and also not in literary form, but require being thought out and written out, I save them for some future time when the work needed on them will be possible.

263

This disjointed style of writing lessens its continuity and thus limits its readership. It seems regrettable but I have had to accept it.

264

The paper lies passive, waiting to receive the inked symbols of rational thought, or, with luck, of intuitive thought.

265

I put down phrases and paragraphs in a disjointed manner, for that is the way in which I can best write. It is like stitching little pieces of cloth together. This is not a good way to write, for it does not give a good smooth result, nor a sustained one. I cannot, like a businessman, sit down at an office desk and work for some hours and then get up. I have to take my thoughts and ideas as and when they come, a little at a time.

266

These are not manuscripts for books but random notes for books.

267

I write in pieces and patches upon a great variety of subjects—mostly short pieces, very short and incomplete patches. However if I did not do so and threw aside the material I would lose the freshness of the impact when the thought or idea came into my mind. Naturally when all these notes are brought together I will find that there is a good deal of repetition and of course a great deal to be thrown out in consequence. Revisions and changes, corrections and improvements will also be necessary. But all that does not really matter so long as the first vital impact of the concept was saved and not lost.

268

I have given a few illustrative anecdotes of cases that are personally known to me, to make plainer the principles taught and to add interest to their expositions. If the names of some persons concerned are withheld, it is for the understandable reason that private confidence must be respected. On the other hand, I have also included a few historical and biographical references from the annals of famous names—whenever I have found them peculiarly apt as definite examples.

269

At odd times and in different places I had developed a habit of turning time into thought and thought again into written phrases or manuscript articles which were jotted down on paper but never got sent into the world. Friends who had been allowed to read some specimens of these scraps had persisted, like Oliver Twist, in asking for more. The availability of a better medium would enable me to melt those words into the leaden slugs of linotype and thence enflesh them in a new incarnation in the printed pages of a stitched periodical, thus extending their circulation to a wider audience than one. But apart from that, each issue would always contain two special articles from my pen. The first would be the leading editorial and of an inspirational character; the other would be definitely instructional.

270

The task of keeping personal news or instructions to friends distinct from the more general communications and the teachings for correspondents, readers, and strangers could easily be achieved by separating the essentially private pages from the rest of the matter and printing them as a small special bulletin to be loosely enclosed only in those copies of the journal which were addressed to friends.

271

To put them into acceptable form, I have strung these sheets together as on an invisible thread, by their harmony of subject rather than by their date or place of birth.

272

This repetitiousness is a fault, I fully agree, yet its aim, being clearer definition of obscure subjects, is paradoxically a merit.

273

I have given a glimpse of myself in some of my books, and that must suffice.

274

I could, indeed, have penned it in the stately style of the Victorians, but that might have proved rather slow for our quick age.

275

Those who complain that there is nothing new in all this, who look for sensational and novel revelations but find none, may be answered with the words of wise Goethe: "The truth must be repeated over and over again, because error is repeatedly preached among us; . . . everywhere error prevails, and is quite easy in the feeling that it has a decided majority on its side."

276

My unfortunate tendency to labour a point too long has irritated some readers but helped others. The intention of all this repetitive statement was to present the same idea in its various aspects and thus help to make it clearer. Where such difficult and subtle metaphysical ideas as mentalism are in question, this clarification is needful.

277

It is thought proper and respectable by many, if not most, writers to emasculate their pens before putting them to paper. I am not of such a way of thinking. I possess a heart as well as a brain, whatever those gentlemen may have, and I will not approach the modern horrors of materialistic civilization with kidgloves.

278

I jot down the ideas that come into my head. But they come when I am relaxed. I cannot force them by concentration, by sustaining a unifying theme. I must let them arrive in their own good time, not mine. As a result, they are independent of each other, separate and unrelated.

279

Repetition may give boredom to a reader, but it may also give what it is intended to do—not only emphasis, not only importance to an idea, but also suggestive power and even hypnotic rhythm.

280

Buddha and Jesus deliberately preached to the unlettered mass of people. This is one of the reasons why Gautama repeated himself so often and why Jesus used simple parables so much.

281

To put a large world-view into a little phrase may puzzle some readers but will enlighten other ones.

282

It may not be prudent to write down statements which may be negatively received by the reader or which may be over-emphasized to a degree that upsets his or her balance.

283

Sustaining the effort to make a consistent single whole which is a book is not in my temperament, not one of my skills. I have written several books, but they are really a number of ideas linked together, ideas which emerged at different times and at varying intervals.

284

Unless one made an immediate note of his words—and too often that was emphatically not possible—some of the material would be lost.

285

If memory has not failed me, this is what he said, but not only memory is at stake here. There may be some rightness in Hazlitt's assertion that "authors in general are not good listeners."

286

It found its way to the crumpled pages of my much travelled notebooks.

287

Repetition is not without value in an exposition of subjects which are exotic, unfamiliar, new, or obscure, as most of those about which I write are to most general readers.

288

My chapters were not dogmatic. I tried to write so as to *lead* the readers by a chain of questions or analysis or reasoning to the truth.

289

The pen trembles in his hand when he thinks of that humbling moment and tries to find a fitting sentence for his private journal.

290

If these thoughts seem much too ragged and imperfect, why, blame my pen which put them down, for its nib is grown somewhat cross and no longer interprets the mental messages I send as once it did.

291

I begin to write something which any other capable writer could turn to good account, when lo! my pen runs into wide generalities and leaps up to airy abstractions; so my scene is forgotten amid the philosophical implications into which it has landed me. However, by a frequent retracing of steps I eventually make some amends, though never sufficient to restore my literary self-confidence.

292

I consciously developed the habit of turning all that happened in life to philosophic analysis and literary purposes.

293

Those thoughts could no longer be contained within my own mind. I was forced to express them. No sooner was a meditation ended, an intuition formulated, a vision completed, or a communion consummated, than I was driven to reach for my pen and put at least some fragment of it down on paper. I went fishing with a long rod in philosophic waters, with what results my readers may themselves gauge from the catch here presented to them.

A sacred vocation

294

We who struggle to put the Wordless into words, driven by memories of a single glimpse or illumined by an overwhelming revelation, are blessed by the mere effort alone.

295

This strange thing I found—that my writing not only recorded spiritual experience which had been mine but also creatively contributed to forming new experience.

296

I work at research because destiny has guided me to it and temperament has fitted me for it, not only because of outer compulsion but also because of inner fascination.

297

Some of us have literally written our way out of ignorance to some sort of knowledge, if not truth. Perhaps this was why we were so happy when actually working?

298

Writing is not only the medium in which I can best express myself but also the one in which I *must* express myself.

299

The vocation was there. I *had* to write, however badly. I was driven to it in childhood and now, in old age, it is more than a mild pleasure.

300

There are times—and they are the times when, looking back, I love my profession most—when writing becomes for me not a profession at all but either a form of religious worship or a form of metaphysical enlightenment. It is then, as the pen moves along silently, that I become aware of a shining presence which calls forth all my holy reverence or pushes open the mind's doors.(P)

301

Writing, which is an exercise of the intellect to some, is an act of worship to me. I rise from my desk in the same mood as that in which I leave an hour of prayer in an old cathedral, or of meditation in a little wood.(P)

302

May this book be as moving a reading experience as it was a writing one.

303

I do not wilfully neglect correspondence, it is that I am *unable* to attend to it when my heart is forcefully pulling me in a different direction—toward creative literary writing.

304

When I look at all these manuscripts, I am reminded of Shakespeare's exclamation: "Words, words, words!" Millions after millions of them have flowered out this past half-century yet mankind continues the downward and perilous course. Of what use to add more? "Why do we write books?" Wei Wu Wei asked me one day. I can reply only that it is my profession to do so. But the truth is really different: I *have* to write them and would produce them even if I were a baker and not seeking publication. Their creation gives me intense satisfaction. Through them I feel that I have justified my existence. Through them the thought is now there on the mental plane for my own benefit. If sensitive minds can come to its acceptance later, let it be so: perhaps it will be for theirs, too. If not, then that is its fate.

305

Even if, when I put pen to paper, a spiritual belt sometimes seems to drive my mental engines, and even though I have tried to unchain the pen that once served Mammon alone, I still write to fill the pantry!

306

Sometimes his mind is flooded with divine images that bubble up from some secret depth and crowd the tip of his pen, trying to find themselves fair bodies of words.

307

This inky but attractive profession to which I have committed myself has helped my intellect become more active, has both retarded its subsidence and yet encouraged it, too!

308

I want to write. I want to set down those wonderful swinging rhythms of the soul that leap up so joyously in my heart.

309

Perhaps I have too generously given away counsel which I need myself!

310

I amuse myself with penning these thoughts in an age which can barely understand them, and with publishing them to an epoch which is unlikely to accept them. If I derive no profit and gather no audience, at least I derive some entertainment and gather some smiling hours.

311

In the actual work itself of writing down such spiritual thoughts, I find its finest reward. This explains why my work is superior to myself.

312

My head is filled with thoughts and ideas. I am never discouraged when confronted with a piece of blank writing paper. For there is always something that I have to set down and communicate, if not to others, then to my ordinary self from my Other Self.

313

Perhaps I am too preoccupied with ultimate issues: I have not that smooth onward flowing facility which can come only to a mind simple enough to fling aside the fascinations of intellectual bypaths and patterns, and confident enough to write without wondering at every line whether it was written truly enough. Where this strange hankering after abstruse and difficult philosophizing has come from, I do not know.

314

What does it matter whether I write books or whether I permit the white paper to remain blank? The world struggled on for quite some time before I appeared, and I am not vain enough to imagine that a few words of mine will ever cease its struggles appreciably. If it were not partly for the necessity to subsist and to gain a livelihood, and partly for the pleasure I get from phrasing my thoughts, I doubt whether any volumes of mine would ever have been born.

315

My interest in mystical studies has never been a professional one only. It is true that as a writer I could have made myself equally at home in several other subjects and indeed did so in my earlier years. But none of them could so engage my heart, so fascinate my mind, as these. I wrote about them out of love for the research into them.

316

People tell me of the mental benefit they have gotten from reading my writings. It is encouraging to hear them. But not one of them has so benefited mentally from this self-expression as myself!

317

Writing is my life-work. I had to play the scribe in modern Euramerica as I once did in ancient Asia because I could not think of doing otherwise.

318

All the learning was not on one side. From the responses which came to my writings, the narratives, the spiritual autobiographies, the praise and criticism, I gained a larger view of the subject, confirmations of truth and corrections of error.

319

Up to the last few years I have philosophized but little on paper, preferring to write my thoughts with the pen of action.

320

Mystics do not usually possess the hands of Midas and therefore we do not look forward to much monetary return for the time and labour put into this work.

321

Writing is not really my professional career. It is my God-given avocation. I am compelled to write by an inner necessity, not by any outer one. Fame, money, or power are not the baits. This necessity itself arises out of the profound dedication to human enlightenment which has burned like a flame in my innermost being for nearly thirty years.

322

Writing is a sphere of activity which now assists and does not hinder any pursuit of self-realization. When a man's work is absolutely congenial to him, it becomes a channel of creative art; but when it is repulsive, it becomes a sin in which he engages at his peril.

323

I write to instruct myself, and if the world gets instructed in the process, it is well—but if not, no matter, for that is not my main intention.

324

We writers are privileged persons. We ourselves benefit by the mental effort needed to see clearly or think logically while expressing ourselves. But we writers are also in a perilous position. For life tests us by our words and matches them against our actions.

325

Writing is in my blood. Consequently, when duty demanded that I share with my fellows such little knowledge as I have attained, the logic of temperament pointed out a single way alone and I naturally began to set down this knowledge on paper.

326

I live with words: they make me happy or tense me with truth; they give peace or excite with discovery.

327

I have long carried certain thoughts in the pockets of my mind which I wanted to embody in ink.

328

If some report that I have written a helpful message without preaching a ponderous sermon, that would be nice to hear but it would not represent my primary aim. As my slow pen plods over the white sheets—unconscious symbol of my ruminative mind—I am aware of but one driving impulse. That is simply the desire to play with thoughts as they arise and to print such of them as seems pleasant to me.

329

I began to ask whether I had written myself out and whether my writing days were no more. The making of a book was not all: the making of a man was more. Had I reached a maturer state where what mattered was life itself, not the recording of life?

330

I feel happy when writing some lines of higher interest, something touching the philosophical plane, but happier still if the pen falls to rest leaving me transfixed, as it were, by a sacred power which commands both stillness of body and silence of thoughts.

The contribution of silence

331

I prefer the pleasure of having become an obscure writer to the earlier rewards of being a famed one. I am happier under the comforting shelter of anonymity than in the open arena of public turmoil. The promptings of personal ambition fail to move me; serenity is worth more to me than success. But although the publishing period of my life seems to have ended, the writing period never did. My jottings continue. I have become insignificant but not idle.

332

My books were written for and served their generation. Now they are dated and so unwanted. But a time will come when they will find fresh readers. If I have not published for twenty years it is in part because I write now for posterity.

333

What does it matter if the words I write are published now or after my death? Why must I hurry them into print and thus blindly imitate every other contemporary author, whose ego is irritated by the criticism which follows the appearance of his work, or inflated by the praise?

334

During my intermittent disappearance from the Western world, I gained a theoretical knowledge and practical experience of the processes by which the soul could be brought within the field of awareness.

335

If there is any regret to be mentioned, it is that despite my desire to help, clarify, and warn those who follow this way, some things have perforce to remain unsaid. Only those who really understand the nature of human nature, as well as the true character of our times, can understand this silence, as well as the total silence into which I fell for so many years.

336

The fear of professional oblivion does not touch me. The silence of modest retirement is now welcome, but I remember what an expert reader of handwriting said to a chance Indian acquaintance who knew P.B.: "P.B. is over a thousand years ahead of his time. Follow him blindly."

337

I deliberately sought obscurity without and oblivion within.

338

Whether I shall, at a later time, retire from this retirement, is something that I do not at present know. I am not a rigid dogmatist, so this is a possibility.

339

It would be understandable if anyone found the wrong reasons for my long silences, but it would be unjust.

340

One day I felt impelled to ask myself the questions: "What have I to say that has not already been said?" and "To whom am I to address these writings?" When I worked out the full implications of the answers, I stopped writing for publication in print, and continued it only for my private files and pleasure.

341

During more than sixty years, so many scattered observations and reflections were left unfinished or undeveloped, so many insights were gleaned in the quarter century since my retirement but deliberately left unpublished, that the appearance of these pages is self-explanatory.

342

I have to laugh sometimes at this situation: for many years now I have been putting down these ideas of mine with a view to non-publication. Time enough to print and publish them after P.B.'s passing away. The joke, which at decent intervals provokes this laughter, is that it won't be long before I shall return again and then, since I am attracted to such reading material anyway, and will certainly be more than attracted to—in fact will be swept off my feet and become an ardent follower, advocate, and propagandist of—the posthumous P.B. books, holding so much that I will agree heartily with—yes, the joke is that I shall be my own reader for certain even if no one else will care for them. I shall enjoy the printing format and the cloth binding just as much as P.B. himself might.

343

I have retired but my mind has not. It is active. These pages are the fruits of solitude.

344

I have since wandered through many lands, a few of which are not even on earth.

345

I have waited many years to write this book [*The Spiritual Crisis of Man*—Ed.]. I have been silent for several years, not because I was indifferent to the mental difficulties of others nor because I was unable to help them, but because the proper time had not yet come to do so. I waited in inwardly commanded patience, but it is with some relief that I now find I need not wait any longer. Those years since December, 1942, when I wrote the last paragraph of *The Wisdom of the Overself*, may seem to have been totally unproductive. But in reality they were years of hidden gestation. I remained silent in obedience to this command, but not idle.

346

Those who thought I had written myself out may be surprised by the appearance of this book.

347

I spent a long time following my return from the Orient in organizing a large bundle of scattered notes.

348

I worked at this book so intermittently and so slowly that some thought it would never be finished at all. But remembering how I wrote *The Secret Path* in four weeks, *The Quest of the Overself* in four months, and *The Wisdom of the Overself* in fourteen, I smiled. For what lay behind this seeming procrastination was not to be told and had to be left a mystery.

349

I would love to retire into the peaceable life and obscure name of an unrecognized writer. Fame, like other things, must be paid for: the rewards it brings are not exempt from penalties. But they are penalties only to a certain type of person, to the possessor of a certain temperament. Such a type, such a possessor am I.

350

The Writer who sometimes sits behind the writer of these lines smiling at my puny attempts to translate the Untranslatable, once bade me put away for an indefinite period the thought of any future publications. I obeyed and there was a long silence in the outer world—so long that two obituary notices were printed by newspapers! I had enough leisure to discover the faultiness of the earlier work and felt acutely that the world was better off without my lucubrations. But a day came when I felt the presence of the Presence and I received clear guidance to take the pen again.(P)

351

To the outside observer, my declining years have been dead ones, apparently spent in inactivity and futility. But this is only one side of the picture. For they have also been spent in a hidden activity on a higher plane, as much for my own spiritual growth as for the world's peace.(P)

352

I consider myself fortunate to have experienced in my own career and not after death the evanescence of fame and the ephemerality of success. There were other lessons, too, that I was able to gather from this occurrence, so that, all told, the spiritual profit far outbalanced the material loss.

353

I could not remain silent any longer as it would then be inferred that I had taught a doctrine which had no basis to withstand criticism.

354

It must not be taken to mean that I accept and endorse whatever people tell me, merely because I listen quietly and make no criticisms. I have learned to keep my judgements to myself.

355

I looked around for my pen and was about to take it up when I realized that it was better to contribute my silence than my thoughts.

356

These writings were kept from publication deliberately. Now, after a quarter century, and during the last lap of physical existence, the writer releases them. Some of the ideas will serve younger persons and some will offend older ones.

357

The results of my twenty-year-long researches are not to be published during my lifetime, but this does not mean the work is wasted. It is probable that some portion of them will be made public by me but how little or how much or when I do not know.

358

Jonathan Swift wrote, "I resolved to exceed the advice of Horace, a Roman poet, that an author should keep his works nine years in his closet before he ventured to publish them."

359

By deferring publication until some later year, I am able to write without the pressure of a contracted dateline, in freedom and satisfaction, what and when I like. Perhaps later the fates will grant me a secretary and a suitable home so that no time need be given to household chores and office correspondence but only to creative work, research, and meditation—which are basic. It would then be possible to organize book production. Until then let me enjoy these necessities.

360

Rather than suspend truth it is better to suspend publication. Rather than expound versions falsified or perverted to suit certain interests, it is better to keep silent.

361

I am forced to cover my present residence and future movements because there are too many persons who are either half-mad or unmannered enough to force their presence on me whether I invite them or not, whether I want it or not.

362

He is not *necessarily*, as most people seem to believe, an uninterested non-observer of his time and therefore standing quite aloof from it. He may be, but he may also be concerned enough to make a personal contribution to it.

363

Most of my life has been hampered by unsatisfactory surroundings and inferior service. Its work has needed uninterrupted quiet but seldom found it. It has often had to accept uncongenial meals. Yet these needs are important to the inner research after truth and outer confirmation of its findings. I have now reached an age when nothing must be grudged to produce the best results.

364

The restraint in expressing my private experience, which has governed my writing, was imposed on me by the particular conditions of my time.

365

I once wanted to adopt as my profession the same avocation which Voltaire took up and which he described in these inimitable words: "My trade is to say what I think." But time has taught me wisdom and I discovered it is well to reserve your best thought.

366

My biographer will arrive with the cremator and attempt to portray my soul which, unfortunately for him, will already have fled. He will write about incidents in my external life, no doubt, and analyse my works with his dissecting knife, but my soul will be beyond him.

367

Such are the thoughts which come shyly out of the winding convolutions of my brain. I have no intention of pouring out my mind on paper: rather do I desire to set down a few hints only, and to reserve all else.

368

Shall we reveal our spiritual thoughts to a sensual world, or shall we slip a few robes of metaphor upon them, wherewith to cover their fragile bodies?

369

"Silence is golden" is a common proverb with most nations but has been a common practice with *true* mystics only. There was and is a necessity of reserving as well as of publishing many things. The great mystics have often lived in secrecy and solitude because of the defamation that greeted them whenever they ventured out of their hermitages. But I hope in this more spacious and more tolerant century their thoughts can find safer harbourage when expressed to the world than they did in former times. The urgent needs of this sorrow-stricken age call for a bolder dispensing of the sweet waters of true life today. Ridicule will come but it must be risked; I for one, though but the humblest of their pupils, intend to annihilate the future malice of detractors by present scorn.

370

Those books represent a part of the history of my mind and a fraction of the record of my activities, but after all they are only a part. There are things which one does not utter in the street.

371

Has anyone ever known enough about anyone else to write his true biography? I completely doubt it.

372

When, with such dawning perceptions and advancing years, I saw all this, the desire to write left me, the urge to help others ebbed away. It was not that my craftsmanship had failed me but that the will to exercise it had ceased to exist. I realized that it was better to be silent, better to leave others to God's care, than to speak so faultily and to meddle so clumsily. I had to separate myself from the self and work of the younger Brunton. I must refuse to identify myself with them any longer. I could never again go to their defense. There was now an indefinable opposition between us. It was certainly the end of an eventful cycle; it might be the end of all labour for me. I had nothing more to give the contemporary world, but if I studied patiently and attentively why this situation had come about, I might have something to give posterity.

373

When a man's fame has stretched across five continents, he has a better chance to evaluate its real worth than do those who live outside its glare. I personally would be more content and more comfortable without it.

374

Does anyone ever reveal all the truth in an autobiography? Or even is what he does reveal the whole truth about each matter? I could never accept "Yes!" as the answer to these questions.

375

There are some things which are better left a while in sacred silence, and that is where they must be left until the appropriate hour for speech is indicated on destiny's clock.

376

So much deliberately chosen evil prevails in human character that I would like to resign from the human race!

377

If I fell silent it was partly because I found speech deceptive in promise but futile in performance.

378

Zangwill's belief that biographies are never true, and his consequent refusal to permit one to be written about himself, is a belief which I share. Zangwill entered into the public life and affairs of his time, which I hardly ever have done, so his experience and observation, his knowledge on this point, are far wider than mine.

379

When a man loses his literary ambitions and deliberately drops out of public notice, it may be because he has heard another, perhaps higher, call.

380

If he is to be reproached for not having given out enough to readers, he must plead a necessary prudence.

381

I am happier when I attract no attention at all. I enjoy being quite anonymous. That was one, but only one, of the reasons why I published nothing for the twelve years between *The Wisdom of the Overself* and *The Spiritual Crisis of Man* and nothing during the more than a quarter century since then.

382

People who ask pertinent or impertinent questions shall receive Ramana Maharshi's answer: Silence. Or I may reply, "My biography is irrelevant."

The value of solitude

383

In my early efforts to advance, I withdrew frequently from the world and lived for several months at a time in cave or cottage. The time was well spent in meditation and study. Such retirement was not selfish. It was absolutely indispensable to further advancement, which in its turn was indispensable if my ideal of serving humanity was to be better realized.

384

Solitude is a necessary condition at this time of my life, in this phase of my career. Nobody must claim my time or person: it belongs to me now, my inner life and written work. Nobody is thrown out—everyone is still there within my goodwill—but too much of high importance needs to be done and time is too short.

385

The presence of another person becomes an invasion of one's own being and creates a nervous situation between us. This is intensified when, usually at the very beginning of the encounter but sometimes during the course of it, he betrays himself as a neurotic by showing compulsive habits. I then have to deal not only with the matter he has come for but also with the other's troubled self-consciousness—a generator of negative feelings and thoughts which impinge themselves on my peace and disturb it. Is it any wonder that I find solitude more enjoyable than its contrary state?

386

There are certain disadvantages in being a literary celebrity. The first is the multitude of letters readers feel swayed to write the author, nearly all demanding an answer. The second is the readership's curiosity about the author.

387

The telephone is an instrument which renders useful service in bringing together, with miraculous swiftness, one man with another whom he needs. But if it also brings him together with an unwanted person, a demanding person, an obnoxious person, or a pestering person, then it becomes a scourge at the worst, a harassment at the least. Robert Louis Stevenson detested the telephone; I merely dislike it. "The introduction of the telephone into our bed and board partakes of the nature of intrusion," he wrote in a letter. "I dare never approach this interesting instrument myself." His words, written at least half a century ago, may sound too extreme, old-fashioned, and out of touch with present-day living. But allowing for this, and recognizing the useful service of this device, there remains an echo in my heart of what Robert Louis Stevenson felt. Much of my time is devoted to long stretches of intensive research on a high impersonal mental level, or to absorbed writing, or to deeply relaxed meditation. When I formerly permitted the noise of a telephone bell to burst in abruptly, unexpectedly, or violently upon the silence without or the stillness within, the effect was to give a harsh shock to my nervous system. Nor was this all. It dragged me out of my delicately poised concentration, wasting the time and effort needed after every interruption to work my way back again and to re-adjust myself again. Let all this happen over and over again throughout the day and a state will be reached where the mere sound of the telephone bell will be like the sound of doom.

388

When my writings became known, a large financial burden was added to me. The expenses of secretarial correspondence and the loss caused by time given to numerous interviews drained away more of my income than I could afford.

389

I dislike being pressed into too intimate and too immediate a friendship, more especially where personal revelations are made and then demanded in return.

390

To secure privacy and protect solitude—two essentials for the research, writing, and meditation which fills this period of my public retirement—I have only a postal address.

391

A withdrawn temperament keeps me from easily made and easily dropped friendships.

392

My inability to answer letters is a serious defect. Ramana Maharshi had it, too. But my justification was not the same as his. Attention to a world-wide correspondence would leave no time for other work.

393

My correspondence is so often conducted with long intervals of two or three years between my letters that it is an off-and-on affair, never a regular one. This is one reason why it is often fated to wither away.

394

The researcher and writer concerned with such topics as I deal with must reject the social obligations of convention. His time is too valuable to be wasted and his personal contacts must be carefully limited if he is to do his work properly. Therefore, he guards both freedom and independence despite the disapproval of those who would rob him of one or the other.

395

The solitary hermit's life, where no telephone bell rings, no visitors call, no engagements need be made, and no problems come up to disturb, is for now my personal ideal.

396

If my communications are rare and their length is short, please understand that they must be so out of necessity.

397

My lifelong reluctance to be put in a false position cannot be abandoned at this point of time. I do not wish P.B.'s name or person to be put forward whenever this can be avoided. I myself cannot avoid having it put on the books. Please help me to protect my privacy.

398

He really is content at heart to live alone. But it is imprudent and unwise for a man so old to do so as completely as he does and as far distant from friends as he is. It seems perhaps somewhat cold-blooded or unkind to maintain this situation. A change may soon be due but will not be easy for him to make.

399

When people become too intrusive and make unreasonable demands on one's time, work, and privacy because they have read one's book, they must be firmly brushed off, however politely or gracefully the firmness is covered up.

400

I need leisure in my daily life, space outside my windows, quiet from my neighbours, and privacy—obscurity even—as defense against invading crackpots. Yet how little I have these conditions.

401

Many days pass when I have not spoken to a single human being. This does not depress me in the slightest way. I have become well-accustomed to seclusion and find it quite acceptable. The feeling of boredom and loneliness are alien to me.

402

He will not care for the formal and public character of a reception, dinner, or party in his honour, but will much prefer a simple and private meeting with one or two persons at a time.

403

Because of this detachment, not a few will judge him to be a cold man. They will not be entirely wrong, nor will they be right.

404

I must avoid letting readers maneuver me into personal relationships. This is what they want; it would serve their interests but would be against my own. I need freedom to serve many thousands who would be robbed of this service if I gave the same time to a single person. So I ask them not to write asking for this.

405

The high priest's Buddha saw much Siamese history in the making in his time, heard many important conversations and confessions in that far land. Now he hears little talk, for I am mostly alone; but he does sit in on all my meditations.

406

Theoretically I would like to reply to every letter received promptly and fully, but actually I find this impossible. Yet I acknowledge that all those who write are not members of the lunatic fringe, that many are sincere seekers. Although too often with inadequate equipment for the search, they are searching and need encouragement—for the world around them has if anything an adverse effect. The mere fact that I have placed my ideas and experiences before the public through the medium of a book makes me a public servant, and if the kind of book I wrote inevitably produces the urge to write a letter to the author, I have no right to complain and no right to ignore those letters.

407

Prudence. It is a matter of forethought not to get mixed up in unwanted obligations just as it is a matter of care not to get mixed up in unwanted friendships or acquaintanceships. In both cases, because of my public standing, people will try to push personal responsibilities off their own shoulders and on to mine.

408

Owing to the shortness of time and the pressure of inescapable urgent or important activities, I am compelled to write the replies to letters in telegraphese style, as if I were merely putting down the headings, the subjects, the principal points of a rough draft in order for a secretary to compose a letter.

409

It is unfortunate that my chosen profession of authorship mocked my inherent dislike for personal publicity.

410

The exertion needed to write personal letters irks me, whereas the exertion needed to write philosophical notes inspires me. Why wonder that I neglect the one and cultivate the other?

411

The burden becomes so heavy that sometimes I wish myself back in the eighteenth century, when people sent few letters in a year because paper was costly, postage expensive, and facilities for transmission slender.

412

How pleasant it would be, after paying fame's penalties, to creep back into the grey anonymous obscurity of earlier years!

413

If I meet a man who comes hoping that I will impart something to him, I counter his hope with a similar one on my own side.

414

I look around and see only a rare few of my compeers drawing their life's breath from the diviner heights.

415

It comes to this: because of the tremendous returns he is drawing from his solitude spiritually, mentally, and emotionally, he must be content to be an exile from his neighbours and expatriated even whilst living among them.

416

What is he to do with these persons who penetrate his privacy by means of unsolicited and uninvited letters? If he refuses to answer them, the writers will be hurt and he himself may be accused of rudeness. If he answers them, he will be disloyal to his own inner guidance to maintain the flow of outer creativity and inner deepening.

417

I am wary of those who make overtures for better acquaintance. There is not much time left, and life's demands are heavy. I may not waste these few years which could be so fruitful if I stand firm—and alone.

418

I make no promises and enter no commitments. This is better for both parties in the end where one of them—namely myself—is such a fierce lover of independence.

419

I want nothing to do with those who jar my nerves, who create physical worldly or personal problems or seek to involve me in their own, or who would involve me in gossip or any other form of wasting time which I desperately need for my work or personal activities. I don't want to get immersed in other people's auras. Theirs are different from mine; they are comfortable in them. I ask only that I be allowed to have the comfort of my own which has taken so many lives on earth to fashion. The others have other attributes which jar on me, which are abrasive to my temperament and habits. All this is not only because my personal history is different from theirs, but primarily because the practice of meditation and the inner-outer work of refining consciousness and tastes, of acquiring culture and improving character has made me feel almost as if I belong to a species apart—so few are those who care for the same things, whose manner, speech, courtesy, and inner calm betray their real caste. So I am compelled to seek solitude, to reject intrusion on my privacy, to ask to be left alone to enjoy a little space around me when travelling, dining out, or resting in a park. The spiritual doctrine of unity with all mankind does not appeal to me; let those seek its realization who find it to their taste. The ethical doctrine of goodwill to all mankind *does* appeal to me and I try to practise it. But this can be done without having other auras foisted on me. I must not only follow Shakespeare's dictum "Be true to thyself" but must go farther and be myself. Those religions and teachings which tell us to destroy the ego do not appeal to me. But if I am asked to destroy the tyranny of the ego, to make it subservient to the Overself, it is certainly my duty to try and do so. Yet I consider that this is not the same as destroying my individuality.

420

I must escape these loud, noisy, and talkative neighbours. This is negative, but it is an essential need for a writer, a meditator, and a lover of good literature. If I could sit down facing a window with a long view where I could admire the sunset in peace and solitude, I should call a halt and not demand much more. The immense volume of undone work presses upon me but needs a settled and suitable home. Will karma permit me to have such a home at last with no more wandering from place to place?—a home where there is a vista across a lake and a picture window overlooks the scene from a hillside or from outside a city? I prefer the Mediterranean warmth and dryness and perhaps I shall return there, but meanwhile I must accept the Swiss snows and Alpine peaks to greet me with the cold winds that blow so often in such areas. There is, of course, good spiritual instruction in my situation, for the duality of life, the mixture of good and evil, is reminding me of its existence through everything—whether in nature or in human experience. It is yin and yang again.

6

THE PROFANE AND THE
PROFOUND

A sense of proportion

We cannot communicate the incommunicable. The absolute reality is outside our finite thoughts; all philosophic writing must fall short of bestowing truth upon its readers. At best it can prepare the way for an attainment which must always be individual. Therefore, we who record the activities of our brains in these directions should not take ourselves too seriously. The printed paper will remain but paper, and readers will still have to take up the quest for themselves though we write a thousand pages. So I make this apology for my occasional light treatment of heavy matters. I am unable to share the illusion of many writers, that a few paragraphs may suffice to convert someone's materialistic darkness into spiritual light. I am well aware, however, that the pen can indeed cast plenty of *mental* light upon the problem of truth; but since I regard this as a buyer of gold regards brass, please pardon me if now and then I remember the futility of all our writing, when judged from the highest standpoint, and if, therefore, I break into irreverent chuckles in the midst of a grave paragraph or link up the profane with the profound in incongruous manner.

2

Why do I let my pen slip sometimes into frivolous conduct, though dealing with the most serious of subjects? My reply is to ask another question: Why should fools be the only persons who can be flippant? Why should not the serious and thoughtful likewise toss words without apparent intent? Yet, in the latter case, you will likely find a tasty kernel of wisdom inside the husky shell of frivolity. Why should a spiritual truth conduce to the incapacity to perceive a joke?

3

The secret of it is that the sense of humour is really the sense of proportion. Those who possess an understanding of the proportionate values of life often throw that understanding into the cast of humour, which becomes *one* of its natural expressions. So the eagle who has dived deep into the profound waters of Reality, when he returns to the surface again and resumes his breathing, can take a peep at the life around him and tell his friends: "Do not take the vicissitudes of life so seriously, O! Earnest Ones."

4

It only remains for me to remember that the inspired portion of this book has been written by my subconscious self, according to the psychologists. I have, therefore, to tender my best thanks to that kindly though vague entity for its cordial existence. Readers who may happen to take pleasure in this volume should address their compliments to it, and not to myself.

5

I take comfort in the continental proverb, "A hundred years hence we shall all be bald!"

6

Not every man who has been in Hell carries a face like that of the exiled Florentine. I like Dante and take pleasure in his work, but after all, I need not follow him into melancholy.

7

I felt the presence of a spirit and, acting under an inner impulsion, took up my pencil and rapidly wrote down the message which immediately flowed into my mind . . . Almost exhausted by the effort, I put down my pen and looked at the written words. "XXX," I read.

8

Why should the witless be the only possessors of Wit; why should they make more enjoyable company than the wise? Must a man forget how to laugh because he has remembered how to live and love aright?

9

The only proper way to treat this idiotic age, when one puts pen to paper, is with irony.

10

Let us seek the profoundest wisdom by all means but let us also carry it lightly, aye even with a smile!

11

Why should we not pour the scalding water of satire upon the feeble shibboleths which pass muster under the name of modern existence?

12

If it were not for the fact that I have suffered from the disease of Writer's Fingers since I was a boy, it is certain that I would never have troubled to obtrude my private moods upon the public gaze. What? You have never heard of this disease? I beg your pardon! Permit me to explain.

13

Writer's Fingers is a non-infectious complaint which attacks the hands of certain types of people, usually in their teens. The disease grows in virulence as adulthood is reached and passed, and the victim is rarely able to shake it off. Its most common symptom is an inordinate—sometimes feverish—desire to clutch the smooth round barrel of a fountain pen, or to pad swiftly on the keys of a typewriter.

14

I have added the tag that since everything is unreal I might as well laugh at it, because it does not matter. I could just as easily cry over it—only crying hurts, and laughter makes me happier.

15

There is nothing wrong with cutting satire if it cuts some of the false-hoods out of our minds. Only the weaklings and truth-fearers can object to it. Skin-puncturing is often as useful as soft-soap.

16

Since I did not seem to make myself understood, I bought a new pen and procured different paper. Now, I thought, surely they will grasp my meaning.

17

Those who walk from Edgar Wallace straight into these pages, who have never learned from him that other and more spiritual sleuths exist who devote their days not to tracking down crime but to searching for God, will find my writing a mere riddle. But if they will have the patience to read farther, they will fall into a half-sleep; and if they will then do me the kindness of bravely continuing, there is no doubt but that a complete coma will supervene. When, however, they emerge from this mysterious state later, they can take it as a warning that the bright and breezy adventures of their favourite crook are better suited to such delicate constitutions as theirs must obviously be.

18

Every reformer drives the camel of compulsion before him—which may explain why so many of us get the hump when we see him. But all I ask is that we sit down and try to see straight, to think a thing out impersonally, forgetting for a while the reformer and the evil he wants to reform and the way he would make you do it.

19

I have somewhere quoted the sage saying (with which I fully agree) that "to be great is to be misunderstood." But sometimes I am amazed at my own achievement in being misunderstood without achieving greatness!

20

It is not because I think life to be so meaningless that I write so lightly at times, but because I think it to be so purposeful.

21

Scathing satire is the only way in which I can applaud the achievements of modern man.

22

It is better to meet an author of spiritual writings on paper than to meet him in person. For in the first case you will always meet him at his best, whereas in the second case you might meet him at his worst. In the first, mind meets mind unhindered but, in the second, his body, his speech, or his mannerisms may offend you and thus prevent such an inward meeting. Thus there was a woman who for some years kept one of my books on a shelf of honour where it might be easily accessible and often read. But one fateful day we accidentally met each other on board a ship for the first time. A single glance was enough for her to make up her mind that she disliked my face, as it was enough to convince her henceforth that she disliked my philosophy! I hope that the next author she meets will be better looking so that he may fare better than I did. For I fear I have little to offer such seekers in the way of hair on the head and less in the way of tallness of the body. As for my features, Venus was too busy elsewhere to give any attention to them when they were formed! Thus a woman may reshape her world view if she is attracted by the shape of an exponent's ear or impressed by the grandeur of its advocate's physical height. I tremble for the guru whom Nature has adorned with a pair of bandy legs. No matter how impeccable his teaching may be, many will come but, being more repelled by his legs than attracted by his logic, few will remain!

An unorthodox yogi

23

So must I move through the world, "a paradox to those who know you and a puzzle to those who do not," as a certain psychologist once remarked.

24

I like a quiet, lamp-lit room. I prefer a vista of red-tiled roofs which are sloping on whitewashed cottage walls to a vista of steel-framed blocks of flats. I retreat from gas-heaters, but am charmed by wood fires. I love to tread grass-grown paths, but quickly tire on properly paved streets. I am old-fashioned.

25

When the hour of passing comes, what better mode for me—as a writer—than to be found dead at my work, pen still in hand, or even better—as a mystic—to be found seated under a wide-branched tree in a little wood, rapt in a meditation so deep that I shall never again return from it to this dark world!

26

I preferred the perils of a casual existence and let the thought of security disappear into remote recesses of my mind. The world wants to feel safe and aims at a sizeable bank account, not to speak of a place in society. And the world is right. But I was born with a truculent nature and obstinately burned my incense in the haunts of Bohemia when all reason and prudence held up warning fingers.

27

I could easily console myself for this shortness of height by remembering that everyone has some physical shortcoming of one kind or another. I believe if the matter is sufficiently investigated this will be found universally true. But such consolation is not really effective. Better to apply philosophy.

28

I am a quiet inoffensive man desiring only to live and let live. Nobody is ever interfered with by me—no neighbour can complain about my habits or my noise, except that I keep to myself. And yet when sometimes I agree to the request of a reader and let him come to see me—"for a single meeting," I always emphasize—he or she is surprised to find that expectation is not fulfilled. From the tone of my writing, a strong personality and a big tall body should appear at the door. Instead there is a little figure, a bald head, a low soft voice . . .

29

I was not only a popularizer, but also an epitomizer.

30

I can work in no other way than the one which befits my temperament. I must spread the truth in an unorganized way and let it take root in the individual hearer of it.

31

I enjoy being studious, without being scholarly in any academic sense.

32

At different times and places, confronted by different persons and authorities, I have called myself scholar, researcher, traveller, writer, and even entered one official document as "without profession," for I dislike being labelled, "placed," or restricted.

33

Must a well-ordered meal, dining with linen, glass, and silver, not be for me? Servantless and cookless must I remain because I am a would-be mystic?

34

The advantage to a hermetic philosopher of being short is the advantage of being inconspicuous in a crowd or a street, especially if he dresses modestly. Deemed insignificant, being ignored, the better he can pursue his strange ways. Blessed are the anonymous and obscure, for they shall be least interfered with.

35

It is for some only a matter of personal refinements but the psychically sensitive person does not like to be touched and, therefore, does not like to shake hands. It is for him a matter of preserving psychic purity. For in every handshake there is a mingling of the magnetic aura emanating from and surrounding the hands and body.

36

It is not all nonsense to say, scientifically, that the eyes have special power, in some persons good but in others evil. It is not mere superstition to shrink from the habit of shaking hands with others. It is more than medical knowledge which kept Brahmins for thousands of years from eating food handled and cooked by non-Brahmins.

37

Because of physical sensitivity to auras, I dislike shaking hands and try my utmost to avoid it, which is too often not possible. A woman may wear gloves, sometimes, but a man must show himself holding many papers and things in both arms if he is to escape the conventional social duty.

38

If you wish to speak distinctly you must speak slowly. This clear slow articulation is the only way whereby those with weak voiceboxes can make themselves properly heard without having to repeat their words.

39

There is no merit in me for whatever I have done of good. I simply obey the tendencies which I found already present within myself, but there is much demerit in me and I am very conscious of it.

40

It is easy to be a monk who keeps nothing beyond what he needs and who needs nothing beyond a robe, a girdle, a bowl, sandals, and food. It is a complex and harder problem to be what I am—a mixture of several types, including a kind of monk, amalgamated into one.

41

Cynicism corrupts man. I am not a cynic. I am an optimist who prefers to face the facts.

42

I am neither a preacher nor an educator, yet something of the activity of both has inevitably filtered into my own.

People and places

43

It is not usually the nonentities of this world who accomplish things that will benefit, change, lead, lift, or better the world.

44

The years confirmed my interest and faith in two of the magnetic personalities among others—Krishnamurti and Steiner. I met both of them many years ago and recognize that Krishnamurti lived in truth and love, Steiner in knowledge and perception. Each was unique and admirable. Steiner, however, had his limitations—chiefly because of his lack of personal experience and knowledge of the vital Eastern traditions.

45

A score of years ago in Europe, during a private talk with Ouspensky, he confessed that his own effort to open up the mystery of man's inner being had ended in failure. He had been Gurdjieff's star pupil, until he broke away. A.R. Orage, who established the school in America for Gurdjieff, died of a broken heart, one of his biographers told me, because of disillusionment. Both these men fully deserve our admiration, the first for his qualities of head, the second for his qualities of heart, and both for their literary gifts. Yet neither had established himself in the Soul-consciousness towards which they proposed to lead their students (the first in his school and the second in his lectures).

46

I take pleasure in the remembrance that I encouraged Vera Stanley Alder to start a writing career and that I recommended the publication of individual books by several other authors, now well known.

47

There was a certain house in Grosvenor Square, London, which was a meeting place for many of the most distinguished men and women of the time. If you were fortunate enough to receive an invitation, you were sure to meet the latest "lion." You would most likely be introduced to famous personalities whose achievements entitled them to your respect, if not to eulogy. And probably you would also meet one or two persons who counted for nothing in the list of the world's great ones. If so, it was well not to ignore them. For tomorrow you might find their names inscribed in the freshest of inks upon that list. For the titled lady whose salon it was took keen pleasure in the discovery of unknown talent or unrecognized genius.

48

On Alan Watts' eating habits—ham (pork). How can such gross food and sexual intercourse give purity necessary to see truth so delicately as it is? But determination may give Truth, yet only flamed, hence distorted, blocked in parts. Make pure food a qualification for the quest. It is not merely a humanitarian act to abstain from eating meat.

49

Mr. Howard Begbie, the gentleman who dusted the mirrors of Downing Street so anonymously yet so effectively, once wrote down a biting phrase. "Our curse is not original sin," he declared in *The Glass of Fashion*, "but aboriginal stupidity!"

50

The English mentality abhors the abstract, prefers the concrete. It is averse to metaphysical principles. However, as a result of its struggle against Nazism and its groping amid crisis, it is now beginning to find a factual content in such principles.

51

A man may look at his own history as if it were a stage-play and find it a comedy, but another may find it a tragedy.

52

The voice of reason is stifled by subtle hints about adeptship and sly innuendoes about apostleship.

53

They prefer to follow Pope's idiotic advice: "Be not the first by whom the new is tried. Nor yet the last to lay the old aside."

54

The American people want its thinkers to form clear conclusions.

55

I find pathetic and poor comfort in the knowledge that Saint John of the Cross was as little a man physically as I am.

56

It was said of Allan Bennett: "His mind was pure, piercing, and profound beyond any other in my experience. His fame as a magician was immense." He carried a glass rod, potent with magical power. Bennett was tall, stooping, with raven black wild hair, a high broad forehead, and a pallor on his face. An expert in electricity and mathematics, Bennett was "one of the most valuable lives of our generation."

57

An hour before he died René Guénon exclaimed: "The soul is quitting the body!" And when the final moment came, he murmured: "Allah, Allah."

58

Without any training but quite naturally a man I knew had the psychic power of knowing at once if a person told him an untruth. Yet in a certain racial matter he was prejudiced and fanatical, that is, accepted an untruth.

59

Yeats-Brown told me that he wrote the entire first script of *Bengal Lancer* in a month and a half, so excited was he with its theme—his life in India. Of course he was dissatisfied with the finished result and spent several weeks revising and rewriting it.

60

Solzhenitsyn senses a calling to share his insights with the world but feels he may not be able to cope . . . there may be too little time.

61

The man who finds in his declining years that he seems to be no closer to the illuminative experience than he was a couple of decades earlier, that the Real apparently refuses to obey his call despite his practices and disciplines, may also find himself suffering emotionally from sadness, frustration, pessimism, or irritation. Such moods explain why, for instance, a man like Aldous Huxley turns first to a drug like mescaline and later to a cult like Subud.

62

G.K. Chesterton: A giant in body, a child at heart. The ample and spacious folds of his flesh enclose a soul untouched and untainted by the sordid world. A double chin and a double talent—deadly seriousness with witty absurdity. I found him at his home in Beaconsfield one Sunday, pottering around his garden. He was the humblest of men as we talked: was this modest figure the great G.K.C., dreaded figure of his literary opponents, more dreaded foe of pretentious people? He spoke with a pronounced Oxford accent.

63

Marcus Porcius Cato: "I had rather men should ask why no statue has been erected in my honour, than why one has."

64

I am certainly not one of those who despise Americans for their materialistic money-making ways, their pursuit of material possessions. America enjoys the highest standard of living in the whole world. What is wrong with that? And money, as the symbol of power, is really pursued everywhere.

65

The Beatles have carried to the whole world and brought in particular to the younger generation the important news that there is such a thing as meditation. That their first experiment in trying to learn it under a guru ended in disappointment does not obliterate the service they rendered. For they made it clear that it was not meditation itself which disappointed them, but the human person, the teacher, to whom they had submitted.

66

One may admire Dr. Johnson as a maker of dictionaries but one cannot admire him as a would-be metaphysician. For he composed definitions by the use of his head whereas he argued against idealism by the use of his foot.

67

The French were remorseless idol-breakers in an age of unbelief and overthrow.

68

When royal persons become stiff robots or smiling wax figures with no special quality of real superiority or worthwhile kind to distinguish them from ordinary people, they become unneeded and dispensable.

69

"I have never myself had what are usually called mystical experiences," confessed the Very Rev. William Ralph Inge, but this did not prevent him from writing much about them.

70

We are apt to assume a man's greatness from his talent. We confuse the tool with the workman. But a witty pen may contain no wisdom, a bewigged judge may be quite at a loss outside the law court, and a politician proposing to govern an empire may be utterly unable to govern his life!

71

J.V. Kapila Sastri said, "Let me look into your eyes." He took my head between both hands and gazed for a long time into my eyes. I felt that he was reading something there which no ordinary psychologist could ever read, that he was ascertaining the depth of my soul and not the characteristics of my personality, that he was measuring my potentiality for final liberating enlightenment.

72

André Malraux drank rather heavily—but it was only tea! Yet it was fitting that he did so for had he not penetrated to the culture of Asia, and especially of China?

73

We see this nostalgia in the face of Marcus Aurelius, this ruler of an empire who felt it was not his true home, who practised Christian virtues while persecuting confessed Christians, who warred by day through most of his life but meditated at night on the lofty notions of Stoic philosophy. His rebellious subjects did not let him live in outward peace so, wistfully, he ever aspired to it inwardly.

74

The United States of America is truly a country today where too many babble of their rights and demands, too few of their duties and responsibilities.

75

Howard Hughes, brilliant designer and financial success, was one of the most secretive men known. He went mad through excess, through hiding from other people, keeping all affairs veiled, remaining a personal mystery.

76

Your letter of May was read with interest and although I don't really have the time to develop correspondences, I will make an exception in your case by answering your questions.

Your friend last year found his spiritual affinity in the teachings called Transcendental Meditation, which have been put out by Maharishi Mahesh Yogi. He joined the society with great enthusiasm and devotes his studies to their teachings—in fact, intends to become one of their teachers when he is sufficiently qualified. He came and informed me about this. I told him I was delighted at the news, since he had tried meditation for many years and never succeeded in getting any result from his efforts.

Now that he is getting some kind of result from the new methods which he is practising, he blames his former method (Who Am I?) for his failure. He also asserted that it was a wrong method and criticized Ramana Maharshi for teaching it, but I assume that Maharshi did so because, as he himself describes, it was the way he used to come into his own illumination, so it was not wrong for him. Moreover, some years after I met Maharshi I discovered in an old Sanskrit text the same Who Am I method. Whether Maharshi knew of this text or not, I do not know. Since it existed in this text, it was therefore one that had the authority of tradition. It is hardly likely that it would have been given out in those days among the students of Advaita if it had been useless. The real mistake your friend made was to cling for so many years to something that was not helpful to him when so many other ways are easily available. This is a well-known fact.

I am happy that he is now happy himself, since there are many paths to go, as Krishna pointed out, and many ways of reaching the goal of yoga. I have always taken an interest in all the different ways and always said and written that a seeker should try whatever attracts him until he finds the one with which he feels an affinity and from which he gets help. It is true that I gave the Who Am I method in the first book about meditation, which was *The Secret Path*, but I did that to honour Ramana Maharshi. My own personal path which I used before I ever went to India was quite different and one which I had not learned from anyone else. This student ignored these statements of mine that most of the different yogic paths are valid for different persons, and if he had told me that Who Am I did not suit him, I would have immediately suggested that he look for something that did suit him. I do not know where he got the idea that I was wedded to the Who Am I teaching alone. I don't know of anyone else who thought so. He visited Anthony Damiani at Wisdom's Goldenrod a year or two ago and he must have seen that various teachings are being studied there.

Your inability to accept your friend's persuasions to join Maharishi Mahesh Yogi's society is nothing you need worry about, but follow your own intuitive feelings in the matter. It is true, as your friend told you, that I approved of his having joined them, but it is not true to say that I advised him to join. It was only after two or three months of his membership that he even came and told me for the first time about his interest in the Transcendental Meditation teachings. You ask whether I advise you to do what he has done and join them. My answer is that you should feel perfectly free to do whatever your reason, your personal feelings, and your own knowledge, so far as you have studied philosophy, altogether tell you to do.

Finally, your friend knows that very many years ago, I spent a day and a half watching the work of Maharishi Mahesh Yogi, at Mahesh Yogi's request, that he asked me to write a book about him and I refused, and that since that time Mahesh Yogi tells people that I became his disciple, which, of course, is not true. But the work of introducing mantram yoga to the world is one he's successfully doing and I acknowledge that. He is to be admired for this. On the other hand, I do not wish to have any personal connection with him.

The feeling of unsettlement, oppression, and depression which this episode with your friend has caused you, is quite unnecessary. He is entitled to go the way which is helping him but you must find your own way which helps you and you need not imagine that what is suited for him must necessarily be suited for you. That you must ask yourself. Be true to yourself. I am not a personal guru and have no personal pupils and I can look at all these happenings impartially. Anyway, don't worry since both of you are seekers.

> With Peace,
> Paul Brunton

77
As genial Charlie Chaplin remarked to me once, "It is good to know that there are a few people like yourself in the same sub-stratosphere, as it were, with oneself."

78
Plutarch could write only of public men, warriors, and politicians in his "parallel lives" because, he said, he could not conceive how any "gentleman nobly born" could even wish to be an artist, whilst as for being a philosopher he praised Lycurgus and sneered at Plato for "while the first stabilized and left behind him a constitution, the other left behind him only words and books."

79
He recalled the questioning Greek sage, though his fate was better than that of Socrates for his own wife was kindly and his end was natural. He was unknown to fame but I, knowing him well, knew his value.

80

Even great men are not all great. How saddening to watch one fall into some negative feelings, born of the ego's limitations, into quite unnecessary embitterment, and pay for the fall with impaired health or personal trouble!

81

Many poor sick souls have crossed my orbit who became neurotics and psychopaths only because the spiritual tendencies with which they were born could not adjust themselves to a materialistic environment or a misunderstanding society. The consequence has been business failure, nervous breakdown, shattered lives, chronic melancholia, madness, or suicide. Neither they nor those amongst whom fate had thrown them could help being what they were. None was to be blamed.

82

When I read Heisenberg's reflections in a small book, I noticed that he used the word "poetry" almost interchangeably with "mysticism" (obviously to protect himself among fellow scientists against the accusation of having become woolly-minded). It prompted the remembrance of two things: first, Carl Jung's statement (in a conversation we had at his home in Küsnact) that he kept his mystical belief and experience secret in order to preserve his scientific reputation; second, Matthew Arnold's prediction more than a hundred years ago that religion would be displaced by poetry, and William Butler Yeats' statement in a conversation at his London club that the poet and the artist were taking over the work of the priests.

83

When the Mongol hordes of China threatened a second attempt at invading and conquering Japan, the priests of all the religious sects prayed feverishly to avert the calamity; but the regent Tokimune, who was a practising Zen adherent, remained calm, firm, and imperturbable, merely waiting on events. The invasion came but failed, defeated by a providential typhoon.

84

The key factor in Joseph P. Kennedy's success was his superb *sense of timing*. He harnessed his fortunes to the momentum of events. He jumped clear of the crashing stock market. Experience, shrewdness, ruthless detachment enabled him to detect warning tremors and shift his ground before it was too late.

85

The Americans, with their perfectly machine-tooled minds, tend to a gregarious conformity.

86

The Buddhist sees only suffering in life whereas the Christian Scientist denies it.

87

I know, from glimpses gained of my contemporaries, that I share this shortness of arm and stature with other authors—notably with the late H.G. Wells, an immeasurably more talented and better endowed writer.

88

Chaplin, when working out an idea, would become utterly absorbed, gazing into space; then, writing it down, he would remain unaware or indifferent to surroundings.

89

The picture of Solzhenitsyn as inaccessible is widespread. He occasionally explodes out of irritation with persistent interference with his work. The pressures of writing restrict his schedule of time drastically. After a few minutes of conversation he excuses himself and hurries away.

90

History has never provided such a wide publicity for meditation as the Beatles' acceptance has. The Beatles, in themselves a sign of the world's governance by youth, declare that they have finally found a meaning and purpose in life, through meditation.

91

The chill manner of a Mejnour encases him like a suit of armour and makes frailer mortals wonder whether it would be possible to find some vulnerable link.

92

If some persons found him withdrawn into himself, so difficult to know, so reticent in speech, others found him friendly, amiable, and considerate.

93

One may not agree with all of his views and believe some of them mistaken, but this need not diminish the regard, the admiration, one has for his character and his ideals.

94

Our respect for such a man is a personal one. It does not mean that we have also to show the same respect toward his world-view and his conduct of life if the gap between our ideas and behaviour has gradually widened.

95

The sage's talks on education made a deep impression. He felt turned inside out. He came back with an attitude to life that was entirely strange to him and he felt rather foolish about it. He has no plans nor aims and no inclination to make them. He does not know what life will bring him and in a way he does not care. But when his friend told him that with this attitude the Overself has a much better chance to come through and lead him on his way and that it was really a positive one, he understood at once and was very glad with this new insight.

96

Dr. Samuel Johnson loathed vegetables although, to his credit, he loved tea. But may it not have been the washed-out, flavourless, boiled corpses of cabbage and the like which repelled him? The Chinese and Indian cooks make vegetables quite attractive.

97

I admire the mind exemplified in the writings of Plato, in the questions of Socrates, in the thought of Spinoza, and in the plays of Sophocles.

98

As one who has travelled around the world and as one who has endeavoured to apply the philosophical attitude towards life, he tries to keep his thinking about political international questions not narrow and partisan but global and impartial.

99

In these short studies of men without ordinary minds, in these impressions of their personalities and records of their sayings, I have tried to see the whole picture, not merely a biased part.

Happenings on the way

100

What a multiplicity of images the past brings to mind if the search after truth has been its chief preoccupation and subsequent realization! Images which are dark, bewildered, despairing, arise alongside of others which are radiant, teeming with luminous hopes, ethereal with unearthly experiences.

101

The Latin poet Horace talks quaintly of travel as changing our sky. But the experienced wanderer whom Destiny has taken to distant lands knows well enough that he is beholding the same sky, whether it canopies waving palm trees or sturdy oaks. Yet I propose here to show how a man may really change his sky, though it be by a somewhat new sort of travel. Hitherto he has been going outwards to this or that place; I propose that he shall now travel inwards and find that centre whence all places radiate.

Then indeed will he see strange sights, for the old sun and moon will fall from their places, and he will behold a new heaven.

102

The years filled with so many widely different experiences could easily have made one cynical. But they have not. But neither have they left one naïve and unsophisticated. One finds oneself sufficiently blasé to be unsurprised at any human villainy, unshocked at any moral deflection. The philosopher within oneself is patient to an extreme point. He recognizes that the mysterious alchemy of life, working with the reincarnations, will take the most abandoned wretches and turn them into admirable creatures, although a few monsters of iniquity may be self-hurled into the outermost region of hell, and be annihilated.

103

New Zealand probably waited longer for the appearance or evolution of human beings than any other currently inhabited area of this earth. I thought it might therefore have a purer aura, less polluted by human evil. But alas! I found that it slaughters more animals than any other inhabited country, leaving the atmosphere no less polluted than elsewhere. Thus a golden chance to establish a new and better way of life was passed by.

104

For years I have wandered in self-sought anonymity save for an occasional brief splurge of press interviews in benighted countries where I sought to awaken people to what philosophy could mean to them.

105

I am a citizen of this land by personal choice but a citizen of the world by wide experience and inveterate travel.

106

As a modest public figure, I have met with so many hundreds of people in the course of time that I was prevented from entering into too personal a view of friendship. Destiny forces me to move and travel constantly, so that the opportunity to take roots is not permitted and the dreamlike character of these contacts begins to intrude itself. I could not help gaining some of the detachment which an exiled and wandering life can give to a person. But this said, I still am human enough to have some feeling about these matters even though I do not allow any feeling to sweep me away and indeed cannot if I am to be true to the philosophic path.

107

For too long I have been accustomed to the fluid inconstant life of a gypsy, for too many years I have wandered from city to city, village to village, continent to continent, gaining my experience of human existence in a variety of places—some quite jungle-like and primitive, others completely metropolitan and sophisticated. Glamour lies no longer in the unknown unvisited district but in settlement for the ageing body, in taking root and gaining refuge from the burden of ever packing and unpacking.

108

There are plenty of reminders that this is the twilight of my existence.

109

When life took me to the end of the inhabited world, to New Zealand, and set me down there for a couple of years, I had a chance to review these past contacts with seekers and their teachers, with doctrines and practices.

110

It is more than seventy years since I came to this planet. The move was a foolish one, for I know now that it was mere curiosity masked as a search after knowledge. For I exchanged a tranquil existence for a troubled one.

111

Some years ago I found myself in the position of having to establish a home. This was a new move for me and one that I had hitherto avoided. The reasons were varied—a nomad's temperament, the wide area of my researches, and a sensitivity which pushed me to get away when negative characteristics in my surroundings pushed themselves to the front. It was agreeable to remain footloose.

112

I remember the fallen autumnal leaves of plane trees on Adelphi Terrace, the thrusting shaft of Cleopatra's Needle nearby, the Adam architecture of so many houses around my office, and the wide tidal water of the Thames beneath its windows.

113

I have no fixed permanent home, no real abiding-place in this world, and wander like the Bedouin. Yet even he has his desert. I never stayed long enough in any one town or village to be absorbed by it: this enabled me to live my own life, follow my own way. Inclination began this unsettled existence and destiny sealed it.

114

Those men and women, teachers and taught, of my generation have mostly disappeared from view: the smaller number who remain are dying off with startling frequency. Having reached the span of years which the Bible allots to human life, we seventy-year-olds have to prepare ourselves for the worst, albeit some of us have learned how to convert it into the best.

115

For more than forty years I moved like a vagrant from country to country, or from place to place. This kind of restlessness is not conducive either to meditation or to work, but it is helpful to detachment or to material-gathering for work.

116

I live in Switzerland, Greece, and nowhere!

117

The remembrance that I am too old to squander time comes back periodically but always it is confronted and defeated by the realization that I will be reborn again, that in these future embodiments I shall have all the time needed.

118

How many happy minutes I spent, in those leisurely Indian years, watching little birds building their nests!

119

Writing short memos to myself and long notes for my instruction are procedures to which I have become an addict.

120

There is no mission that I feel or that I would care to undertake, nor indeed is there any sense of such a thing. Moreover, at seventy, time is running short, is the enemy of mission.

121

I love to listen to the chiming of old bells.

122

I have kept a deliberate and studied silence for many years on the subject of the past and present history of Ramana Maharshi's ashram. Not even the strange claims and stranger teaching emanating from there since his death have provoked me into breaking this silence.

123

The first book which brought me into mystical ideas was a curious fictional composition by Abu Bakr Ibn Ab Tufail. The title was *The Life of Hai Ebn Yokdan, the Self-Taught Philosopher* [also known as *The Awakening of the Soul*—Ed.]. Ibn Tufail flourished in the twelfth century in Spain and Morocco. He was a practising physician, a mathematician, and a Sufi. The book opened my knowledge in a vague general way to the possibilities of meditation, so I embarked upon the practice—unguided, uninstructed, groping my way in what, at first, was absolute darkness.

124

What more does a writer need than a fat notebook in his pocket and some ideas in his head?

125

I lived once, in my early manhood, in what was then called Highgate Village but now is alas! swallowed up in London's great hungry mouth. Coleridge had lived there too a century earlier, an ornament to English literature.

126

It is difficult to settle down to work when moving from place to place or country to country. Yet I wrote ten books in the same number of years while living just like that. For I found that travelling fed my writing. I not only met many who were seeking God, which allowed me to observe their struggles, but also some who had found God, which allowed me to profit by their experiences.

127

When I think back to those days, I remember when Michael Juste shared an apartment with me on Tavistock Square in a massive eighteenth-century late Georgian house with lofty ceilings and thick walls, where two or three years later Leonard and Virginia Woolf turned the rooms into a publishing office for "The Hogarth Press" and helped to foster the so-called Bloomsbury Tradition in English literary life, with its high rationality, fastidious stylistic prose and irreverent youthful and unconventional criticism. Juste wrote brief inspired verses. His first publication, a yellow-covered little booklet, aroused the London *Times* reviewer to enthusiastic appreciation. He had extraordinary genius for poetic creation connected with spiritual sources, but turned his head to other kinds of work. He published an occult periodical for a few years and I know that he opened a bookshop near the British Museum.

128

I drink tea so freely and so frequently that sometimes I think it is a relic of that fifteenth-century Chinese incarnation of mine—more especially since I deserted the stronger brew of India's Darjeeling for the milder one of Cathay-grown leaves.

129

If a lifetime given to spiritual research and spiritual adventure bore no more fruit than the keen interest generated during the endeavour itself, I would now judge it well-spent. But the result has fortunately not been so barren as that.

130

I do not agree with Thoreau's ascetic assertion that "water is the only drink for a wise man." It is a good drink for all, yes, wise and stupid alike, but it brings no such cheer to the heart as tea.

131

I stood atop the high and lonely lighthouse which itself tops the rocky promontory of Cape Saint Vincent and watched greenish Mediterranean waters meet bluish Atlantic rollers. It is the most southwestern point of Europe and the windiest point of Portugal. Here fish-eye decorated Phoenician ships, Visigoth vessels, Roman galleys, and Moorish sailing boats came with their crews of traders, warriors, pirates, or settlers. The waves dashed themselves in wanton fury upon the rocks, or crashed in suicidal exits from this world.

132

No flesh food passes between my lips, and no smoke passes out from them.

133

In all my world wanderings and quests, I met very few who demonstrated completely in their lives the loftiest teachings, though many could talk marvellously or write skilfully about them.

134

I feel that, in an overpopulated world, it is no longer a duty to leave a brood of still more humans behind me at death. And I feel too that in an overly materialistic age, it is nobler to beget true ideas and divine inspirations for others than to beget children.

135

It is not unreasonable to suggest that if we are now beginning to find our way to other dwelling places of other inhabitants of the solar system, some of them may be finding their way to us. The suggestion may even be extended to the possibility that they have done so in past centuries and that what they saw of this planet's population was not to their liking.

136

In the Jain monastery at Shravana Belgola, the largest in South India, the abbot showed me his rare, treasured, ancient palm-leaf manuscripts where numerous symbols were beautifully drawn and their meanings or effects explained. In Bombay, the most learned of all Jain pundits gave me lengthy instruction in the Jain secrets which he had gathered by travelling throughout India for many years, going from monastery to monastery and copying or collecting rare, little-known volumes which are still in the unprinted unpublished state.

137

More years ago than one cares to remember, some of us, some enthusiasts among us I should say, proposed the creation of a periodical to be called *The Philosophic Life*. But the cultured Cambridge University graduate among us objected to the proposal. He pointed out that such a publication would be mostly for the use of beginners because articles would necessarily be short and compressed, and philosophical subjects with their mystical profundity and metaphysical subtlety could not be adequately treated within such limitations; further, the pressure of preparing material for a dateline would mean hurried writing—also an unphilosophical procedure. So in the end the proposal was dropped.

138

It is not only the American business executive who often prefers to be designated by his initials alone. Far from him in geography and interests, it was also preferred, or rather enjoined, by the Imaginists, a group of French and English poets and writers who delighted in a half-spiritual but somewhat obscure symbolism.

139

Those experiences which now seem to have happened to another man and to belong to another age, did in fact happen to me.

140

An old gypsy once taught me a few scraps of Romany philosophy, and among them she put this one first and foremost: "A trotting dog finds a bone." I was put in mind of this saying while contemplating today the devious wanderings we Western aspirants must endure before we can even discover in what direction the Bone of Truth lies.

141

It is not too far off—not farther perhaps than a little beyond the time I became initiated into these studies—when they were as unfamiliar to most people, and as distant, as Cathay was a thousand years ago.

142

I have almost reached the Biblical age allotted to a man. Whenever I bid anyone farewell, whether at the end of a personal meeting or in one of those rare letters I sometimes write, I never know whether there will ever be any contact between us again.

143

I am without plans for the immediate future and even without a home for the actual present. Let the World-Mind make the first and find the second!

144

The snowy peaks redden in the evening's last light as I muse over old age in my Ticinese half-Swiss, half-Italian retreat.

145

In the little mountain train I travel in twice each week in order to purchase food and other supplies, a neighbouring passenger asked, in the friendly, well-meant way of village folk, what was my work? I usually rebuff such intrusions, but something influenced me to reply, "I have none."

146

I find myself in my last years and have tried to find the proper way to deal with them. First, I must forgive everyone (which includes myself) their past mistakes. Second, I must prepare properly for the coming event—death. Next, I would look into what others have found, if anything, of what recent knowledge says concerning those who have already striven to open the gates of the half-passing which precedes a full movement away. Ross, Stevenson, other medical writers like Lewis Thomas, and some of the parapsychologists also have some useful information.

147

I lived among the shady chestnuts on one of the hills overlooking Lugano.

148

An inward glow comes from the small coloured lamp which rests in the corner of the otherwise darkened room. It provides a kind of mystic beauty and a pleasant comfort.

149

A writer is instinctively interested in the study of human nature, but a writer on spiritual self-improvement is doubly interested.

150

Both His Holiness Shankaracharya of Kanchi and Ramana Maharshi were met within the same month of 1930. I had prepared myself by nearly two years' intensive study, principally with the help of the secretary of state for India's library in London. Now more than fifty years have passed and there has been sufficient time to get a little more knowledge and understanding of these two sages and to watch the effects of their persons and teachings upon others.

151

I was given Holy Communion by a Greek Orthodox priest who later became archbishop of all Greece. Did his sacrament of grace create in me that interest and study of Orthodox Mysticism which arose soon after? Did my personal contact and repeated good wish bring him this promotion over the heads of several senior Bishops?

152

The ritual of tea-making begins with the hissing of the kettle and ends in its festival of bodily refreshment and mental stimulation.

153

After all, it was southern China which raised tea to its higher importance; it was Lao Tzu and Bodhidharma, the Taoist and the Zennist, who allied it with contemplation and inspiration, who made its drinking a sacrament, its effects a refined poetic joy.

154

Superior beings have come to this earth planet since ages ago; but, their work completed, they have gone away again. Since then, other visits have been made from different parts of outer space. It would be surprising if the technological developments which have enabled human beings to probe other bodies in space were to pass unnoticed by these distant inhabitants.

155

The precious quiet which surrounds me is not hurt by the tick-tock of a grandfather clock. The sound of the swinging pendulum is so gentle and so rhythmic that it soothes the ear.

156

I love to wander around old-world villages and faded cities whose narrow streets and cobbled squares carry my memory back to a time of periwigged old gentlemen and the powdered Venuses with whom they joked. It is true that the sedan-chair was a poor substitute for the Buick sedan, but the century of the latter kills many true thoughts, whereas the century of the former gave one time to create them. Keep your automobile if it must murder my best hours, and leave me to a more leisured life, wherefrom I hope to draw the honey of diviner joys.

157

He walked out into the street and thus unwittingly walked out to his fate. For when he reached the traffic-laden crossing a few blocks away, a car drew up to the curb, a quiet voice hailed him, and the most extraordinary pair of dark eyes he had ever seen riveted his own gaze.

158

We were walking through one of those attractive pillared arcades so often found in Italy, Portugal, and other Mediterranean areas when we met him. As we approached from opposite directions I recognized his face and greeted him.

159

When I walked the sacred, hilly, Grecian ground where once the Delphian inscription "Know Thyself" met the pedestrian's gaze, I felt the melancholy peace of this glen-like scene. The fragments of carven stone seemed to reproach the warring races of man, steeped in self-ignorance still.

160

It does not really matter whether he believes in the four Archangels or not as it is not of importance to anyone unless he has advanced far enough to have made contacts with such beings.

161

When after the act of dying I shall be carried away to my own star, to Sothis of the Egyptians, Sirius of the Westerners, I shall at last be happy.

162

I found this path of philosophy most interesting and mentally exciting; but many, if not most, will probably find it dull and boring.

163

I have lived to see strange things. The name "Fakir" applied to a German carpet cleaner! The name "Yogi" applied to an American sweet!

164

Large cities are also large concentrations of all that is bad in human nature. Whether by falling into temptation or by picking up psychic infection, men are always exposed to moral degeneration in such cities. This is why so many mystics and most ascetics have refused to live in them.

165

The crinolined dullness of early Victorian women compares strikingly with the vivacious brightness of the modern miss. Two or three generations have sufficed to knock man's stuffy and stupid notions of women on the head.

166

Sirius, called the Dog Star in antiquity, has a symbolic meaning: it stands for the hidden knowledge of hidden truth.

167

The horrors of the vivisector's table create an equal karma; moreover, instead of yielding truth, as he thinks, the practice blinds him and yields illusion instead. The motive may be good but the method is wrong, for a right end cannot be achieved by a bad means.

168

He takes the situations in which he finds himself, the circumstances that surround him, either with instant decision and subsequent action to improve them, or with cultivated serenity—for he is unwilling to suffer the miseries of unsatisfied desire.

169

If he looks back at his past history, he wonders how he came to give so much importance to so many things, persons, events, and circumstances for which it does not now seem worth disturbing his peace of mind.

170

From time to time I need to consult some old text, Oriental or Occidental, for the purposes of research, study, or writing. Therefore it is useful to live not too far from a great city or university library.

171

It was only after the nearly two years which were needed to get rid of the blackwater fever with which India had dragged me down that I was able to begin work on *A Search in Secret India*. For this purpose I retired from the noisy metropolis to a little village in Buckinghamshire which I knew could give both beautiful wooded landscape and peaceful residence and from where I could attend, Sunday after Sunday, the old Quaker meeting-house nearby where George Fox and William Penn had established the Society of Friends in its first abode. It was in the Buckinghamshire woods, too, that another kind of book was born and finished: *Of Everlasting Mercy* by John Masefield. It was a spiritual glimpse-inspired, vividly written poem.

172

We authors are in the paradoxical position of being both known and unknown to our readers. That is to say, they know a part of our mind, the expressed part, but they know little of the unexpressed one, and probably nothing of the physical part, the body.

173

This huge freighter bore down upon our little ship when it was too close and therefore too late to avoid a collision. In the rending crash which followed, I was thrown from the bunk-bed to the floor.

174

Buckinghamshire was my favoured English county so perhaps it was fitting that, after my first return from India, I went there to write *A Search in Secret India*. The two rooms over an ancient village inn gave an open view of quiet countryside. The buxom, red-faced landlady brought up the simple and rather plain vegetarian meals every day—how deliciously garden-fresh they were! On Sundays, I walked over to a neighbouring Quaker village and sat with those grave sober and pious figures in the morning service at the seventeenth-century Meeting-house. Sometimes I would wander through beechwoods, cross streams, look at the graves of William Penn and George Fox, ruminate over America's unique history and England's religious background, and finally return to the table where the book grew.

175

When I visited England some years ago to see the old village where I wrote *A Search in Secret India* and where I went Sunday after Sunday to the old Quaker Meeting-house, I found much to disappoint me, alas!

176

I am not the only vegetarian inhabitant of this room. There is a second party across the room, a long-whiskered creature against whose presence I make no objection, even though he is a mosquito. This may seem strange, as also my indication of his dietetic preference, but it is a fact that the male of the species is quite harmless. The sharp painful incision made daily in the skins of so many million human dwellers in tropical regions is made, I regret to state, by the female mosquitoes. This is because the mouth of the male mosquito is unadapted for this purpose. He dines only on fruits, pollen, and nectar.

177

I love flowers but only when they are in gardens or in pots. For then they are living things but, cut, they are decaying, dying ones.

178

Two worthy people may become quite unworthy if thrown together in domestic harness or business association. Every quality in one person seems to stimulate the undesirable qualities in the other. There is constant discord and friction, disagreement and irritation.

179

Lord Byron refused to let his friends constantly use the formal terms of address or his title. He told them he was content to be called Byron and he would also accept even the initials L.B. alone that some of them chose to use. If therefore, he, a poet and an aristocrat, did not think he was demeaned by such acceptance, I, a commoner, am surely not demeaned by preferring the use of the impersonal initials P.B.

180

I was told that this area, this canton of Vaud, has a long winter and a short summer. Now I have verified the statement by my own experience. It is an aesthetically pleasing experience to look across Lake Leman and see those huge French Alps rising from the water and the land or to turn in the opposite direction and to see the Swiss Alps jutting upward, but it is not an enjoyable feeling to have their cold icy winds blowing down on and cutting into one's body.

181

When I was quite young, I became enthralled by poetry to the extent that I studied the laws of composing it and once succeeded in writing nearly eighty poems in a single month. To make those verses as beautiful as possible, I composed lists of beautiful words and put them in a small red notebook where I could constantly read and reread them, linger over their beauty, and eventually bring them into my compositions. There were such words as azalea, azure, nectarine, eventide, chimes, and so on. But alas! with the passing of youth the fascination of poetry faded away and the fascination of the scientific attitude took its place. There was nothing wrong in this, except that I failed to keep the two by maintaining a balance between them; instead, I foolishly adopted a one-or-the-other attitude. To the scientist, the Himalaya Mountains cover an enormous graveyard filled with fossilized animals; but to the poet, how grand and how unearthly a sight is the dawn sun rising over the Himalayan peaks!

182

Dear X:

Many interesting works have been published since Adamski started writing. As for my opinion, there are two types of UFO. There are the saucers, and there are the ships. Having had personal experience of both these saucers and ships, I cannot deny their existence, but too much unreliable fantasy has attached itself to the subject.

I regret that I am not in a position to discuss it any further. Advanced age has made retirement necessary. Inner needs have compelled a retreat from personal correspondence and interviews.

Thank you for the interest in my books; I hope you keep investigating still further and deeper—not only on the mystical side, but also on the philosophic, for which you have a wide field dating back many centuries. You should also not neglect the ancient Greek and the Chinese. It is not enough to limit oneself to Indian sources. [This was a standard response to queries about UFOs.—Ed.]

183

There were times when Ramana Maharshi actually appeared before me, advised or discussed. Death had not ended our relationship or barred our communions. He still existed in my mind, life, as a veritable force, an entity bereft of the flesh but clearly present at such times. And then one evening which I shall never forget, about a year and a quarter after his physical passing, he said that we needed to part and that he would vanish from my field of awareness. He did. I never saw him again. If it was his spirit, as I believed, it was either no longer able to maintain communication with this world, which I did not believe, or had withdrawn because the next step in my own development imperatively called for this freedom, which subsequently proved to be the case. [In 1981, P.B. said more about this "next step." He said that while the inner contact had never in fact been broken, he had lacked the ability to recognize that at the time. He had to stop looking for the contact through any sort of imagery, and learn to recognize its presence as pure essence rather than personalized image. —Ed.]

184

In my search for the truly wise as well as in my mission for the master, I led the wandering life of a dervish for many years; perhaps the time for final settlement is near at hand.

185

Alas! I can say with the Syrian poet, Abul Ala, "The years have gone like water."

186

There have been too many lectures and too many books in our time. In the East of long ago, students were not allowed to have the most important books. The teachers alone possessed them. They would bring one of these books out during a lesson and expound a few paragraphs and then put the volume away again.

187

Closest to the human stage of intelligence comes the ape; then, in descending order come the monkey, the dog, the cat, and the elephant.

188

There are times when we know that declaration can only lead to disappointment, when feelings must be kept secret and thoughts left hidden.

189

What wrong is there in seeking sufficient financial resources, sufficient good health, and enough of the pleasant things of this world to make life physically endurable?

190

Because I usually greet pastel colours with delight, this is not to say that I do not recognize that stronger colours have an appropriate use and place in the scheme of things.

191

We have lived to hear disembodied voices speaking to us through radio broadcasts, and to see faithful images of the bodies themselves not only speaking but also moving and acting just like them—and all this at several thousand miles distance. We must be more cautious before we deny a miracle.

192

The horrors of those prehistoric periods when grotesque gigantic monsters existed, as revealed by the nightmares of drug addicts, the vision of past births by Buddha, are confirmed by science. These reptilean creatures who emerged from the slime, these ichthysauruses and dinosaurs, were unbalanced, small heads set on immensely disproportionate bodies.

193

I have tasted the teas of a dozen different countries on their own soil, from the youthful green plant of Japan to the hard compressed brick of Tibet, and from the mellow mature herb of China to the mild soft growth of the Indian Nilgiri hills. We would have done well had we travelled together, Chang Tai—my fellow scribe across the centuries—and myself, for we could have matched tastes and scribbled lines with mutual understanding and inborn passion for this nectar of the gods. But why, in the pages of what purports to be a philosophic writing, do I thus refer to tea?

194

Such was my former fondness for tea that I lamented at times over the wasted years when misguided persons filled me with nothing more appetizing than cocoa, most uninspiring of drinks.

195

It is unfortunate for me that so many believers, because of the number of editions of my books or because I travel so far and so wide or because of my reputation or because I am a celebrity think that I must be rich. They think wrongly. I have stretched the pound and the dollar, the rupee and the piastre to their extreme limits of spendability.

196

My personal competence in financial affairs is nil.

197

P.B. called to see Mr. H.B.W. at his office on legal business. He offered to take P.B. to his hotel, as he was travelling home in the same direction. At a very busy intersection, the back of another car got in the way of our taxi. It would not or could not move and soon we were caught amongst and surrounded by a number of other vehicles. We were jammed on every side. Our driver became very angry with the man whose poor driving had created this awkward situation. He shouted imprecations in a loud voice. After two minutes the taxi was able to free itself but, throughout all that period, a volume of vocal abuse poured out uninterruptedly in a strong Brooklyn accent. H.B.W. got tired of hearing this and turned to P.B. and criticized the man. There was no partition between the driver and his passengers, so he was able to overhear them. P.B. replied: "What is the use of criticizing this man? His nerves are upset, his emotions are excited simply because he does not know any better and cannot help being what he is. What is the use of expecting him to behave like a philosopher and become detached from the troubles of the passing moment? He has never even heard of the existence of philosophy." The next morning the lawyer telephoned to P.B. and said: "I thought you might be interested to know that after I dropped you at your hotel the taxi driver turned to me and said: "Say, who is that guy who was with you just now? Is he some kind of monk?" H.B.W. asked him why he wished to know. He replied: "I heard what that guy said to you, and when he finished speaking, something changed inside me. I did not feel mad at the other fellow any more. I seemed to get very calm. I never had such an experience before. I can't understand it. Its wonderful!"

198

A little brook meandered by the cottage where I made both that world-forgetting retreat and this book. On its green narrow bank I sat for meditation every day at the sunset hour. Within hearing of its tinkling gurgling progress over rugged stones, I prepared the material that was transferred by pen, pencil, and typewriter to these sheets. The brook's waters gave me a rich sustenance.

199

The object of these pages is to tell the Western world about this spiritual light to which the gods led my feet in India; I seek to share with others, so far as the secondhand medium of writing can do so, this rare blessing of contact with a God-Man.

200

Chao-Chou, the ninth-century Master of the Ch'an School in China who was gifted with extraordinary spiritual perception, lived till he was 120 years old and travelled about till he was eighty. I follow his illustrious example whenever I say, "Have a cup of tea," to enquiring seekers after truth.

201

The cottage has been born. All newborn things should be given a name. What can I give mine? Let it be called "Desert Peace Cottage"—a place where a tired soul may periodically return and weave fresh webs of truths for busy men.

202

A sight of the worn brown cover of Bulwer Lytton's *Zanoni*—I think my copy is the second edition for it is dated 1853—brings back to me strange yet delightful memories. With what eagerness did I first peruse its quaint double-columned pages! How it opened a new and eerie world for me, a stripling yet at school! It gave me dark brooding ambitions. I, too, would take to the path of the Rosicrucian neophyte and strive to fling aside the heavy curtain which hides the occult spheres from mortal gaze. I could not keep this newborn enthusiasm to myself but was compelled to attempt to communicate it to a vivacious lady I knew, whereat she recoiled in philistinic horror and threatened to have nothing further to do with me if I persisted in trying to become a wizard. Alas! she kept her threat; we began to drift apart and many years ago she came to bid me a final adieu before putting a vast ocean and a great continent between us forever.

203

I hope the jinns of the ink-well will favour me this day, and let my pen flow fluently.

204

Nature has made me an exceedingly quick thinker but an excessively slow writer; the years in journalism brought my unwilling hand to keep a better pace with my thoughts.

205

The difference between journalism and literature is that the productions of the time-pressed journalist come out of his head, whereas those of the leisurely litterateur come out of his heart.

206

Dr. Roy Burkhart, an organizer of the United Christian Youth Movement, an author of books on psychology and Pastor of the First Community Church of Columbus, Ohio, suffered at night from psychical persecution by an unseen spirit trying to get control of his body, so that he was able to get very little sleep. At last he spoke about this trouble to P.B. and requested help. That night the persecution stopped and he enjoyed a full night's sleep for the first time in several years. The cure was maintained permanently.

207

"I felt such an outpouring of God's compassion towards your child and I am sure something wonderful is being set into motion. I do understand the nature of this searing problem. The only real answer, in the end, is total dedication to the Father and an opening of God's healing love to bless the wounds of soul and body. I just *know* deep inside, that it is a yearning for a total clearance and it is this inward readiness that we must speak to. We call for the Living Christ in him; we reach into the deeps of his soul and behold it awakening in the immaculate spirit of God; we enfold him in the love for which his soul yearns until he truly awakens to the highest and noblest and best! This letter comes forth on the wings of love and prayer to help him. . . . I was a *real* disciple of Dr. Paul Brunton when I was a young man and devoured all his wonderful books."—Brother Mandus

208

If he should ever see these pages, as I hope he will, may he take them as a tribute from the Western student to whom he opened darkly curtained doors.

209

When I first went off to India, it was at a time of widespread and massive rioting. It is not surprising that the British Government Foreign Office told me that it was necessary to keep my researches unhindered by irrelevant matters and myself unclouded by suspicion and that I had to satisfy these conditions by keeping rigorously aloof from both political controversy and propaganda in my writings and from political leaders in my travels. The undertaking along these lines which I was asked to give was faithfully kept during all the years of my personal contact with the Orient. Not only did I refuse to write a single page that could be regarded as other than non-political but I also refused tempting offers of personal interviews with men like Gandhi. Yet such is the perversity of human character that in the end and to my disgust, because I did all physical exploring in my own unconventional way, I was an object of unfortunate misunderstanding to both sides!

210

In the twelve years that passed afterwards until his death, I never saw Ramana Maharshi again. At least a half dozen times I passed within a few miles of his ashram during the part of that period when I was wandering in India. A lump would come into my throat and a choking sensation would seize me as I thought how close we were in spirit and yet so harshly separated by the ill-will of certain men and by the dark shadows of my own karma. For inwardly I never broke away from him.

211

The complete misunderstanding by this ashram of my character and motive, my outlook and purpose, was of itself sufficient proof that their path did not necessarily lead to true knowledge, however much it led to inner peace.

212

That I was most unfairly treated by one ashram in particular and many Indians in general is a shameful fact, but nevertheless it was a fact which helped my own emancipation.

213

I travelled in the Orient not only geographically but also mentally. I absorbed its ancient wisdom from books, men, monuments, and atmospheres.

214

I am humbly aware that the bulk of my writing is only journalism in book form. It is certainly not literature. This consciousness tames my vanity and mocks the hopes which I nurtured in youth of becoming a creative artist. And yet I know that I was not built for journalism. Its never-ending haste and its intrusions upon the affairs or privacy of other people are repugnant to my taste and repulsive to my temperament. And I know, too, that few journalists have dealt with such unworldly themes or written for such aspiring readers as I have.

215

I enjoy the old tree under which I am squatting and hear the birds' song uninterrupted by human crows croaking.

216

Unintelligent, impractical, and unself-reliant men proudly announce their possession of a degree. The worship of degrees often makes me laugh. An education which mistakes books for facts, words for things, and talk for action has produced individuals who over-value degrees and under-value life. I have met too many academic nonentities to be much impressed by an academic qualification. I do not have to have a diploma. There is no academic or professional post which I would accept were it to be offered me. I am in a position where I do not need the honours or even the emoluments which the world can give. I cherish my independence and freedom. I do not share the superficial joy of the typical hunter of academic distinctions any more than I share the infantile elation of the average climber in the social pyramid. My heart is elsewhere and my head is otherwise occupied. With mystical knowledge and experience of an unusual character already in my possession, with an assured place in world literature, there was no need from the point of view of personal advantage to trouble to secure a scholastic honour. Nevertheless I know that while conventional society believes and accepts such values, I can use them for the advancement of true ideas where I would not lift a finger to use them for the advancement of P.B. This is sufficient justification for not discarding the title derived from the college degree which I hold. I sought and

obtained this degree for one reason alone and that was for the benefit of
the backing of such a weighty academic honour as a Ph.D. For then people
will think that the man who holds it has some brains at least and that if he
takes up the teachings there may be something worthwhile in them after
all. This is quite apart from, and has nothing to do with, the fact that the
possession of this degree is an indication to the reading public that I have
at least the mental equipment to handle properly the subject of philosophy. And this indication remains and is even strengthened by the further
fact that it was granted not on the basis of examination, but partly on a
philosophical thesis submitted which was judged as showing capacity for
original research and as making a contribution toward existing knowledge
and partly in recognition of distinguished service to the cause of Oriental
research. And I became a candidate specifically for a doctorate of philosophy because this would be a recognition of attainment in the field wherewith my future publications would be most concerned.

217

I learned anew the ancient lesson which one learns in every land, that
human nature is, basically, everywhere the same, that it runs eternally
around the triangle of self, money, desire and especially sex-desire, with
religion as the fourth dimension which holds this triangle.

218

In these ashrams I witnessed at first hand what I had perforce hitherto
taken at second hand from history. For I witnessed the spectacle of myth-
making which turned a human being into a remote idol, the process of
building up the legendary figure of a god out of a man. Although the
master himself personally protested against the practice, he did so vainly.
Incense was daily offered to him in a ritual of perambulation and worship-
pers prostrated on the floor before him amid cries of "Lord! Lord!"

219

What joy came to my heart, during the years when I could wander this
earth, each time I met one of those rare spirits who had liberated himself
from common prejudice! What ease to be able to exchange thoughts in an
atmosphere of perfect equity!

220

Does Europe need a new evangel?

221

When I suggest a simpler mode of living, I am not preaching neo-stoic
gospel. I believe that man was born to be happy and that he need not
disdain the things of this earth in order to attain some supramundane bliss.
I refuse to make my philosophy a torture for myself and a nuisance to

others. These thoughts coincide with my instinctive tastes and I am well content if the rest of mankind refuses them hospitality. What I do suggest is that we call the bluff of that bully, Mammon, and stop to enquire whether we really need all the things we desire, and whether all our consequent slavery is worthwhile.

222
Three more letters will turn man into maniac.

223
Among two or more men silence can be without any significance at all or it may express mere boredom. Still more, it may even be ugly and sinister. Rarely, it may denote spiritual harmony.

224
The removal of forests leads in the end to the removal of rain. This, in turn, converts flourishing farmland to alkaline deserts. Nature does not ask man to deny himself some land but only not to take all, as he does.

225
The embryo formed in the womb is in a helpless situation, half-grown and half-conscious, cut off from past incarnatory memories, having no post-natal identity, prisoner in a solitary cell, fearful and anxious.

226
We overwork the past if we drag it constantly into the present. And this is true not only if it appears in the shape of negative broodings and lamentations but also of intellectual beliefs and views.

227
It is no doubt hard for the working man to follow this quest, but experience has shown that it is hard for rich people to follow it also. The only difference is that the particular difficulties—such as lack of time—which stand in his way do not stand in theirs. On the other hand, the particular difficulties which stand in their way do not stand in his. However, it is a fact that the hindrances which a poor man has to face are on the whole greater than those which the rich have to face.

228
The mason's hammer, splintering the aeon-resting rocks for the sake of intruder man, echoes no more. The bricklayers have gone and he with it. The carpenter's saw has ceased its rough music. At last the place has become quiet again and no doubt Nature will absorb this artificial structure of my cottage in her landscape and may lay it in time with part of her own variously coloured phenomena.

229

The wanderlust which led me from place to place, from land to land, for more than thirty years, led me also nearer and nearer to the work which is fitly mine. Thus it had an undeclared purpose, and was not mere wandering in a circle.

230

A woman who was P.B.'s London secretary for a time tells the following story. One day P.B. needed some letters in German translated into English. The secretary offered to ask an Esthonian girl, who was living in her house and knew the language, to do the job. It was done and P.B. sent his thanks to her. The girl's people had been taken away in the war by the Russians and were never heard of again: she herself had been in a displaced persons' refugee camp for some years and had become epileptic, with horrible fits. The secretary occasionally told this girl a little about P.B. and about spiritual things, but only a little because she was not ready for more. One night she awoke from sleep in a kind of nightmare and both sensed and saw a very evil creature in the corner of the room. It horrified her. Then she became aware of another presence, whom she felt was or was associated with P.B., who bade her not to be terrified but to drive it away by her mental command. She did this and it vanished. Then this good presence advanced and said, "Just as you have the strength to overcome evil spirits, so you can overcome epilepsy." After that night she never again had a fit; the cure was permanent.

231

What a disgusting spectacle these humans, with their incessant disputes and wars, must present to the higher beings of other planets.

232

With what pleasure do I put the dry green or black leaves of Chinese tea in a little earthen pot when the daily rituals of leisurely relaxed refreshment come round! How pleasant to balance in one's hand a cup of the delicately aromatic and fragrant liquid! I have long since lost the taste for Indian Darjeeling, Ceylonese, and Japanese teas, finding satisfaction only in those which come from Cathay or Taiwan—young Hyson green for breakfast, semi-black Oolong for mid-morning, smoky Lapsang or flowered Jasmine for mid-afternoon.

233

As I sit, bending over a desk, writing these thoughts, there comes to memory a sentence from a Chinese classic. Was I in a previous incarnation, the author of that sentence? I have reason to believe so.

234

Being in possession of other people's books always disturbs me. I have no rest until they are returned.

235

Much that I have written in my notes about the Himalayas can quite truthfully be written about the Andes. Both are the world's longest and highest mountain ranges. Both stick a galaxy of snow-capped steeply rising peaks like towers and spires into or through the clouds.

236

Chinese saying: "The taste of Ch'an (Zen) and the taste of Ch'a (tea) are the same." This is applied to the power of tea to render the mind clear and to refresh its power.

237

I would like to ask what Europe was drinking during all those barbaric centuries before it first tasted tea in the seventeenth one.

238

Living in so small an apartment yet having so large a number of possessions, it is needful that the most be made of every bit of space. Everything must be readily accessible, and its whereabouts known or inventoried. Books, office equipment, stationery, domestic items, clothing—all must be put away in an orderly and efficient manner, as the ancient Phoenician sailors stowed things on their far-voyaging ships.

239

Those immense silences of the Himalayas were like living in a completely soundproofed room. They helped me to quieten the mind as nothing else. And there was more. The sharp air freshened the mind, the endless spaces gave it new perspectives.

240

I have travelled the world and though I found some countries, some cities, some rural areas better than others, I did not find any place that I could feel was the ideal. Indeed, the conclusion was forced on me that this place was nowhere to be found except within myself. And even there I had to find my way to it by the hardest of explorations.

241

A journalist travelling in India, and a rationalist sceptic and cynic withal, I received my first lesson in an unforgettable philosophy from this strange little man. He showed me that much of our life is written beforehand.

242

"Why go off to the East for light? If you believe in a World-Soul, then it should be possible to sit down even in a town like Dublin and look within until you contact that World-Soul and so gain all the spiritual light you seek. But perhaps your destiny compels you to go, for I foresee that you have an exceptional work to perform in threshing the corn of Eastern wisdom for the sake of Western students." This was the advice tendered me by my beloved friend, the distinguished Irish poet "A.E.," a few weeks before he died. It was sound advice, as I found to my cost. Yet the force which drove me to disobey it was overwhelming. It was, as "A.E." rightly surmised, my personal destiny.

243

The incense began to affect me no less than the staring eyes of the fakir. The room swam before me, all power of movement seemed to desert me, and I stood as one paralysed.

244

I wander farther afield and, overcome by a feeling of fatigue, throw myself upon the ground and listen to the hum of insects. The minutes pass and then I slowly become aware of a second sound. It is a kind of gentle swishing, yet so faint that it could be easily overlooked. Certainly if my corpse-like position did not bring my ears close to the ground, I could never hear the noise. I sit up suddenly and gaze around in circular fashion. Through the bushes comes a gliding snake. The glittering, baleful eyes stare coldly and petrify me for a few moments. Why has Nature cursed this country with sneaking, crawling things? And then I remember the Buddha's injunction to be compassionate, to live and let live. Was he himself not shielded from the hot mid-day sun by a cobra which formed its hood into a canopy over the sage's head? Has not Nature provided a home for this snake equally as for me? Why need we look at each other with such trepidation? It rises from the ground in magnificent malignity to the height of my own head, a venomous and vertical creature whose neck gradually spreads out into a narrow hood marked with coloured spots. Instantly I direct my thought toward that Overself which pervades the creature confronting me no less than this body of mine. I perceive that this Self is one and the same and that the two forms appear *within* it. I sense that it is binding me to the other form in universal sympathy. My separateness, my fearfulness, even my repugnance and hatred, melt away. In that sublime unity, there is no second thing to arouse enmity . . . The snake passes on its way, and I am left safely alone. How much higher is this than the snake-magic which I learned in Egypt, how much more worthwhile! For the dervish who taught me his arcana of conquering cobras by occult powers now lies in a sandy grave outside Luxor, his face distorted by the agony of snake-bite, his twenty-year immunity lost in a single moment.

245

Asia is my ancestral home. Wherever my spirit has wandered in the past, it has mostly taken birth in the beloved lands of the East.

246

If the task were not so distasteful to my peace-loving temperament, it would be a necessary duty to write a sequel to that immature book, *A Search in Secret India*, about my later experiences in a country so elusive to a foreigner. The more I penetrated beneath the surface of men and institutions, the more my early enthusiasm evaporated. The better I came to understand the thoughts and deeds of "Secret India," the better I realized how deceptively rose-coloured were the spectacles with which I first viewed them. A truly scientific estimate of such matters would have uncovered the whole picture, the dark side no less than the bright one. The existence of this side is well-known to thoughtful and educated Indians themselves. But the years have passed and I shall certainly never attempt to do work of this unpleasant and unappealing character. Nevertheless it is most needful to the few earnest seekers after truth, as distinguished from the many uncritical seekers after personalistic emotional satisfactions, to know that I have revised most of my former estimates and come to modified conclusions and that, in short, my realization that the West must work out its own salvation is based upon mature experience and profounder reflection. Not by turning solely eastwards, as superficial enthusiasts would have us do, nor by turning solely westwards, as the white-race superiority complex would suggest, but by taking what both have to offer as the starting point only for our own new twentieth-century quest, shall we work out this vast problem of giving a spiritual significance to modern man's life in the most effective and satisfying sense of the term.

247

Somewhat altered to suit our times, a Sufi master's retort to a question motivated by suspicion is quoted as "Enlightenment is not to think that because a man is a professional writer he is not enlightened."

248

If this planet's inhabitants can send space vehicles as far as the moon, let it not be denied *as a possibility* that some other planet can send them *here*. And if that planet is evolutionarily more advanced, let us grant the likelihood that these missions of exploration are based on deeper knowledge and a higher morality than our own.

249

How could I live in a house where the view is shut off by ugly walls? I have done it many times when homeless and I had to wander from hotel to hotel, but this was mere existence and was not adequate living. It would be delightful to have an adequate home where all the necessary conditions for a sensitive person's outward surroundings were available. But alas the ideal residence of that kind does not exist—at least not for those of modest incomes like myself. I have to accept surroundings which however imperfect are at least more tolerable.

250

It was pleasant to recline on a comfortable divan, harmoniously patterned and coloured, with a small table at its side bearing an oriental teapot containing a favorite infusion of delicately fragrant tea.

251

I see dead races of men rise from their dust. Atlantis has vanished into watery oblivion.

252

It was one of those delightful sunny days which on occasion, and by contrast, light up the greyness of London.

253

I am quite content to rusticate amid old villages and decaying windmills.

254

When I lived in that little Connecticut cottage, the water I used for making the cups of jasmine tea which warmed me in the early mornings and slaked my thirst in the mid-afternoons, came from a spring close by. It had a neighbour, a brook that leaped after rains from stone to stone but sometimes dried up completely. The spring itself never went dry, never stopped giving its beneficent draught. My happiness was just like that spring. It bubbled up all the time, unfailingly fresh.

255

I love these quiet beech woods which lie close to my cottage in South Buckinghamshire.

256

The twilight wind moving through the leafy trees sighs out a requiem for the dying day. So to those who have ears to hear all the universe is forever in mourning.

257

I may only be a writer. I shall certainly be a sage.

258

It has not been easy to revive these memories, some from a very remote past. Any mind which has become deeply mystical and habitually metaphysical tends to value timelessness more than time, to discard what has gone before as mere pictures vanishing from the world-illusion, and to cling to what is eternal.

259

I know now after long and varied experience that the place I sought, Home, had no physical existence, only a spiritual one.

260

With filial joy I offer you this flower of days that whatever fragrance it may have shall tell of the days I spent at your side. My head was heavy and bowed with the sorry burden of earthly life; my feet had wandered long among the rocky places and then grew tired as a sleeping man, when your great love shone down upon it and warmed it into life until it took strong root in some soft earth. Is it not appropriate then that I cull the first blooms for your table? I count it one of the great things of my life that I am privileged to call you Friend. And I know if I know you at all, that I can do no greater deed in return than to speak to my fellows of the unforgettably beautiful stream into which you turned my little boat, broken and halting though the words of my stammering lips must needs be.

Index

Entries are listed by chapter number followed by "para" number. For example, 6.242 means chapter 6, para 242 and 6.54, 64, 74, 85 means chapter 6, paras 54, 64, 74, and 85. Chapterlistings are separated by a semicolon. Please note also that, for the reader's convenience, the first number in the right-hand running heads throughout the text indicates chapter number.

A

G

Gandhi, Mahatma 6.209
Gaudapada 5.209–210
Gethsemane 4.124
gifts 4.143
glimpses 1.2 (p. 8), 1.2 (p. 11), 1.2
 (p. 13); 2.82; 3.21, 26, 28, 33, 52,
 56, 60, 62, 65, 67, 71
Goethe, Johann Wolfgang 5.275
grace 1.2 (p. 10), 1.2 (p. 14); 3.88;
 5.204
Greece 6.159
Greek Orthodox religion 6.151
Guardian Angel 5.155
Guénon, René 6.57
Gurdjieff, George I. 6.45
guru 4.29–104
 definition 4.60
Guyon, Madame 5.155
gypsy 6.140

H

handshake 6.35–37
Hazlitt 5.285
Hegel, Georg 3.131
Heisenberg, Werner 6.82
Hidden Teaching Beyond Yoga, The 1.1
 (p. 3); 2.208; 3.72; 4.5, 174;
 5.114, 132, 201–209, 211–213,
 216, 218–220, 222–223, 248
Hildebrand 5.112
Himalayas 1.2 (p. 18); 6.235, 239
Hindu philosophy 5.89
Hinduism 6.71
Hinton, James 3.131
history 4.10, 20
Hitler, Adolf 5.101
Horace 5.358; 6.101
Hughes, Howard 6.75
Huxley, Aldous 3.131; 6.61

I

Ibn Tufail, *Awakening of the
 Soul* 3.141; 6.123
imagination 1.2 (p. 10), 1.2 (p. 13)
Imaginists 6.138
independence 2.136–137, 178
India 2.144, 172; 5.80; 6.136, 209
Indian texts 2.173
Inge, Rev. William Ralph 6.69
initiations 1.2; 2.73, 200; 3.39, 60,
 84, 127
inner guidance 2.144; 3.5, 18, 63
Inner Reality, The 5.194, 199
insects 4.189
insight 5.214, 216, 218
Interior Word 1.2 (p. 12), 1.2 (p.
 16); 5.238
intuition 1.2 (p. 12)

J

Jains 6.136
Japan 6.83
Jeans, Sir James 4.8
Jesus 1.2 (p. 18); 4.148; 5.199, 247,
 280
Joad, C.E.M. 2.2
John of the Cross, Saint 6.55
Johnson, Dr. Samuel 6.66, 96
journal, philosophical 4.64; 5.269–
 270; 6.137
journalism 6.204–205, 214
Jung, Carl G. 6.82
Juste, Michael 6.127

K

Kabbala 1.2 (p. 19)
Kabir (*Shabda*) 5.238
Kennedy, Joseph P. 6.84
Khmer adepts 3.61
King, Bishop 4.143

The 28 Categories from the Notebooks

This outline of categories in *The Notebooks* is the most recent one Paul Brunton developed for sorting, ordering, and filing his written work. The listings he put after each title were not meant to be all-inclusive. They merely suggest something of the range of topics included in each category.

1 THE QUEST
*Its choice —Independent path —Organized groups —
Self-development —Student/teacher*

2 PRACTICES FOR THE QUEST
Ant's long path —Work on oneself

3 RELAX AND RETREAT
*Intermittent pauses —Tension and pressures —Relax body,
breath, and mind —Retreat centres —Solitude —
Nature appreciation —Sunset contemplation*

4 ELEMENTARY MEDITATION
*Place and conditions —Wandering thoughts —Practise
concentrated attention —Meditative thinking —
Visualized images —Mantrams —Symbols
—Affirmations and suggestions*

5 THE BODY
*Hygiene and cleansings —Food —Exercises and postures
—Breathings —Sex: importance, influence, effects*

6 EMOTIONS AND ETHICS
*Uplift character—Re-educate feelings —Discipline emotions —
Purify passions —Refinement and courtesy —Avoid fanaticism*

7 THE INTELLECT
*Nature —Services —Development —Semantic training —
Science —Metaphysics —Abstract thinking*

8 THE EGO
What am I? —The I-thought —The psyche